101 ADVENTURE
WEEKENDS IN EUROPE

SARAH WOODS

NEW
HOLLAND

First published in 2009 by
New Holland Publishers (UK) Ltd
London • Cape Town • Sydney • Auckland
www.newhollandpublishers.com

Garfield House
86–88 Edgware Road
London W2 2EA
United Kingdom

80 McKenzie Street
Cape Town 8001
South Africa

Unit 1, 66 Gibbes Street
Chatswood, NSW 2067
Australia

218 Lake Road
Northcote
Auckland
New Zealand

10 9 8 7 6 5 4 3 2 1

ISBN 978 1 84773 415 0

Senior Editor: Sarah Greaney
Designer: Roland Codd
Cartography: Stephen Dew
Production: Marion Storz
Publisher: Ross Hilton
Publishing Director: Rosemary Wilkinson

Reproduction by Modern Age Repro House Ltd, Hong Kong
Printed and bound by Times Offset (M) Sdn Bnd, Malaysia

PHOTOGRAPHY CREDITS

p9 © Imagebroker/Photoshot; p10 © www.ibatour.com; p11 © Kay Nietfeld/epa/Corbis; p13 © Ruben Adalia/www.kayakdmar.com; p14 © xtremegene; p15 © www.madsegs.com; p16 © www.rocksportmallorca.com; p17 © Ted Levine/zefa/Corbis; pp18, 19 © EFE/UPPA/Photoshot; p20 © Marcin Ratajczak/www.tarifaocean.com; p21 © www.tourspain.co.uk; p23 © Galen Rowell/Corbis; p24 © Frans Lanting/Corbis; p25 © Oceans Image/Photoshot; p27 © Patrick Ward/Corbis; pp28, 29 © Oliver Relations; p30 © Gail Mooney/Corbis; p31 © Kawasaki Motors; p32 © Ric Ergenbright/Corbis; p33 © www.euromast.nl; pp34–5 © JUPITERIMAGES/Creatas/Alamy; p36 © Michael Busselle/Robert Harding World Imagery/Corbis; p37 © www.gthq.co.uk/LeMans06; p39 © Franck Seguin/TempSport/Corbis; p40 © Office de Tourisme de Lourdes; p41 © 360 Expeditions; p43 © Gareth Brown/Corbis; p44 © Charlie Munsey/Corbis; p45 © AJ Hackett, Normandie; p46 © OTC Pau/DG & DR; p 47 © moodboard/Corbis; p49 © Organizing committee, Mille Miglia 2008; p50 © Owen Franken/ Corbis; p51 © De Agostini Picture Library; p52 © Tony Gentile/Reuters/Corbis; p53 © Mauritius-images/Photoshot; p54 © Owen Franken/Corbis; p55 © Brenda Tharp/Corbis; p56 © Jan Drbal; p57 © Vito Arcomano/Fototeca ENIT; p58 © De Renzis/ANSA/PAT/Corbis; p59 © Vito Arcomano/Fototeca ENIT; p60 © Imagebroker.net/Photoshot; p61 © Ashley Cooper/Corbis; pp62–3 © Emmanuel Lattes/Alamy; p64 © Steven Robertson/iStockphoto; p67 © PICIMPACT/Corbis; p68 © Dean Shults/Alamy; p69 © www.bodyflying.ch; p71 © ONT; p73 © OPT; p74 © www.lazef.be; p77 © World Pictures/Photoshot; p80 © Cees van Roeden/Syddansk Turisme; p82 © German National Tourist Office; p83 © Presseamt Stadt Münster/Angelika Klauser; p84 © German National Tourist Office; p85 © Imagebroker/Photoshot; p86 © German Tourist Office/Sylt Marketing/Georg Supanz; p87 © Schlegelmilch/Corbis; p89 © Ed Kashi/Corbis; p91 © World Pictures/Photoshot; p92 © Irene Ascher/TVB Innsbruck; pp94, 95 © CzechTourism.com; p97 © World Pictures/Photoshot; p99 © Zamberlan Adventure Trophy; p100 © Atlantide Phototravel/Corbis; p101 © Mauritius Images/Photoshot; p102 © Terta Images/Photoshot; p105 © www.kopos.lt; p107 © www.adventurerace.lv; p109 © Estonian LR Off-Road Club; p111 © Wulf Pfeiffer/dpa/Corbis; p113 © Dimitri Iundt/TempSport/Corbis; p115 © Boris Bajzelj/Slovenian Tourist Board; p117 © Croatian National Tourist Board; p119 © Nik Wheeler/Corbis; p121 © Romanian National Tourist Office; p123 © Nenko Lazarov/www.imagesfrombulgaria.com; p125 © Eye Ubiquitous/Photoshot; pp126–7 © Aliki Sapountzi/Aliki Image Library/Alamy; p128 © Walter Bibikow/JAI/Corbis; p129 © Paul Taylor/ExtremeCY; p131 © audi_insperation; p133 © Kinnaird Estate; p134 © Andy McCandlish/www.visitscotland.com/adventure; p135 © Beattie Communications/ Blue Planet Aquarium; p136 © The Photolibrary Wales/Alamy; p137 © Honey PR/Go Ape; p139 © victoriapeckham; p140 © NONSTOP Sail Adventure Sailing; p141 © David Lyons/Alamy; p143 © Robert Harding Picture Library Ltd/Alamy; p144 © Jonathan Hession/Tourism Ireland Imagery; p145 © Chris Hill/Tourism Ireland Imagery; p147 © Atlantide Phototravel/Corbis; p148 © www.blacktomato.co.uk; p150 © Nancy Bundt/Innovation Norway; p151 © Jes-Peder Lokke; p153 © www.asunden.com; pp154–5 © Henrik Trygg/Corbis; p156 © Nordicphotos/ Alamy; p157 © Zak Waters/Alamy; p159 © Kristiina Leinonen/CharismaPR

CONTENTS

CONTENTS

101 ADVENTURE
WEEKENDS IN EUROPE

FINLAND

101

RUSSIA

99

071
ESTONIA

070 LATVIA

072

LITHUANIA

069

RUSSIA

067

066

BELARUS

POLAND

068

065

UKRAINE

064

SLOVAKIA

073

077

MOLDOVA

HUNGARY

ROMANIA

IIA

OATIA

BOSNIA
HERZE.

SERBIA

BULGARIA

075

MONT.

078

MACEDONIA

081

37

ALBANIA

083

GREECE

TURKEY

080

079

CYPRUS **082**

PORTUGAL

TIME DIFFERENCE GMT +1

TELEPHONE CODE +351

CURRENCY Euro

LANGUAGE Portuguese

POPULATION 10 million

SIZE OF COUNTRY 88,889 sq km
(34,667 sq miles)

CAPITAL Lisbon

WHEN TO GO Mainland Portugal's winters are
exceptionally mild, especially in the Algarve region.
Cooler inland temperatures typify inland provinces,
with snowfall in the Serra da Estrela mountains.
Autumns are pleasantly warm, turning steadily
cooler into December. Islands offer year-round
temperate conditions – 18°C (64°F) in winter and
22°C (72°F) in summer.

TOURIST INFORMATION
Portuguese National Tourist Office
Tel: 0845 355 1212
Fax: 020 7201 6633
Email: tourism@portugaloffice.org.uk
www.visitportugal.com

On the west of the Iberian Peninsula, Portugal's 830 km (515 mile)
Atlantic coastline flanks the nation to the south and west, with the
Spanish border to the north and east. The River Tejo provides a neat
division across the country, stretching out to meet the waters of the
Atlantic in Lisbon. Portugal's 17 islands and atolls include the
archipelagos of the Azores and Madeira. Many of Portugal's sleepy
fishing villages of brightly painted sardine boats, cobbled streets and
whitewashed houses sit alongside pristine beaches. The rugged,
windswept coastline is renowned for its world-beating windsurfing,
big game fishing and waterskiing in a nation famed for over 300 days
of sunshine a year.

TREKKING MADEIRA

The flora-rich hill trails of the small Portuguese island of Madeira are renowned for their jaw-dropping views across vineyards and bird-filled valleys out to dramatic cliffs. The island's ancient water channels slice through vegetation-cloaked terrain, moulding the landscape with dome-shaped 'riverbanks' that provide ideal hiking paths. Known as *levadas* – a Portuguese word derived from the word 'levar', meaning to carry – a rough translation is 'carriageway' but it is more correctly defined as a mini-canal. Used to distribute water from the rain-nourished northern regions to the dry and dusty sun-baked south, the 16th century *levadas* provide much needed irrigation to Madeira's wheat fields, maize farms, banana plantations, vineyards, fruit orchards and vegetable gardens. A crisscrossing network straddles the mountains and stretches around 1,550 miles (2,500 km) but don't be tempted to drink the water – it's untreated despite its sparkling depths.

If you have a pair of decent boots and a head for heights, trekking in this region is a must. A guide in Madeira costs 30–35 euros per person, including transport and maps. Some of the finest treks flirt around the sleepy settlement of Arco de São Jorge, protected from the east winds by scenic slopes and to the west by the Boaventura

Mountains. Year-round, a comfortable steady stomp from Boaventura to Arco de São Jorge takes around three hours. Gentle ascents and descents wind through ancient gullies overlooking a wind-carved cliff shaped like sugar bread ('Pain de Sucre'). The trek down to the ramshackle ruins of a fishing hamlet adjoins a plummeting zigzagging trail with a sheer drop into the sea – with no handrail. Journeying from Boaventura via the ultra-green 'Levada de Cima' burrows through lush shrubs and clusters of chestnut trees, with trails that look out over pretty red-roofed houses and church spires. The nestling Porco (Pig) River joins the ocean on a small rocky beach protected by two islets where contrasting geological formations range from red basalt to inky-black volcanic crags. Crystal-clear springs run from Boaventura to the Laurel Forest, the most impressive being the flora-edged Levada Grande, Levada dos Tornos and Levada da Achada. Those seeking a truly challenging trek should head to the Levada da Central da Ribeira da Janela, in the northwest of the island – it journeys through eight pitch-black oppressive tunnels (one over a kilometre long) under cascading water. Don't forget to pack a torch and some waterproof gear – but, if you're claustrophobic, give it a miss.

GETTING THERE
Hire cars from the airport (and taxis) are the only option to reach Arco de São Jorge from the airport, a 60 minute drive.

CONTACTS
Madeira Tourism
Tel: +351 291 211 900
Fax: +351 291 232 151
Email: info@madeiratourism.com
www.madeiratourism.org

Madeira Levada Walks
Tel: +351 291 763 701
Fax: +351 291 761 464
Email: info@madeira-explorers.com
www.madeira-levada-walks.com

Ancient water channels slice through thick vegetation and arid scrub.

Killer waves pound the coast, attracting world-class boarders.

BODYBOARDING SINTRA

Lord Byron once described Sintra in verse as a 'glorious Eden' but today's poetry-inspiring Atlantic coastline attracts more surfers than literati. As home to Portugal's 'water sport capital' Praia Grande, Sintra's bodyboard Mecca is aptly named, for it is just that – a big beach. A large sweep of stunning sand sits underneath ancient clifftops on a prehistoric fossil bed imprinted with visible dinosaur prints – yet Praia Grande is no elderly clapped-out relic of the past. Host to numerous modern local and international water sport championships, including the prestigious Bodyboard Pro 2007 World Bodyboard Championship, Praia Grande attracts the best boarders in the world.

Surfers wax lyrical about the constant waves at Praia Grande, citing its ability to keep pumping, even when other beaches around sit flat. Swells come in predominantly from the north, ensuring that Praia Grande is perfectly positioned to receive a pounding every day of the year. Waves tend to be fast and hollow with shifting peaks and good tubes. The hard paddle out is worth the effort for rides of up to 200 m (656 ft), meaning that few boarders need to trifle with ankle-busting waves. Successive sets of waves (as many as four and five) – from both left and right – are commonplace in the central triangle. The left hand side of the

sand is extremely popular, but when the beach gets overcrowded simply shift along to the right, past the rip – or arrive early as the Portuguese don't tend to get up before 9am. Even swells and plenty of heavies (big waves) on a sandy bottom make Praia Grande a popular choice with bodyboarders keen to make the most of a long summer season – but with 340 days of annual sunshine there's very little need for neoprene other than on January's chilliest days.

The beach is home to a couple of surf schools with several hire shops nearby, and those new to bodyboarding will find no shortage of good, practical tuition. Once your body weight is in the right position, the key is to paddle well using kicks, arms or both. A duck-dive is the next basic move to master, allowing the rider and board to get under the turbulence of a breaking wave. When you're ready, pick a nice looking wave and paddle out towards it. Then catch it, turn around to face the shore and begin to kick hard – the wave will start to push you along. As you gain momentum, move down the face of the wave to attempt a bottom turn – another boarding staple. Praia Grande's hollow, tube-like waves are favoured by both dropknee and prone (stand-up) bodyboarders – with many riders switching tactics for the sake of a killer wave.

KITEBOARDING PORTO

The surf-pounded Costa Verde coastline is renowned Portugal-wide for its health-giving attributes in a region blessed by embracing scenery and pure, fresh air. Mountains and sea nestle along the River Lima in Portugal's lush, green, sporting haven where every pursuit from walking and horse riding to a healthy dose of adrenaline on the peaks is within easy reach. Dozens of unspoilt, natural beaches – many completely free from resort-style tourist trappings – boast excellent surfing swells throughout most of the year. At least 40 great surf spots from Miramar and Matosinhos to Moledo dot the shoreline, while jet skiers, sailors, canoeists and fishermen favour the languid currents of the River Lima. One of Portugal's most memorable panoramic views can be enjoyed from the top of Monte de Santa Luzia, a 3.5 km (2 mile) uphill slog from Viana do Castelo's historic city centre.

A barely-suppressed surfing mania engulfs the beach scene in and around Viana do Castelo, long a Mecca for the region's urban and rural coastal sporting nuts. A late winter and early spring ensures a long watersports season, with the best swells found on the Praia do Cabedelo's vast sandy arc-shaped stretch, about 5 km (3 miles) east of the city's old town. Accessing it via the river on a five minute ferry trip from the pier south of Largo 5 de Outubro is the easiest option. Departures run hourly from around 8am to 7.30pm daily from May to September (and often later in July and August) – and increase in frequency to accommodate arrivals for the kiteboarding crowds in the summer highs.

Ask surfers what's great about the water at Viana do Castelo and they'll cite the sheer versatility of its waves. An expanse of flat between the piers at the entrance of the harbour allows boarders to let rip with some spectacular blasting. On the left, at the beach, a point break right with side-off shore winds provides waves that are rideable for 300 m (984 ft) – maybe more. Plenty of jumps ensure lots of aerial action at the Praia do Cabedelo on this more or less perfect beach, characterized by a horizon-stretching curved sand carpet on a coastal stretch that continues northwards, virtually unbroken, to the Spanish border at Caminha and south to Póvoa de Varzim.

Several companies rent out equipment and offer windsurfing and kiteboarding lessons. A handful of cafés cater for a relaxed beach-bum crowd in summer, but it may pay to take your own drinks and snacks with you in the off-peak season.

GETTING THERE
Located 60 km (37 miles) from the Francisco Sá Carneiro International Airport, Viana do Castleo has excellent communication and rail networks linking it to the rest of the country. Car drivers should join the IC 1 that links Porto to Valença via Viana do Castelo.

CONTACTS
Viana Castelo
Tel: +351 258 809 300
Fax: +351 258 809 341
www.cm-viana-castelo.pt

Region Tourism Department of de Turismo do Alto Minho
Tel: +351 258 820 270
Fax: +351 258 829 798
Email: info@rtam.pt
www.rtam.pt

The open, unspoilt beaches boast strong gusts and powerful swells.

SPAIN

TIME DIFFERENCE GMT +1

TELEPHONE CODE +34

CURRENCY Euro

LANGUAGE Spanish

POPULATION 40.4 million

SIZE OF COUNTRY 504,782 sq km
(196,865 sq miles)

CAPITAL Madrid

WHEN TO GO Spain is generally divided into a
temperate north and a hot, dry south, with April to
October the most popular time to visit. In the
height of summer (July to August) temperatures
soar to scorching highs inland. Coastal regions
remain pleasant year-round but are prone to wet
weather in winter.

TOURIST INFORMATION
Spanish Tourist Office
Tel: 020 7317 2010
Fax: 020 7317 2048
Email: londres@tourspain.es
www.tourspain.co.uk

Spain has at least a dozen personalities, from the desert-style plains
of Almeria and silver-sand beaches of Formentera to the curvaceous
hills of Catalonia and the deep ravines, stalagmites and caverns of
the Balearics. Away from the rapid urban development of the
Costas, Spain offers plenty of unspoiled swathes of forest and
coastline. Vast highland plateaus are segmented by spiny
mountains, while low-lying narrow coastal plains run like ribbons
throughout the southwest. Dramatic cliffs are home to hook-clawed
raptors while bears, lynx, and wolves roam mountain woods and
streams. Vines, olives, figs and orange groves flourish in the fertile
soil of the foothills, and two rivers – the Ebro and the Guadalquivir –
provide a natural habitat for trout and barbell, with surrounding
marshlands rich in butterfly species.

CONTACTS
Catalonia Tourist Office
Tel: +34 93 484 97 55
Fax: +34 93 484 98 20
Email: turistex@correu.gencat.es
www.gencat.net

Paddle along between jagged, grass-fringed cliffs, caves and outlying islands.

SEA KAYAKING BARCELONA

In sea kayaking circles, the Catalonian coast just north of Barcelona is considered the Holy Grail, blessed with calcareous caverns and untamed waters. Numerous excursions depart from umpteen points along this languid Mediterranean stretch. A spine of jagged, grass-frayed cliffs hide myriad secluded coves embedded with mysterious caves. A rich variety of marine life includes bream, sea stars, sardines, mullet, groupers and many other fish in shallow waters, while scrawny inlets offer an off-the-beaten-track ocean journey only accessible to those in a kayak, allowing privileged views at a paddling rhythm.

What's great about sea kayaking in Catalonia is that it can be enjoyed at a leisurely pace in good weather with calm seas, requiring minimum effort under cloudless skies. Easily accessible waters offer kayaking conditions suited to every fitness level with plenty of demanding routes on choppier sections, if more strenuous excursions are your style. The type of gear required depends a lot on weather and location, although the canoes are very different to those used on interior waterways. Sea kayaks are longer, more stable and almost unsinkable, thanks to bulkhead design. Built-in hatches provide great interior loading capacity, while comfort features ensure that a cruise can last for hours.

Catalonia's specialist sea kayak tour operators are skillful in rescue and self-rescue techniques. They also monitor the region's coastal breeze regime to determine the optimum time to depart the shore. Most offer 2–4 hour itineraries to cover around 10–15 km (6–7 miles) without the need for clock-watching. Others run full day and two-day kayaking through untapped watery labyrinths inaccessible by land. Due to its close proximity, the central coast (straddling north and south of Barcelona) is popular with weekenders. Large, sandy stretches and scenic rocky formations punctuate the coastline around El Garraf, Sitges and Vilanova i la Geltrú, and cliffs and solitary inlets intersperse the shoreline around Torredembarra, Tamarit and L'Ametlla de Mar. One real not-to-be-missed highlight is the Illes Medes (or Medes Islands, a pinprick archipelago of seven islets some of which are merely oversized bumps). Kayakers traversing the islands' bath-warm outlying waters will paddle through a sparkling broth of varicoloured fish. Once a hideout for pirates' buried treasure, today it is the islands' undersea riches that lure visiting vessels to an ecosystem blessed with 1,350 marine species.

005

GETTING THERE
Xtreme Gene is located 20 minutes
from the city of Cordoba.

CONTACTS
Xtreme Gene
Tel: +34 957 63 54 37
Email: debbie@xtreme-gene.com
www.xtreme-gene.com

Cordoba Tourist Office
Tel: +34 902 20 17 74
www.turismodecordoba

*Hit speeds of 40 kph (25 mph)
on rolling reservoir wakes.*

WAKEBOARDING CORDOBA

As a wild and wonderful muddled mix of snowboarding, surfing and skateboarding, wakeboarding has been born out of a melting pot of cross-over disciplines. As an exciting derivative of intertwined techniques, wakeboarding allows plenty of freedom for individual interpretation and is exciting to watch – and even more fun to perform. Over the years, the sport has evolved along with board shape. Today's symmetrical 'twin-tip' design with a fin on both ends is standard throughout wakeboarding circles. Unlike the old surfboard shape, this board allows a centred stance to ensure equal performance, whether the wakeboarder rides in the forward or switchstance (fakie) position. Greater buoyancy also offers riders a quicker, 'looser' feel and aids softer landings from sky-high wake jumps.

Spain's wakeboarding centre sits on the banks of the resplendent Embalse de la Brena, a reservoir close to the picturesque town of Almodovar Del Rio, 15 minutes from historic Cordoba. Stretching over 15 km (9 miles), the lake boasts plenty of sheltered areas for slalom courses and also has space for endless runs. As one of Europe's premier wakeboarding destinations, the Xtreme-Gene centre offers professional coaching run by resident trainer Andres Alijo, whose clients include members of the Spanish National Team. Super Air Nautique 210s – the wakeboarding world's boat of choice – are used as standard to pull riders across the reservoir at speeds of up to 40 kph (25 mph). Each is equipped with a aluminium wakeboard tower which places the 'pull point' about 2 m (6.5 ft) off the water's surface, providing the rider with greater control.

State-of-the-art boards are coated with fibreglass, with small, moulded fins that create less drag. Choose a smaller wakeboard for lighter, faster spins at the expense of an easy landing, or ride a larger board for a slower, smoother style. Jumps involve hitting the wake and launching into the air, where tricks can be added as skills progress. A three-stage rocker offers plenty of height off the water – the ultimate 'pop'. At the Xtreme-Gene's Wakecamp, riders of all ages studiously perfect their tricks, including the 'raley' (when the rider hits the wake and allows their body to swing backwards), the 'batwing' (a toeside raley perpendicular to the water), the 'butter slide' ('snapping' the board sideways to slide on top of the wake) or the dramatic surface 360, when a rider spins the board fully around at speed.

SEGWAY MADRID

For seven days a week, Madrid plays host to an unusual style of sightseeing, as tourists take to the city's historic streets using futuristic-looking self-propelled contraptions. Since being unveiled in 2001, the Segway PT (personal transporter) has been hailed as a pedestrian speed-freak's friend. In Madrid, this gliding, spinning self-balance stand-up scooter whizzes around the city's elegant paved plazas, scattering pigeons up into the balconied eaves above. Designed to mirror human body mechanics, the nimble Segway hurls itself around ornamental fountains and monuments, speeding along city centre sidewalks, backstreets and alleyways.

Tours begin with an introduction and training session. Lean forward on a Segway and it gently rolls ahead; lean back and it moves in reverse. To bring it to a halt, the rider has to stand perfectly upright: a valuable lesson in posture for anyone prone to a lazy stoop. Acceleration is straightforward, once the human tendency to overcompensate in a shifting stance is mastered. Tipping back and forth in a series of jolting, erratic movements is a rite of passage on a Segway. It feels precarious, but rarely is it enough to flip a rider face flat. Within a few minutes, most riders can roll forwards and backwards and turn in a complete circle. The learning curve may be steep, but it's mercifully brief.

Many of Madrid's Segway operators set off from the elegant Plaza de España, the city's main gathering point at the end of Gran Via's arterial stretch. Routes encircle the Plaza Mayor, wind along the Teatro Real (Royal Opera) and glide by the Templo de Debod – an eye-popping 2,200 year-old temple gifted to Spain in gratitude by the Egyptian government in 1968. Then it's on to the Prado Museum and opulent 2,800 room Palacio Real, the largest palace in Western Europe and the official residence of the King of Spain. Next it's the Plaza de San Juan de la Cruz and on to landmarks El Ángel Caído, Fuente de la Fama, Fuente de los Delfinos and the Museo del Arte Contemporáneo al Aire Libre in a crest-shaped sweep.

Any fit, healthy person can enjoy a Segway tour, and riders aged 7 to 84 have sped around Madrid's balconied vendor-scattered plazas to date. Groups tend to be small – up to seven or eight is the norm. Weight restrictions apply, the parameters being between 25 and 135 kg (55–298 lbs). Madrid's skilful guides offer plenty of Segway tips and trickery, so even the octogenarians complete the course, able to weave around traffic cones slalom style. Itineraries run for three hours, allowing plenty of time for tapas and photographs.

CONTACTS
Madsegs Tours S.L
Tel: +34 659 82 44 99 (English)
Tel: +34 669 26 99 97 (Español)
Email: info@madsegs.com
www.madsegs.com

Madrid Tourist Office
Tel: +34 915 88 16 36
Email: turismo@munimadrid.es
www.esmadrid.com

See the city sights on a self-propelled stand-up scooter.

007

CONTACTS
Rocksport Mallorca
Tel: +34 629 948 404
Email: john@rocksportmallorca.com
www.rocksportmallorca.com

Mallorcan Tourist Board
www.majorca-mallorca.co.uk

The Belearic Islands
www.illesbalears.es

*Challenging rock-fuelled
thrills on crags, in gorges
and in canyons.*

CANYONING, CAVING AND POTHOLING MALLORCA

Mallorca's astounding limestone formations, dramatic dusty gorges and jutting corkscrew crags hide all manner of pre-historic limestone warrens, from slither-like gashes the size of a sleeping bag to vast gaping hollows. The island's rugged terrain means that potholing and caving on Mallorca involves plenty of fell walking, hiking and canyoning – both wet and dry. The adhesive grip of Mallorcan limestone makes scrambling a genuine treat, unless, that is, you fall foul of a prickly spine or razor-sharp bush.

The Sierra de Tramuntana runs for 88 km (55 miles) in the northeast of the island, from Andratx to the pretty bays of Porto Pollenca and the rocky outcrops of Sa Dragonera and Cap de Formentor. It features ten peaks over 1,000 m (3,280 ft) including Puig Major (1,445 m/4,740 ft) and Puig Massanella (1,349 m/4,425 ft). While the range contains no rivers, it is riddled by mountain torrents that swell rapidly at the merest hint of rainfall. Just a single tour guide works the sheer vertical slabs of the Sierra de Tramuntana, but Brit John Hind has the pedigree of a caver who knows his stuff. After solo climbing in and around the central Pyrenees and French Alps, Hind is a dab hand at exploring the mountains of Mallorca and runs scrambles, caving, canyoning and other rock sport tours that are 100 per cent custom-made. Physical challenge remains at the heart of all of John Hind's endeavours, but not at the expense of sightseeing in the mountains. Most explorers access the Puig Major and Puig Massanella via an endless succession of gut-wrenching hairpin bends, traversing tunnels and gorges along the way. Circling vultures bring home the peril of this vertigo-inducing climb. This is superb hiking terrain, with a network of well-marked paths to choose from. What's more, they're almost usable year-round, with winter days still warm and almost more suitable for trekking than the searing heat of summer.

Expect Mallorca's mix of canyoning, caving and potholing to provide every rock-fuelled thrill imaginable, from loose-stone scrambles through shallow pools at 1,000 m (3,280 ft) to delving into pitch black gullies and traversing deep-water ravines. Tour prices include all equipment, transport, guiding and maps required, depending on the demands of the tour. Kit can include karabiners, ropes, helmets (with light) and waist harnesses, and waterproof clothing, sturdy boots and sunscreen are essential. Rigging is an option for steep descents into cavernous chambers – rest assured that reputable rock sport tour operators are scrupulous with their safety planning. Prime challenges include the trails of the Torrente de Pareis, the Cavall de Bernat Ridge, 'Puig de Seis Viñes' Ridge and Silla de La Reina, via Directa – each full-on nine hour trips.

GETTING THERE

The Sierra de Béjar–La Covatilla ski resort is accessed from the road N-630 and is easily accessible from Madrid by motorway – only two and a half hours away, Salamanca, Avila and Plasencia are all less than an hour away. Lagun Air connects Barcelona, Malaga and Palma with Salamanca's Aeropuerto de Matacán. Visit www.lagunair.com for schedules.

CONTACTS

Sierra de Béjar La Covatilla Ski Resort
Tel: +34 923 401 141
Fax: +34 923 401 835
Email: info@sierradebejar-lacovatilla.com
www.sierradebejar-lacovatilla.com

Schuss down slopes hemmed by mysterious glacial etchings.

SKIING SALAMANCA

In 2002, a ski resort opened 70 km (43 miles) south of the historic city of Salamanca atop the summits of the Sierra de Béjar after taking an extraordinary 70 years to complete. Since stalling in the 1930s, the project had suffered several major setbacks. Yet when it opened, 10 km (6 miles) from the city of Béjar, the commanding views it offered of the northern slopes consigned the projects' hiccups to the annals of time. Heavily snow-cloaked from the end of October until mid-March, the Sierra de Béjar ski resort's trademark wide runs on low gradients are situated in the midst of cross-country trails. Some 19 km (12 miles) of alpine skiing ranges from 1,990–2,369 m (6,527–7,770 ft) with 19 runs served by a 1,230 m (4,034 ft) four-person chairlift plus a lift for the summit – not to mention a ski school staffed by 40 instructors from all over the world.

The Sierra de Béjar's snow-capped silhouette outlines the southern territory of Salamanca that makes up the western sector of the peninsular Central Mountain Range (described as the 'dorsal spine' of the Castilian plateau). Canchal de la Ceja is the most elevated point in the Sierra de Béjar and is characterized by weird-shaped glacial etchings. Every season adds some magic, from spring's verdant flower season and summer's balmy breezes to the baronial hues of autumn – while winter's snow and ice give the mountains sparkle and pizzazz.

Virtually unknown to international tourists, the ski runs are popular with snow-seeking urbanites who have escaped Madrid, just a 90 minute drive away. Even the King of Spain is rumoured to have joined the throng of salopette-wearing Madrileños to schuss down the Sierra de Béjar–La Covatilla's most fearsome off-piste runs. Costs range from 20 euros for a one day pass to 45 euros for the weekend. Runs can get crowded on Sundays and local holidays, so arrive early for the milk run to avoid a crush.

009

GETTING THERE

The nearest airport to Pamplona is 6 km (4 miles) away at Noáin. International flights arrive in Bilbao (150 km/93 miles away) where you can catch a bus to Pamplona. There are only two buses a day from Santander to Pamplona, and it will take about 3 hours. Many travellers choose for convenience to travel with tour companies, which run fleets of coaches to the event. Most of these tour groups are based at outlying campsites and run regular shuttles into town.

CONTACTS

Pamplona Tourist Office
Tel: +34 848 42 04 20
Fax: +34 848 42 46 30
Email: oit.pamplona@navarra.es
www.turismo.navarra.es

Pamplona Town Hall
Tel: +34 948 420 100
Email: sugerencias@ayto-pamplona.es

RUNNING WITH THE BULLS PAMPLONA

Although it is barely dawn, the villagers of Pamplona are already gathered at a small shrine on the plaza to honour 12th century Saint Fermín, while an excitable crowd chants to an ancient screed, fists waved skywards. Groups of men in traditional garb of white shirts with crimson sashes and bandannas wave rolled-up newspapers in fervour. Prayers complete, the villagers begin to crack open ice-cold bottles of sparkling wine. Several thousand crazed eyes bear the reddish hue of sleeplessness, as exploding firecrackers resonate throughout Pamplona's whitewashed streets. Over the red-tiled rooftops, the sun breaks through the shadow as the town's bull-running festival reaches its ultimate fever pitch.

Pamplona is inextricably linked with Spain's most famous fiesta: a bull-running tradition (*encierro*) made famous worldwide by Ernest Hemingway's novel *The Sun Also Rises*, published in 1926. Each year, 6 July marks the beginning of the Sanfermínes festival; a week-long spectacle that fuses wine-soaked Spanish revelry with an infamous testosterone-pumped machismo pursuit. More than 2.5 million tourists descend on Pamplona to witness or participate in the celebrations, swelling the city's normal population of just 100,000.

Spectators keen to get close to the action will need to muscle into a surging crowd clad head-to-toe in red and white, although upper balconies offer a better view and obvious safety advantages. Every single one of the Cava-swilling throng is jumping, dancing and shouting above the music, crammed into skinny cobblestone streets filled with the laughter of thousands. Strewn party debris litters the streetscape, while family groups lean from windows above, dousing those below from fizzing bottles. Amidst this bizarre chaotic scene, a collection of marching bands add the sound of beating drums, accordions and trumpets to the mix. Cafés and bars overspill for seven straight days around the clock, many removing their doors to signify the fact that they simply never close. On the main square, Plaza del Castillo, former Hemingway haunt the Iruña bar serves up a potent brew in searing, sweltering heat. Folding crowds sashay back and forth on Calle Santo Domingo, as several thousand sweat-beaded bystanders await the effigy of Saint Fermín. A deafening burst of fireworks prompts a frenzied state of terrified excitement, signifying the pen is open – and the bulls are on their way. In a blink of an eye, a deafening boom heralds the arrival of a thunder of bovine fury as Pamplona's narrow streets fill with rampaging wild-eyed beasts. Oily black hides glisten in the sunlight as a herd of bulls with a combined weight of over 3,600 kg (7,956 lbs), charge clumsily past on an unpredictable path, just an arm's length from a hysterical crowd keen not to be trampled by angry beef.

This first stretch heads towards Pamplona's town hall, before racing onto Ayuntamiento Square. Then a short burst along Calle Mercaderes before an abrupt right into long, thin Calle Estafeta. Next it is Calle Duque de Ahumada, a narrow corral that runs down to the entrance of the bullring, a crowded finishing line and a byword for survival, where the relief is palpable. At just 825 m (2,706 ft), the bull run is all over in 220 hair-raising, heart-pumping seconds, but it feels like several hours. Grazed elbows, bruised shins and trampled toes provide the telltale battle scars of bull-avoidance tactics. High-fiving bystanders infused with adrenaline

laugh loudly in shared insanity, surrounded by scenes of joy and verve. Like Hemingway, many tourists visit Pamplona year after year for the Fiesta of San Fermín, despite the dangers. Although purists lament the arrival of cordons and barricades, safety is much improved, with running only advisable for those with local know-how. As a spectator in Pamplona, the bull run is as extreme as it gets: an under-a-minute adrenaline rush of manic mayhem and terror. After pelted eggs and flour bombs, the bedlam continues in Pamplona's matador hangouts par excellence, Hotel Yoldi and Plaza de Toros ('bull ring'). Jubilant runners in frayed red and white booze-stained rags recount endless bull-running yarns, while propping up the bar. After nine days of non-stop partying, the celebrations wind down on 14 July, when exhausted revellers sing a traditional Spanish song as a finale, entitled *Pobre de Mi* ('Poor Me'). Hemingway's old room at the Hotel La Perla is booked solid for the fiesta until 2045 by a Swiss publisher. With laudable optimism, he intends to celebrate his 100th birthday risking life and limb on the bull-run – Papa himself would be proud.

Crazed bulls, firecrackers and wine-soaked machismo: a chaotic scene.

WINDSURFING TARIFA

GETTING THERE
BA flies from London Gatwick and Monarch flies from London Luton to Gibraltar (a 45 minute drive). Monarch flies from Manchester Airport and RyanAir flies from London Stansted to Jerez (1.5 hour drive). RyanAir and ClickAir fly from London Gatwick to Seville (2 hour drive). British Airways, Easyjet, Monarch, Thomson and Flybe also serve Malaga (2.5 hour drive).

CONTACTS
Tarifa Windsurfing Festival
Tel: +34 618 650 496
Email: tarifaocean@hotmail.com
www.tarifawindsurfingfestival.es

Hotstick Tarifa (Windsurf School)
Tel: +34 956 680 419
or +34 647155516 |
www.hotsticktarifa.com

Wind Tarifa
Email: windtarifa@windtarifa.com
www.windtarifa.com

Serious squalls draw the crowds in Europe's 'Wind Capital'.

In the early 1970s, a group of windsurfers discovered the joyous gusts of Tarifa, swearing a pact of secrecy to keep the wind-fanned shoreline free from crowds. Well, guess what? Someone spilt the beans – and today the town is one of the world's most popular windsurf playgrounds. Before the arrival of the surf set, the people of Tarifa used to curse the wind. Today the townfolk burst with pride that their home is the 'wind capital of Europe'. Perched on the southern tip of Spain where the Atlantic meets the Mediterranean, Tarifa is renowned for two prevailing winds that bluster through the Straits of Gibraltar. The *levante* (side-offshore) blows in from the southeast and is a strong, warm, summer wind that can gust 24–7 for weeks. The cooler, westerly *poniente* (side-shore to side-onshore) is most prevalent in spring and autumn, driving in from the Atlantic to bring Tarifa bumpy waves. So reliable are these world-class squalls that two consecutive days without wind is a rarity.

Tarifa's perfect windsurfing conditions are matched in spirit. Mellow surf shops and funky beach bars nestle alongside unpretentious cafés overlooking a trademark year-round jumpy chop and decent swells. Windsurfing hotspots shift in synchronicity with the weather conditions, although prime months are May to September. Board-carrying pilgrims from across the world become slavish devotees of Tarifa's thrilling force sevens, wowing onlookers with an array of backloops, spocks and spectacular slalom gybes. The beach starts in town and stretches for around 6 km (4 miles) then extends around the small peninsula to another 8 km (5 miles) of sand. Tarifa's strong winds rarely rouse themselves until lunchtime, a thermal effect that pleases a late-to-rise party crowd.

Although a destination popular with maestros, Tarifa's large, sand-bottomed bay offers safety for complete beginners as well. Helmets are advisable when the wind is at full throttle, especially for novices. A half-dozen windsurfing centres offer lessons (group and one-on-one) along with equipment hire, sales and spares. Visiting in December? Book early, as Tarifa's hotels are stretched to capacity when the Windsurfing Festival comes to town.

RAPTOR-SPOTTING
SANTANDER

CONTACTS
Teresa Farinois
Tel: +34 943 735 154
Email: Teresa@iberianwildlife.com

Picos de Europa
www.picoseuropa.net

To visit the Picos de Europa is to step back in time. Vast tracts were once the domain of Europe's largest predators, amidst jagged limestone massifs that form a fierce pincushion of knife-edged ridges and pinnacles born out of a glacial era. Rising to 2,648 m (8,685 ft) at Torre Cerredo and split into three distinct ranges – western (El Cornión), central (Los Urrielles) and eastern (Andara) – by a dramatic string of gorges, the Picos de Europa's population of prehistoric bird species is much fabled in sci-fi narrative. Tales of mammoth, hooked-beaked, claw-footed vultures swooping down on ancient deciduous forests remain steeped in local legend – but aren't consigned to the past. These bone-gnawing raptors continue to nest in caves, ledges and low rocks rising from the planes of the Picos de Europa and can be sighted swooping down to smash their prey against rocky ravines, dipping in flight from a soaring position to increase velocity.

Harbouring around 130 pairs of griffon vultures plus numerous immature birds, the Picos de Europa are a breeding ground to a large number of raptors, many with a wingspan of over 2.5 m (8 ft). Egyptian vultures arrive to nest in the springtime where, without a sense of smell, they rely on an almost bionic eyesight to hunt out prey. Using vision twice as refined as that of a human, the Egyptian vulture can spot 4 cm (1.5 in) shrews from a height of 1,000 m (3,280 ft). Over 50 years since the species disappeared, lammergeiers have been successfully encouraged back into the area's sheltered, rocky cavities. Breeding pairs of golden eagle can also be found on limestone ledges, with booted and short-toed species fairly common in summer. Bonelli's are more rare, as are sightings of black vultures, but a reintroduction initiative has reported some notable success in returning the osprey to the Cantabrian coast, 20 km (12 miles) away. Healthy numbers of honey buzzards, goshawks and sparrowhawks are all common in forested areas – in all, 160 bird species have been recorded, including many carrion-devouring scavengers.

Declared Spain's first national park in 1935, this wild 64,660 ha (159,710 acre) expanse of mountainous and wooded terrain remains wholly undisrupted. Notoriously complicated to navigate, the deep hollows and steep rocks of the region are crisscrossed by a muddle of ancient tracks. Raptor watchers keen to unearth the region's bird of prey population should engage a specialist tour guide, such as naturalist Teresa Farinois. A resident of the Picos de Europa, she has been leading tours since 1989. For the ultimate raptor experience, ask about customized weekend tours that take in the bird-rich La Hermida Gorge. This breathtaking, nerve-racking rocky fissure allows good access to some exhilarating upland trails to the domain of Picos de Europa's sinister-looking winged dinosaurs. Dress for a humid, rainy, temperate climate and prepare for heights of over 2,000 m (6,560 ft). Frequent fog banks can present serious hazards in all seasons – as can perilous vertical drops, bears and wolves.

Razor-sharp ledges and deep hollows are home to prehistoric birds.

012

SOS SURVIVAL GRANADA

Remote, harsh and forbidding:
the ultimate survival challenge.

The foothills of Sierra Nevada sit firmly in the aged city of Granada and sprawl out to Málaga and Almería. A vast spine of ridges contains continental Spain's highest peak, Mulhacén, a formidable snow-capped crest that soars to 3,482 m (11,420 ft). Stretching for 80 km (50 miles) and reaching up to 30 km (19 miles) in width, the Sierra Nevada is one of Spain's most impressive botanical enclaves with over 2,000 species of vascular plants (25 per cent of Spain's total plant species, 120 of which are endangered) that includes a staggering array of snow-tolerant endemic species. Over 86,200 ha (212,914 acres) encompasses torrential rivers, sheer-sided gorges, stony scree slopes, glacial lakes, snow-crusted summits and, in the foothills of the Alpujarras, cultivated terraces of cereal crops, olives, grapes, almonds, walnuts, apples and vegetable fields. In Sierra Nevada's southern base, a steamy tropical climate prevails due to a close proximity to Africa, while a dozen peaks reaching heights exceeding 3,000 m (9,840 ft) are snow covered for around 250 days per year. Several long but narrow river valleys lead off towards the southwest, separated by a number of subsidiary ridges. On the steeper and craggier northern side, valleys are dominated by the Rio Genil which starts near Mulhacén, and into which many of the other rivers flow. Arid, sun-baked gullies lead from a thickly wooded mid-region to the frost-blown, spindle-thin branches of the bleak upper slopes. In 1986, UNESCO declared the Sierra Nevada a Biosphere Reserve and it was awarded national protection as a Natural Park in 1989 before being given National Park status in 1998. Today, this epic glacier-hewn rockscape offers explorers a foreboding and dramatic terrain of weirdly-shaped ravines that is home to vultures, eagles, weasels, foxes and Iberian mountain goats.

Sierra Nevada's unique, testing environment makes it an ideal location for survival skills training, and a number of specialist operators have risen to the challenge to offer courses run by guides with an intimate knowledge of the mountains' nooks and crannies. Most are run in the harshest winter months from December to April, but some do run

later. Apart from covering the basics, guides impart a considerable amount of technical knowhow, including essential winter navigation techniques. Itineraries vary, but generally tackle winter hill walking, ice axe skills, abseiling, roping, making emergency snow shelters, hunger management, crampon techniques, avalanche risk, step kicking and cutting and a whole lot more. Training places a strong emphasis on environmental challenges, survival tips and endurance. A study of the park's network of mountain refuges (*refugios*) and rustic stone shacks (*refugios vivacs*) details the shelter available to climbers faced with an unscheduled overnight stay. Other tips include how to keep clothing dry, nutritional advice, how to keep warm, what do to if someone is missing, how to use a compass and some first aid. The course also combines textbook mountaineering skills with a more judgement-based knack for understanding the Sierra Nevada's changeable weather patterns – fusing theory with plenty of practice. Old mining paths from the era of the Santa Constanza copper mines, and the craters of the Alquife iron mines provide a testing training ground, while the hardy, north face routes of Mulhacen and Alcazaba provide climbers with a genuine treat.

Most of Sierra Nevada's high peak ascents are do-able in one or two days, with plenty of high factor sun protection and a hat essential for protection against burning at high altitude. Not all routes are ultra-arduous, but most get the blood pumping, leading through craggy fissures and past plunging dark rock gashes and sprouting alpine scrub. Prices include transport, guiding, camping gear and any other specialized equipment required. Don't miss the long slog to the Mulhacen summit from the south – a full day of 8–10 hours. Local knowledge allows a lesser-known cluster of tracks that skirt the edges of the park's highest ground to be followed, even those deemed impassable due to icy gusts. A two day alternative via Siete Lagunas involves travelling light to overnight in sleeping bags in a Poqueira Hut – a rewarding scramble across a yellowy lichen-clad ridge filled with butterflies, as vultures circle overhead.

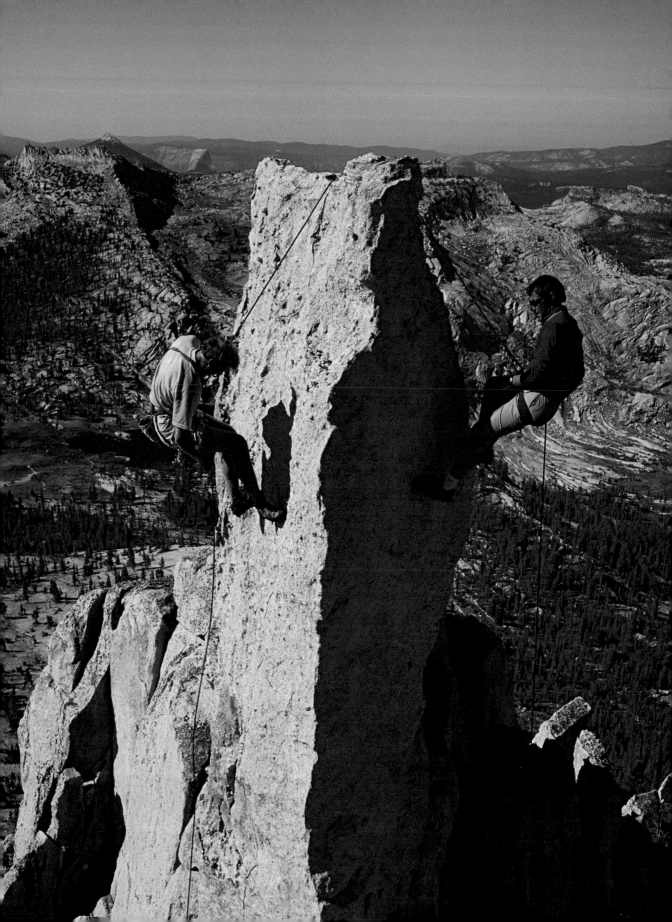

CONTACTS
Tenerife Tourism Corporation
Tel: +34 922 237 889
www.webtenerifeuk.co.uk

Encounter the 'kings of the ocean' in the Gulf Stream's fertile depths.

WHALE SPOTTING
TENERIFE

Expect a strange gurgling in the pit of your stomach as the boat rolls with the swells out in Tenerife's waters. No, this isn't seasickness – it's high excitement as a dozen pairs of eager whale-watching eyes scrutinize the journey out to sea. After chugging out of Los Gigantes the boat gathers real momentum, cranking up a gear or two to bounce atop the chop. Over a crackling loud-speaker system, the captain will inform you that a whale's moan is louder than a 747 jumbo jet on take-off, and that the songs of male humpbacks are the longest and most complex in the entire animal world.

As the 'whale watching capital of Europe', Tenerife boasts no shortage of tours and crafts devoted to this most magnificent of marine encounters, many captained by able seafarers of advancing years. Vessels tend to be modern and purpose-built, with gleaming paintwork, an upper deck and 'submarine vision' from a glass-panelled bottom below. Weather permitting, boats set sail almost year-round from Los Cristianos, Playa de Las Americas, Los Gigantes and Playa San Juan, riding the waves with deft athleticism. Twenty-eight species of bottlenose, common, spotted and rough-toothed dolphins, plus short-finned pilot, sperm, false killer whale and various beaked whales are regularly sighted in the area. The rich volcanic soils of Tenerife's oceanic trench, and the nutritious warm waters of the Gulf Stream, ensure a ready-made store cupboard of squid and vegetative dietary staples, attracting vast numbers of cetaceans to the region.

Almost a third of the world's whale and dolphin species either live or pass through the waters around Tenerife, and most would-be watchers strike it lucky around 45 minutes from shore. Four bottlenose dolphins often bow-ride alongside in sleek synchronization, their grey torpedo-shaped bodies cutting through the swells in perfectly choreographed leaps and dives. Keep binoculars at the ready as the boat lurches to a sudden halt and begins to bob in hypnotic silence. In the hush even the most innocuous splashes attract scrutiny, but there is no mistaking the deafening whoosh as the waters open up. A vast black shadow will lie just under the surface of the water, before it reveals itself with an ear-splitting boom as it pounds the water with mighty swish of a hefty black tail. A forceful eruption of salty spray resonates in the air before the graceful dive back into the deep: few superlatives can match the moment. Then, in a split second, the king of the ocean is gone, a towering spume of misty water all that is left in its wake.

MIDNIGHT SCUBA DIVING
VALENCIA

The underwater scenery of Spain's Valencian coastline is a completely different world once the sun goes down. Nocturnal marine life emerges from daytime nooks and crannies to provide a magical below-surface display as the sun bids farewell and the moon starts to shimmer. Many species of crustaceans and molluscs use the night hours to feed – as do their predators. Although visibility under the water is obviously restricted by the darkness, night clarity is often extremely good. Heightened sensations and torchlit panoramas add to the frisson as fish, plants and coral are showcased by the beam. Dive lights restore the natural colour not visible at depth without artificial lighting – crimsons, yellows and oranges are especially dazzling against the darkened background of nightfall, appearing more intense. Night dives are seldom totally dark; the amount of light underwater can be surprising, with reflected sunlight and shadow from the moon and stars. Strobe-illuminated marker buoys and chemical light sticks add to the glow. To experience Valencian waters at their most unique, allow your eyes to become accustomed to the gloom and permit your senses to sharpen.

More than 112 km (70 miles) of coastline offer countless night dive sites with the biggest cluster around 50 minutes from Alicante, close to Calpe. Divers are spoilt for choice by the first class dives all around the Peñon de Ifach and out to Javea and Benidorm. Choose from depths of 5 to 35 m (16–115 ft) with lots of swim-throughs, tunnels, arches, caves and caverns that provide a wonderfully soothing ambience after dark. Octopi unravel in space-like slow motion, while eels scour for prey and groups of twinkling minute organisms add fairy dust to the sea. Exciting underwater perspectives enter the realms of magnified fishbowl vision, with blurred, misshapen, ghost-like silhouettes and fuzzy manifestations. But don't be afraid of what might be lurking beyond the beam of your dive light – just point it in an interesting looking area and take the time to closely examine it.

Night dives run by Les Basetes Dive Centre are priced at 49 euros per person, including full equipment and torch. Even in Spanish coastal waters, staying warm in the water at night remains a challenge. Sea temperatures don't drop as rapidly as air temperature when the sun sets, but divers prone to feeling the cold should wear additional thermal protection when diving Valencian waters at night.

GETTING THERE
Leave the A-7 motorway at the Benissa/Calpe junction to join the N332. Travel through Benissa and on until the exit junction for Calpe North. When you reach a junction with traffic lights turn left and travel through Calpe and straight across two roundabouts. At the next roundabout take the second exit and cross the next roundabout. Keep a look out for signs for Cala Les Basetes and Restaurant Timon. At the sign for Restaurant Timon turn right and go down the hill. There you will find Les Basetes Dive Centre.

CONTACTS
Les Basetes Dive Centre
Tel: +34 965 835 428
or +34 619 107 806
Fax: +34 965 835 428
www.buceo-costa-blanca.com

TurisValencia
Tel: +34 963 606 353
or +34 963 390 390
Fax: +34 963 606 430
Email: turisvalencia@turisvalencia.es
www.turisvalencia.es

Ghost-like, twinkling organisms can be seen in underwater gardens and tunnels.

FRANCE

TIME DIFFERENCE GMT +1

TELEPHONE CODE +33

CURRENCY Euro

LANGUAGE French

POPULATION 61.5 milion

SIZE OF COUNTRY 547,030 sq km
(213,342 sq miles)

CAPITAL Paris

WHEN TO GO Coastal regions sizzle in July and
August while the French Alps in the southeast of
the country attract skiers in their droves in winter
months. Spring and autumn are ideal seasons for
hiking, cycling, climbing and running.

TOURIST INFORMATION
Maison de la France (the French Tourist Board)
Tel: 09068 244 123
Email: info.uk@franceguide.com
www.franceguide.com

Whether it is the chic tree-lined Parisian boulevards, Burgundy's sun-speckled vineyards or the sun-kissed beaches of Cannes, France's charms are omnipresent, with much of the country and its culture immediately familiar to the first-time visitor. Almost the entire world has in some way been exposed to French influences, be it the wine, the coffee and the croissants or lavender fields and elegant châteaux. Covered two-thirds in mountains and hills, including the mighty Alps, Pyrenees and Vosges ranges, France is also famed for its sun-drenched Mediterranean coast: a sizzling summer beach area and popular wintering resort. For fans of more urban pleasures, Paris is one of the world's most beautiful cities and harbours some fine Baroque architecture and art galleries, set in a sedimentary basin on the banks of the River Seine.

CONTACTS
Bourgogne Tourisme
Tel: +33 380 280 280
Fax: +33 380 280 300
www.burgundy-tourism.com

Air Adventures
Tel: +33 380 90 74 23
www.airadventures.fr

Air Escargot
Tel: +33 385 87 12 30
www.air-escargot.com

Glide over vineyards, spires and lily-topped lakes on a kindly gust, to a gaseous roar.

HOT-AIR BALLOONING
BURGUNDY

Bourgogne is famed the world over for its sumptuous wines and grandiose history; facets that can be truly appreciated while in the basket of a hot-air balloon. Few vine-laden landscapes are quite as stunning as those of the aged Burgundian terrain, an enjoyable prospect for any balloonist keen to explore the country where manned aviation began. Hot-air ballooning itself was invented by two brothers living to the south of Burgundy. Joseph and Jacques Montgolfier developed their first hot-air balloon in 1783, flying just over 2 km (1 mile) at a height of just 2 m (6.5 ft). Today, balloonists attain anything up to 1,200 m (3,936 ft), travelling with burners blasting at a racy 16 kph (10 mph). Apart from a gassy roar every 20 seconds, hot-air ballooning is delightfully peaceful: a timeless, trance-like journey punctuated by thrills.

Getting off the ground requires a pilot to connect propane tanks to the burners. Once the valve is switched on, a flame jettisons into the envelope as it slowly inflates. Ropes untied, a bumpy take-off preludes a rise skywards. At night, this display is especially spectacular, particularly when a multi-balloon launch takes to the skies.

Those fortunate enough to be airborne during the wine harvest will enjoy unrivalled views of world-class vineyards in the full throws of reaping.

Burgundy's ballooning conditions are considered France's finest, with dry weather and light winds aiding control. Although a skilled pilot can influence the height of a hot-air balloon within centimetres, balloons rely on wind for direction. Courses can be altered by changing height, but the balloon will only go where the winds take it. This erratic casting of your fate to the wind is part of the appeal of ballooning. Few travel plans are as fickle as not knowing where you are going, what you'll find and how long it will take. Balloon travel provides the ultimate in joyously haphazard journeying, propelled by kindly gusts and a frisky breeze – all for 180 to 230 euros per person. Drift across the Côte D'Or from Santenay over Chassagne-Montrachet, Pommard, Beaune, Aloxe Corton and Premeaux, across medieval châteaux and ancient market towns. After a couple of hours sightseeing Burgundy, you'll skim across the Canal de Bourgogne and some lily-topped reservoirs before landing with a jolt in a farmer's field.

016

GETTING THERE
Blienschwiller (about 39 km/24 miles
from Strasbourg Airport) is a 45
minute transfer by taxi or hire car.

CONTACTS
Régional du Tourism d'Alsace
Tel: +33 388 25 01 66
Email: crt@tourisme-alsace.com
www.tourisme-alsace.com

Alsace Route des Vins
www.alsace-route-des-vins.com

*Skirt the Vosges Mountains
on the Wine Route's 170 km
(105 mile) trail.*

CYCLING STRASBOURG

The scenery may be postcard-picturesque, but don't let the genteel charm of the Route des Vins deceive you – discovering Alsace on two wheels can be a slog. Top-notch athletes with a fervent enthusiasm for the saddle will find the gentle, sloping stretches a breeze, but in the unrelenting searing summer heat, the route's shadeless climbs are a gruelling test of endurance. Thankfully, a scattering of rustic stone water fountains offer panting cyclists frequent, much-needed irrigation. And if you need more encouragement, few things are as thrilling as free-wheeling downhill at speed just a stone's throw from Germany and the Rhine, past 119 wine-growing, half-timbered villages in a rainbow of bubble-gum hues.

Although it's possible to cycle from Strasbourg itself, the city's traffic-heavy streets and suburbs are worth giving a miss. Instead head to the pretty stone villages around handsome Blienschwiller about 39 km (24 miles) to the northwest. The entire Wine Route stretches some 170 km (105 miles) from Gimbrett in the north to Leimbach in the south, a stretch do-able in a long weekend. A shorter burst from Blienschwiller to Riqewihr is a 60 km (37 mile) round trip – hardly the Tour de France, admittedly, yet almost all of it congestion-free. Yet with the blue-green Vosges Mountains and the crags of the Black Forest as

distractions – not to mention 7,000 winegrowers and 14,500 ha (35,815 acres) of vines – a more intense, cherry-picked Route des Vins snapshot makes excellent use of time for those up against the clock.

More than 8 million visitors make the pilgrimage to the Wine Route each year, not all of them by bike. Those that do, however, will experience some of France's most stunning countryside along with plenty of challenges to conquer. Most tour companies deliver bikes to your door, spokes and sprockets checked and tyres fully pumped. Then, simply unfurl a map to gauge the physical demands ahead: the spaghetti riddle of wiggly lines is testament to an upcoming series of hills. An initial easy stretch through Dambach-la-Ville, Dieffenthal, Scherwiller, Kintzheim and Chatenoise eases cyclists into the saddle, but is merely a light appetizer for a meatier entrée. Yellow-green vines and red-roofed cottages form a checkerboard landscape dotted with Gothic spires and turrets. Forests, ramparts and ancient ruins lie looped by meadows of sweet-smelling wildflowers. It is impossible not to become lost in the rush of scenery as the miles whizz by, such is the heady freedom of Alsace's vine-hemmed open roads. Rorschwihr, a small hamlet, lays down the first gauntlet. It's a skyward climb, prompting a gripping of handlebars, lowering of head and gritting of teeth as the pedals are pounded with vigour. In summer, a field of beaming, weathered farm workers are prone to imparting words of advice on the quirks of the road ahead.

Freewheeling through Kintzheim and Orschwiller and out towards Saint-Hippolyte allows a chance for the adrenaline to surge as the speedometer hits the max. Towards Rorschwhir the road widens and becomes busier as farm trucks and tractors chug and billow past, followed by a stream of slow moving cars. One hilly mile leads to another, yet the constant visual stimulation of the magnificent Wine Route's Gallic-Germanic vine-clad contours helps dull the pain of tiring limbs. Another source of motivation is the super-fit professional road racing cyclists who favour the route, whooshing effortlessly by at bullet-train speed, legs waxed and oiled. Competitive types will find that just the sight of such an über-human species can trigger a surge in natural power, sparking an energetic out-of-the-saddle sprint in pursuit.

From Rorschwihr a leaf-shrouded water pump dispenses an ice cold, gin-clear dousing where the route edges out towards Bergheim. The barrel-fronted Gilbert Dontenville winery signifies that Ribeauville is just a few miles away, along an immaculate tarmac carpet. Only the seriously virtuous will be able to resist the lure of slithers of scrumptious tarte flambé served at the roadside. Negotiating Ribeauville isn't half as troublesome as it looks on the map – simply skirt the outskirts, loop a couple of mini roundabouts and follow the road to Riquewhihr. Free again from the urban mêlée, the route becomes distinctly bucolic, with a light scattering of simple farm buildings on rounded yellow meadows. The long climb to Hunawihr and Riquewihr weaves past the bougainvillea-filled barrels and swaying wrought iron signs temptingly shaped like wine bottles. Stamina and staying power are essential for this final leg, so be sure to have a croissant stashed in a pannier somewhere to help muster much-needed reserves. The ornate archways and fairytale world of Riquewihr provide a strangely magical finale, complete with castles, jutting Rapunzel-style towers and Cinderella spires. A mammoth novelty wineglass (well, we are on the Route des Vins) provides a good place to tether bikes. Seek out a crisp sparking crément at the Au Cep de Vigne to toast tired joints to the sweet-smelling aroma of cinnamon biscuits and strains of Bavarian oom-pah classics.

Strasbourg's city streets can be a starting point.

017 HIKING AVIGNON

GETTING THERE
Most reach the Dentelles de Montmiraille area by car on the A7 (Lyon–Marseille) – both towns have airports.

CONTACTS
Gigondas-les-Dentelles-de-Montmiraille Tourist Office
Tel: +33 4 9065 8546
Email: tourisme.gigondas@hotmail.fr
www.gigondas-dm.fr

Overhangs and spiny pinnacles: typical limestone terrain.

Set smack-dab in the heart of Provence's finest wine region, the Dentelles de Montmiraille (meaning 'admirable mountain') is a climber's paradise woven with well-worn trails. Only the most hard to please hikers can fail to be roused by over 650 limestone climbing routes neatly divided by separate ridges that split the short, tough climbs from moderate multi-pitches. The Chain du Clapis, Chain du Grand Travers, Chain de Gigondas, Chain du Clapis and Roche St Christof are all within a close proximity of each other, comprising striking rock formations etched by time and sculpted by Mother Nature. Rising to over 700 m (2,296 ft) with aromatic plants, shrubs, oaks and pines nestled at its base, the Dentelles de Montimiraille's raw, jagged edges are softened by the curvilinear vine carpet of the Côte du Rhone. Waymarked paths reach out tentacle-style through forests to the village settlements of Gigondas and Beaumes-de-Venise, and steep slabs climb up to demanding overhangs and pinnacles, with the north side popular in summer and the south side ideal from spring until winter.

Choosing a hiking trail is almost impossible, given the sheer breadth of choice, but the long loop between Vaison-la-Romaine and Beaumes-de-Venise offers a first-rate stomp of about 60 km (37 miles). Pick up a IGN 'blue' map (number 3040 ET) from the tourist board offices in either Gigondas or Beaumes-de-Venise. The route is known as both the GR de Pays and the Tour des Dentelles de Montmiraille and is clearly marked, well maintained and most often walked in a counter-clockwise loop. Set off from a trail mouth south of the centre of Vaison-la-Romaine (about 500 m/1,640 ft southwest of the 'table d'orientation') and follow it for 5 km (3 miles) to the west along the edge of the hills, south of the river valley. Pick up the GR4 from the northwest and follow it for 5 km (3 miles) to Séguret, where from the southern edge of the village the 10 km (6 mile) trail leads east of Sablet to the Pas de l'Aigle before taking a sharp southwest turn towards Gigondas. Then in a dramatic zigzag, the path stretches east for 8 km (5 miles) or so in an arc through Beaumes-de-Venise and out to vineyards before heading back to low hills and to Le Barroux past the Sainte-Madeleine Monastery. About 2 km (1.2 miles) north, the path loops to the north for 3 km (2 miles) onto Crestet before turning west for its final leg northwest for 14 km (8.7 miles) to Vaison-la-Romaine.

CONTACTS
Cannes Jet Location
Base Nautique
110 bd du Midi
06150 Cannes La Bocca
Tel: +33 6 2333 9898
Email: contact@cannesjet
location.com
www.cannesjetlocation.com

Blast off full throttle in the bath-warm waters of France's swankiest bay.

JET SKIING CANNES

As the world-famous venue of one of the glitziest film festivals on Earth, Cannes doesn't necessarily spring to mind as a place to chill out on the water in your scruffs. A city synonymous with tuxedo-wearing Hollywood stars and ball-gowned cinematic goddesses, Cannes conjures up visions of A-list glamour and champagne soirées. Yet several miles of beautiful white sandy beaches beg barefoot exploration, lapped by glassy waters that offer some of the finest seaside adventures in France. More than 300 days of sunshine mean mild winters (12–19°C/54–66°F) and warm, breezy summer highs (with an average of 27°C/81°F). An endless supply of boats offer plenty of on-the-water opportunities, from fishing to island hops, while Cannes' ample supply of jet ski schools provides the freedom to explore the warm shoreline waters with the Mediterranean wind in your hair.

Jet skis ('scooters de mer') – or personal watercraft (PWC) to give them their proper name – operate from almost every major beach-front hotel in the Cannes area. Many offer instruction for beginners while some simply hire out by the half-hour, hour and half-day. Others run schools for proper certification and provide tandem jet ski tours. However, all provide a basic safety briefing that covers capsizing and righting, speed control, steering and identifying buoys and markers. Providing riders with a wetsuit or drysuit as applicable, buoyancy aid, goggles, emergency whistle and kill cord (plus spare) is generally standard, but you'll need to pack your own sunblock and foot protection (sea shoes are best).

Wherever you look there's a booking desk, tour agent or flyer in Cannes, so jet ski options are easy to seek out. Regular on-the-water events in summer showcase acrobatic jet ski high jinks, wowing shore-side onlookers with big air, hood tricks and high-tech 360 shenanigans much like those achievable on a BMX. Some of the models available for hire in Cannes are equipped with a handlebar-mounted GPS systems that log upwind or downwind VMG (velocity made good). Others have been calibrated for speedier upright handling, although speed limits mean opening the throttle and throwing the jet ski through a series of full-blast rev spins can only happen a safe distance from shore. Budget for around 80 euros for 1–2 people per half-hour ,or 130 euros per hour – deals are often available for half-day bookings during off-peak times. Online reservations with key operators, such as Cannes Jet Location, are advisable from 1 May to 30 September.

CONTACTS
Circuit des Remparts
Tel: +33 545 949 567
Fax: +33 545 949 566
Email: circuit-des-remparts@
orange.fr
www.circuit-des-remparts.com

Charente Tourist Board
Tel: +33 545 697 909
Fax: +33 545 694 860
Email: info@lacharente.com
www.visitcharente.com

*Two-wheeling against a vintage
backdrop of historic ramparts
and medieval spires.*

CYCLE RACING ANGOULÊME

Draw a line around the route of the Circuit des Remparts in the historic walled city of Angoulême and it forms an arrow-shaped lightning burst, linking the Cathedral St Pierre to the turn at Jerome Tharaud. This world-renowned classic car street race takes place on the third weekend in September each year, on a circuit unchanged in layout since Angoulême first hosted the event in 1939. Located about 45 minutes from Cognac, in the heart of the Charente district, Angoulême's ancient core – the Cité des Valois – is encircled by imposing ramparts and a riddle of climbing, narrow roads. On race day, amidst a flurry of brightly coloured flags and bunting, Angoulême's historic quarter closes off to form a very demanding street circuit. Highly polished classic cars gleam in anticipation at the start line, from the Bugatti, Riley and MG racers of the pre-war category to post-war Porsche 911s and TVRs. Angoulême's fearsome combination of hairpin bends and lightning-fast straights require driving precision on a spine-tingling course, lined by spectators and grand medieval buildings that provide a spectacular throwback to bygone years. Handsome solid stone walls do much to enhance the drama as the blood-pumping roar of resonating vintage exhausts hails the arrival of one of the most perilous races on the planet.

With a per-lap distance of 1.3 km (0.8 miles), the right-angle bends and tight twists and turns provide a decent competitive cycle sprint route. Guided by the ramparts, the infield section of the city maps out as a convenient fast-paced dash. Almost two-thirds of the route runs atop the city to offer striking views of the scenery beyond, while the statuesque cathedral provides an imposing start and finish line. Cyclists keen to race or time-trial should set off early to avoid rush-hour traffic, allowing each rider to swing wide on an eye-popping hairpin bend. The straight run to Jerome Tharaud begs a pedal-pounding mega push, before a death-defying turn on the homeward stretch. A challenging series of frightening crooks scale the ramparts on a gradient. Then it's on to the final strip to the finish line at a tearing pace. Grass-banked verges planted with vegetation add a touch of peaceful calm to a frenetic charge. In the Circuit des Remparts, lap speeds topped 70 kph (43 mph) in the feistiest races of yesteryear. Angoulême tradition dictates a winner's lap of honour is mandatory, and tourists are urged to follow suit, even on two wheels.

HANG GLIDING CAUTINE

The undulating, rolling, wild terrain of the Central Massif is renowned for its soaring birds of prey and is home to large number of swooping red kites. Using wind power and thermal lift to remain airborne for long periods, these majestic fork-tailed birds have perfected the art of harnessing this natural phenomenon to maximum effect, a trick that hang gliders have also perfected. As the ground heats up from the sun, hot air on the surface begins to rise, creating the perfect conditions for man and bird alike. The Central Massif is fanned by soft, steady breezes with sponge-like, forgiving meadows ideal for crash landings and false starts. Forests and mountains edge the scenic valley of the Dordogne, a bucolic terrain crisscrossed by winding roads and sparkling lakes. At between 500 and 980 m (1,640–3,214 ft), the Plateau de Millevaches looks across rounded hillocks and grazing land. The name doesn't mean, as you might suppose, 'the plateau of a thousand cows', but is derived from the world *melo* ('high place') and *vacua* ('empty' or 'abandoned'). The Plateau de Millevaches sits on the source of the River Vézère and attracts hang gliders in their droves. Somehow it seems only fitting to fly like an eagle in the company of gently soaring red kites, with man and avian sharing a bird's eye view.

First-timers gain their wings after some basic training on a 300 m (984 ft) steel wire bana-bana slide. Next it is time for lift-off, flying in tandem with a qualified instructor before moving on to the Pente Ecole Delta, a miniature flying area. Here the rudiments of piloting are covered, from taking off and landing to turning and keeping course. Then you'll enjoy a solo flight, guided by two instructors who spot alongside as you swoop along the slopes. Full contact is maintained with ground staff via VHF radio and seasoned pilots (H3+) can opt for more challenging slots. A late afternoon gently buoyant lift offers gliders extended flight until sunset and beyond. Chateau Adventures in Cautine, 30 minutes from the Plateau de Millevaches, offer a three day hang gliding package (either self-catering or all-inclusive) from 142 euros per person. Solo flights cost as little as 20 euros. Even 'wuffos' (non-gliders) enjoy the plateau's spectacle – composite-framed fabric wing gliders can reach speeds of 70–200 kph (43–124 mph) over the Central Massif, while the red kites circle tirelessly for hours with their 2 m (6.5 ft) wingspan.

CONTACTS
Chateau Adventures
UK tel: +44 1 872 262 985
France tel: +33 555 280 192
Email: info@chateau-adventure.com
www.chateau-adventure.com

Plateau de Millevaches
www.plateau-de-millevaches.fr

Tourisme de Millevaches
www.millevaches.net

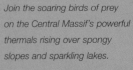

Join the soaring birds of prey on the Central Massif's powerful thermals rising over spongy slopes and sparkling lakes.

TRAIL RUNNING
BORDEAUX

CONTACTS
Bordeaux Tourism
Email: otb@bordeaux-tourisme.com
www.bordeaux-tourisme.com

Bordeaux's wine producers would no doubt shudder at the prospect of the region's vineyards having any use other than spawning the finest vintages on the planet. Yet the vine-flanked trails that swathe the Bordeaux countryside offer some of the most scenic jogging routes as well as world-class wine. Lush, green terraces of saluting vines in fine wine-growing terroir offer jaw-dropping views of handsome, wooden-shuttered châteaux that are home to vintage-stacked cellars. Towns steeped in aged wine growing traditions boast the cobblestone charm of a bygone era, hemmed by esteemed appellations of world repute. On a map that reads like a five star wine menu blessed with the most famous Bordeaux vineyards, the jogging trails of the region provide an exhilarating way to delve into the region's culture. From France's oldest wine town, St Emilion, across the more rugged trails of the Medoc to the region's northwest, enjoy a route framed on the east by the estuary of the Gironde and on the west by the Atlantic Ocean, wrapped in a protective forest.

Sure-footed sand and gravel paths rise and fall with the contours of the vines, stretching across the regional appellations of Medoc and Haut Medoc, Saint Estèphe, Pauillac, Saint Julien, Listrac, Moulis and Margaux. Bordeaux's most important body of water, the Gironde Estuary, opens onto the Atlantic Ocean, after stretching over 80 km (50 miles) from the convergence of the Garonne River and the Dordogne River near Bourg. Jogging – or more accurately, trail running – along the public access bridle paths, you will crisscross some of France's most magnificent hiking country. Most of it is along single track trails, often inaccessible by road except at the trail heads. Almost all traverse varying terrain with stretches that may require hiking or scrambling. For this reason you should opt for a sturdier pair of running shoes, with stiffer, cushioned soles for added protection. You'll need more support than a

pure fell shoe can offer, so look for a lacing system that allows a close, wrap-around fit, as uneven ground requires plenty of grip. Urban joggers used to super-smooth asphalt should be prepared for the thrill of rugged inclines and muddy descents.

A particularly nice 17 km (10.5 mile) morning run leads from the St Seurin de Cadourne, a pretty wine village where Hollywood film star, French-born Gerard Depardieu, owns 2 ha (5 acres) of vines that produce a particularly spicy red with a blackcurrant nose softened by oak. Head off from the village through vineyard paths to the marshy plains that lead to Saint Estèphe, where rolling fields of grapes stretch for 12 km (7 miles) along the banks of the sleepy Garonne. Carry on along the vineyard path before crossing another wetland expanse to arrive at the home of

three of Bordeaux's first growths, Pauillac. As you catch your breath, enjoy stunning views of the resplendent Château Lafite-Rothschild, set on a backdrop of small hills. Gravel-rich soils with a limestone base provide a softer, aromatic flavour to the wine produced here, and also ensure that the vineyard trails are robust under foot – a real boon for runners braving the wet. To add an extra circuit at around 15 km (9 miles), continue out to the charming hamlet of Pouyalet. Then journey along the vineyard-edged paths to the châteaux of La Tour-Pibran and Pibran. A quick detour allows a visit to picture-postcard Artigues, home of the Château Plantey. Continue on towards Châteaux Lynch-Moussas, Batailley and Haut Batailley to reach picturesque Daubos before passing the legendary Château Latour. Rejoin the banks of the Garonne to wind back to Pauillac along bird-filled, vine-rich paths.

Another beautiful wine trail leads from the St Emilion, France's oldest wine town, snaking 12 km (7 miles) on a gentle route. A spider's web of vineyard paths extend from the UNESCO-status medieval town centre, providing a circuit that encompasses châteaux, wine producers and historic sites – the tourist board will point you in the right direction, or look out for the signs.

For a longer, harder blood-rush, try the 23 km (14 mile) run from the hamlet of Grand Poujeaux, passing the Château Chasse Pleen before joining the vineyards towards the Château Maucaillou and the forest to the Château Lafon. A narrow country road connects to the small town of Listrac and the 13th century church that marks Médoc loftiest point. Follow the signs out towards Moulis en Médoc, crossing through the vineyards of Château Lestage and Château Clarcke, before passing the fortified 12th century church. Enjoy the peaceful ambience of the hamlet of Le Petit Poujeaux before passing an old watermill, taking the prone-to-mud forest trail to arrive at the storied Château Citran. Continue towards Tayac and on to the village of Soussans to reach the epicentre of the Margaux vineyard, where Château Lascombes provides a grand and fitting finale for a challenging few hours cross-country on Bordeaux's vine-fringed mixed terrain.

Criss-cross leafy trails through saluting vines, up muddy inclines and down rugged descents.

GETTING THERE
Troyes is an easy 1.5 hour train ride from Paris's Gare de l'est or a 3–5 hour drive from Calais. From there it's about a half hour's drive to the southwestern Côte des Bar area.

CONTACTS
Aube en Champagne Tourist Board
Tel: +33 325 425 000
Fax: 33 325 425 088
Email: bonjour@aube-champagne.com
www.aube-champagne.co.uk

Cobbled streets and sunflower fields in 'Champagne Country'.

ROAD TRIP REIMS

France's fabled Champagne Country makes a thoroughly great place to explore by road, as its 270 local producers are clustered within a beautiful 220 km (136 mile) Champagne Route. Clear signage helps even the most disorientated visitor navigate through a muddle of complex roads and backstreets, from the pretentious undertones of the Rue de Champagne to tiny, family-owned small producers. Wide, open roads hemmed by sunflower fields lead to vine-trimmed rustic villages far from Reims' maddening crowds. Hire a classic vintage open-top car, stick some sunglasses on and switch the radio to 101.4, a station evocatively named Champagne FM. Pull back the roof, settle into a steady cruise and head into Champagne's vine-clad hillsides as a finely-tuned engine gently purrs. Over 30 producers – big and small – offer tasting sessions (*degustation*) and cellar tours, so every passerby can get a bubble-filled kick from Champagne along the scenic Côte des Bars.

The Champagne Route winds along the south of the *department* between Bar-sur-Seine and Bar-sur-Aube and is split into four sections, so there is no need to tackle it all at once. Rich soil, lush forests and undulating pasture contain carpets of vines and ripening fruit. Gently rolling hills lie dotted with water towers and steeples, with sloping, vine-filled terraces that sweep down into cobbled village streets. Deep forests rim a succession of plunging steep-sided valleys on a picture-postcard route laced together by tractor-wide roads. Choose from the Montagne de Reims route (a 75 km/47 mile run that starts in Reims and leads south to Epernay); the 52 km (32 mile) Marne Valley (which starts in Epernay and heads west to Vincelles); the Côte des Blancs/Côteaux de Sézannais (a 100 km/62 mile or more route from Epernay to Villenauxe-la-Grande in the south); and the Côtes des Bar (a stretch between Troyes and Chaumont in the region's southeast corner). Unsurprisingly, after just a few miles, a melodic clinking from the boot marks each pothole, a fitting memento of the region's grand cru vineyards and fine pinot noir grapes.

Visitors that arrive in July will experience the region's fizz-fuelled Champagne Festival, held at the end of the month. Those that turn up unannounced in September should be prepared to roll their sleeves up to help out with the harvest – back-breaking work as all 33,500 ha (82,745 acres) are picked by hand.

INLINE SKATING LE MANS

If 24 hours in a pair of inline skates sounds like a breeze, then maybe it's time to enter the sport's most demanding endurance test. Organized by French inline specialists La Tribu Rollers, the Le Mans Inline Race is billed as the world's most gruelling skating relay (*estafete*), a world-class challenge held on the prestigious Bugatti Circuit across 24 taxing hours. Around 50 million people regularly inline skate worldwide, but only 5,000 feel up to tackling Le Mans. Teams of between two and ten participants are joined by an increasing number of tag-duos (a shared relay pairing), but racing solo is undoubtedly the ultimate test of staying power.

Registered entrants are provided with access to Le Mans's race village, with a nominal fee charged for a commemorative T-shirt, on-course refreshments and race insurance. Although participants aren't subject to a pre-race evaluation, each skater should be capable of skilful turning and braking. Although the course is basically flat, a 3.5 per cent 600 m (1,968 ft) uphill gradient is followed by a 2 per cent 1 km (0.6 mile) hurtling downhill stretch. Gathering speed at momentum can test even the most seasoned skater, as the most innocuous pebble on this snaking course can lead to a pile-up. Skaters should also be confident of racing in a pack, as the 9 m (30 ft) wide track is crammed with racers jostling for position. A succession of bends and lightening run-outs offer few opportunities for bailouts. High velocity propulsion at 40 kph (25 mph) prompts a surge of adrenaline around the body, especially on a floodlit route in the dead of night.

Prior to the race itself, Le Man's competitors complete a colourful 10 km (6 mile) warm-up parade downtown. Inline skates or quads are worn along with a protective helmet, knee pads, elbow pads, wrist protection and optional bum saver (tailbone padding) – a wise precaution on a racing circuit designed for thrills and spills. Pole position is decided by a 300 m (984 ft) sprint, with competitors dashing to the start line to strap on skates and start the race *tout de suite*. Careering down the Dunlop Bridge stretch along a spectacular, languid curve requires a squat position low to the ground in order to gain enough speed to roll onto the following hill. Bunched packs block the way along the early laps, with the circuit also prone to gusts of wind around the clock. Most teams choose to relay one full-pelt lap after another, with the race's top-flight skaters employing strategic rapid-paced swaps. After nightfall, temperatures plummet as Le Mans becomes a monotone blur of whirring, slicing blades. The winners chalk up almost 200 bullet-fast laps totalling more than 900 km (558 miles), before the finishing line and daylight beckon.

CONTACTS
Le Mans Tourist Office
Tel: +33 243 281 722
Fax: +33 243 281 214
Email: officedetourisme@ville-lemans.fr
www.lemanstourisme.com

Le Mans Inline Race
www.24rollers.com

Le Mans is a Mecca for speed-freaks, but only 5,000 dare race on skates.

024

SKIN DIVING MARSEILLE

CONTACTS
Marseille Tourism
Tel: +33 491 138 900
Fax: + 33 491 138 920
www.marseille-tourisme.com

Some of the most fearless, daredevil divers in the world cut their teeth in the sea around Europe's 'diving capital' Marseille, where the sparkling waters have played host to such legends as Jacques Cousteau. Boasting a lengthy diving tradition, the charming bays of the Provençal coast were where the aqualung was first tested. Dramatic rocky massifs are rich in a rainbow of fish and coloured soft corals, with gorgonias, anemones and sea fans prevalent. A fascinating array of marine life ranges from deep water grouper, barracuda, jack, moray and conger eels, to wrasse and octopus. Other underwater highlights include a handful of historic sunken wrecks in over 50 sites that skirt the cliffs.

Tidal currents and good weather directly impact the availability of dive sites, and in choppy waters many of the region's finest deep water caverns are impossible to locate. In and around Cousteau's favourite waters at Le Grand Congloué near Marseille, evidence of Roman artefacts remain, hidden in remote rock-embedded seabed stretches – a memento of a trading era of the past. In this area of pioneering underwater excavation, a seemingly never-ending list of operators offer all manner of dive options, from snorkelling in the shallows to night safaris. All will ask for a valid diving medical certificate or letter and proof of adequate dive insurance – a French legal requirement. Many membership-only dive schools also operate on a club basis off-season for a nominal one-off joining fee. Better still, some offer skin diving in lesser-known open waters to spear-fish for squid and octopus, just a stone's throw from central Marseille.

As the host of La Coupe des Calanques, Marseille is synonymous with free diving, an extreme discipline that relies on the power of breath-holding underwater. In its most extreme form (apnea), divers attempt to attain great depths, times or distances on a single breath without the direct assistance of underwater breathing apparatus. Using strength and skill to achieve a near-perfect balance of buoyancy control, pressure equalization techniques and movement – the disciplines of free diving – skin diving and apnea involve a variety of styles. The body alters to cope with the depth of the water by slowing the heart to about 20 per cent, diminishing the need for oxygen. Blood vessels and capillaries in the limbs constrict to force blood away from the extremities and around the vital organs, especially the brain. Blood plasma fills the lungs making them resistant to collapse – part of the mammalian diving reflex that allows peak-fitness free divers in the 'no limits' category to descend to great depths using a weighted sled, then use balloon systems to return to the surface at speed.

Diving courses run from Marseille explore these extreme disciplines and work on accustoming the muscles to work under anaerobic conditions, boosting tolerance to carbon dioxide and building up increasing distances. All free divers have an accompanying 'buddy' in the water, as safety plays a huge part within the sport. Shorter courses focus on conditioning work to prepare the body for sea conditions. Prime sites are situated in the imaginary triangle between La Pointe Rouge, the lighthouse of Planier Island and the Frioul islands. Be prepared: you'll need to be super fit, as skin diving takes snorkelling to the next level, offering a more free underwater propulsion that requires considerable swimming strength and agility, often used in scientific and military exploration to depths of more than 91 m (298 ft). Excellent visibility at up to 25 m (82 ft) offers world-class summer diving before mistral winds begin the make sea thick and lumpy. For the best diving conditions arrive June to September – but be sure to pre-book. Marseille is asserting itself as France's diving capital, and this is luring divers from all across the world. Those seeking master diver certification will find courses run by the French Federation for Underwater Sports and Studies, and the National Professional Divers' Institute, the only organization in France authorized to issue diplomas to diving instructors. Bring your own gear, or arrange to hire equipment locally – prices are keen and kit is widely available from reputable operators awarded the tourist board stamp.

Deep-water dives push the human body to the limit in Europe's 'Diving Capital'.

025

HIKING LOURDES

GETTING THERE
Tarbes-Lourdes-Pyrénées airport is 10 km (6 miles) from Lourdes. It has a direct exit on the RN 21.

CONTACTS
Office de Tourisme de Lourdes
Tel: +33 562 42 77 40
Email: info@lourdes-info
tourisme.com
www.lourdes-infotourisme.com

A divine forest landscape.

Lourdes was once a simple market town without much to shout about in the foothills of the Pyrenees. Then in 1858, the apparition of Our Lady of Lourdes to Bernadette Soubirous caused a stir in a strange-shaped shallow grotto. Ever since, the town has been a major focus for Christian pilgrimage, attracting six million devotees and spawning the second-greatest number of hotels in France. Today Lourdes remains synonymous with religious tourism across the globe, with Virgin Mary pendulum clocks, icons and deities sold by hawkers throughout the town. Cynics may think it trite, but Lourdes has a Disney-esque feeling of goodness – even well away from the miracle worship. A trio of summits – the Béout, the Petit Jer and the Grand Jer – rising up to 1,000 m (3,280 ft), shimmer with an ethereal haze. Not only do these cross-topped brows overlook the town and boast the finest panoramas of Lourdes, but they also offer a compact series of robust hikes along peaceful trails.

From the summit of the Pic du Jer (890 m/ 2,919 ft) follow a 17 km (10.5 mile) or four hour network of paths above the east side of the River Gave du Pau, before dropping down to the attractive spa town of Argelès-Gazost. Here, visit the tourist office for a map of more than 90 km (56 miles) of signposted local trails, from loose-stone ridge paths and forested tracks to blood-pumping uphill climbs. From the edge of Argelès-Gazost, take a tree-hemmed path up through a dense mixed deciduous forest to open grazing land above, complete with boggy marshes. Follow the unmade tracks and quiet roads that lead to the cobblestone streets of St Savin and on past the Chapelle de Piétat to take the steep trail to the former hermitage of Chapelle de Poueyaspé. A descent through beech trees leads to a well-prepared cycleway that stretches through a tunnel to the town of Pierrefitte – all in all a 14 km (8.7 mile), three hour trek. Almost all of the trails are way-marked with distinctive white/red/white GR (Grande Randonnée) signs, in accordance with the map. The route is clear and straightforward, although a compass (and the skill to use it) may help to pinpoint one or two debatable turns en route. Those keen to avoid the steady seven hour return hike will find that frequent buses connect Pierrefitte with Gare de Lourdes bus terminal; alternatively, you can grab a taxi for around 35 euros.

GETTING THERE
Toulouse and Pau are the closest airports to Papilio – both are accessible by train or are a 1 hour, 45 minute drive by hire car. Biarritz and Carcassonne (about 2.5–3 hours' drive) can be reached by rail via Toulouse.

CONTACTS
360 Expeditions
Tel: 020 71 834 360
Email: info@360-expeditions.com
www.360-expeditions.com

Luchon Tourist Office
Tel: +33 561 792 121
Fax: +33 561 791 123
Email: luchon@luchon.com
www.luchon.com

ICE CLIMBING LUCHON

Ice climbing addicts rave about the soaring craggy Alpine peaks around Luchon, hailing them as some of the most challenging in western Europe. Ultra-tough ice-clad ascents require axes, crampons, helmets, mountaineering boots, thermal clothing and ice protection – not to mention brute strength, agility and stamina. Harnesses may also be required along with optional head lamps, karabiners, rappel devices, ski poles, altimeters and goggles. A bandana and baseball cap protects the skin from sunburn, while a fleece hat covers the ears. Keep fingers warm by wearing a pair of mountain mitts, but have a thin pair of gloves as well for dexterity. Stay cool and calm under pressure on ice-covered verticals without handholds by breathing deeply – and not looking down.

Ice climbers should have a good basic level of fitness, so if you're a little out of shape, prepare with some cardiovascular training for a few weeks in the run-up to the climb. Weight training will help improve the upper body, required to carry a pair of ice axes used to gain purchase on the route. These are usually leashed to the climber's wrists, to make it easier to maintain a grip on the axe for long periods of time. Axe attachments are common, such as an adze (a wide cutting surface)

and a hammer depending on the route and weather conditions. Independent adventure tour company 360 Expeditions runs a thrilling two day course across various locations in the Pyrenean Mountains. From a 'base camp' in the sleepy village of Montauban across the river from Bagneres-de-Luchon, the programme is aimed at people who aspire to climbing steeper snow and icy routes, led by Australian-born resident of the Pyrenees, Rolfe Oostra. As a member of the United International Mountain Leader Association (UIMLA), Oostra's CV is impressive, having led expeditions to Everest, Aconcagua, Kilimanjaro, Mount Kenya, the Sahara, the Amazon, Patagonia and Bhutan. He is also a fully qualified first-aider and a keen Alpinist who knows the Haute Pyrenees better than most. Key components of 360 Expeditions' ice climbing weekend skills course include crampon usage techniques, ice protection, rope management, rappelling and multi-pitch climbing techniques, hazard assessment (avalanche danger, rock and ice falls), survival skills and Leave No Trace ethics. Instructor–student ratios run at a maximum of 2:1, with courses from January to the end of March. Expect to pay 200 euros per day plus accommodation and flights, and to bring your own equipment.

Demanding Alpine peaks require strength, agility and stamina – and a head for heights.

027

PARKOUR PARIS

GETTING THERE

To reach Lisses, take a train from the Gare du Nord in central Paris to Evry Courcouronnes, then the 53 bus to the Dame Du Lac stop.

CONTACTS

Parkour Network
Email: contact@parkour.org.uk
www.parkour.org.uk

Paris Tourist Board
Tel: +33 892 68 3000
Email: info@parisinfo.com
www.parisinfo.com

David Belle, the acrobatic star of an awe-inspiring BBC TV ident, thrust 'le parkour' into the mainstream spotlight. As the acknowledged guru of the world's newest urban sport, Belle hopes it will make it into the Olympic schedule given that this part-extreme sport, part-gruelling meditative challenge encourages discipline, self-improvement and interdependence – admirable qualities in a hard-paced modern world. Wisps of eastern philosophy permeate the ethos of this obstacle-coursing phenomenon. Practitioners (known as traceurs and traceuses) come in all shapes, ages and sizes but share a common desire to run free, unencumbered and unhindered. Psychologists would say that Belle and his followers are expressing a basic human urge for freedom in an oppressive suburban environment. Most traceurs would simply admit to having a lot of fun, moving fast in the least energy-consuming way, to crisscross the city. The skill is to seek out the most efficient way to get from A to B using just the abilities of the body and an awareness of its limits. Over time, these movements become so adept that they recede into the subconscious to form an instinctive quasi-commando system of leaps, vaults, rolls and landings in order to avoid or surmount anything in your path. Customary hurdles are fences, walls, railings, stairwells, rubbish skips and rooftop chasms, in an exhilarating sport that is an urban, rather than a countrified, pursuit. In the James Bond film *Casino Royale*, a thrilling parkour chase forms the centrepiece of the opening sequence, with hair-raising jumps from the boom of one tower crane to another. Yet those who dismiss it as a madcap excuse for acrobatics, stunts or recklessness are doing parkour a serious disservice: safety is paramount in this test of mind and body in which mastering the metropolis is the goal.

As the birthplace of parkour (in the suburb of Lisses in the 1990s) the city of Paris remains a global focus point for traceurs from every corner of the planet. Free running meet-ups take place in several Parisian hotspots with local authority consent. Well-organized events include tuition for beginners in parkour's fluid combination of movements. Exploration starts with a full stretch and warm-up at the Dame du Lac monument in Lisses, before a series of body rolls and reduced-impact landings. Next it's a trio of energetic stairwell jumps, before a succession of propelling climbs and crawls using highly controlled movements to follow a pre-defined inner city route. Careful practice can soon perfect parkour's ultra-graceful cat jump (in which the exponent places two hands on an obstacle and then leaps between them) and tic-tac (a kind of push-off made mid-movement from a wall or other hurdle). Speed vaults, trash cans, turn vaults, under bars and monkey vaults are other tried and tested staples. More adventurous 'grunts' (parkour newbies) may also attempt to conquer some of the more complex movements, such as swanton bomb flips (full body spins) and wall runs (running vertically up a tall object) – both high-energy precision moves of gasp-inducing agility that epitomize fluid grace and ease. Parkour is a word that can't be found in the dictionary, but Google it and more than seven million results are testament to the reach of this adrenaline-pumped pastime. Video-sharing sites reveal new extreme flips, while dedicated clothing stores hail the latest in gravity-defying super-grip sneakers. More than 15,000 clips showcase a host of potential parkour paths in Paris, while dozens of glossaries surmise that the term derives from the French word *parcours*, meaning route.

The age-old adage 'practice makes perfect' could have been invented for parkour, as flawless movements only come with sharp, exacting precision. Parisian parkour aficionados ooze with the honed confidence born out of ardent training. They rock back onto one foot with bodies poised to snap into action, fingertips hooked onto a high-rise ledge atop the built-up backstreets of Lisses – their urban playground. Hand over hand they climb steel fences with dance-like fluidity before making breathtaking building-to-building leaps using footholds where none appear to exist. Tumbling rolls and crawls elude the boulders and barriers of the city, while elegant vaults are absorbed by the shadows of the metropolis – this is an urban pursuit you'll relish mastering.

A quasi-commando series of leaps, rolls, vaults and landings masters the metropolis.

CONTACTS
Lyon Tourist Board
Tel: +33 472 77 69 69
Fax: +33 478 42 04 32
Email: info@lyon-france.com
www.en.lyon-france.com

Ride the wave in Hawaii sur Rhône, for some of the most exhilarating urban kayaking on the planet.

FREESTYLE KAYAKING
LYON

To the French it is La Feysinne; to the rest of the world it is dubbed 'Hawaii sur Rhône' – a huge, perilous, crested wave that is mixed with chasms over a vast expanse. One of the most exciting urban freestyle kayaking venues on the planet, the River Rhône's natural standing wave attracts extreme paddlers from all around the world. Downstream tidal surges and the river's sheer girth and vast dimensions make it off-limits for the easily intimidated novice. Like specks in an unworldly mass of water, kayaks do battle with an unpredictable force, conscious that the shore – a distant shadow – is too far away to be easily reached. Only the foolhardy dare to paddle here alone, as flips can easily happen in an unexpected power swell. Difficult to control, tricky to understand and impossible to tame, Hawaii sur Rhône has claimed its rightful place in kayaking legend as host of the Lyon River Festival, a thrilling extreme sport challenge that attracts top-flight paddling champions in their droves.

The unreadable character of Lyon's stretch of the River Rhône is undoubtedly part of its mystique, although lower water levels from the end of August to late September mean dicey waters (eddies) on both sides of the wave. Higher water levels bring huge upstream surges that require considerable technical skill. At all water levels, a hole on the extreme river-right demands maximum caution – even schooners would want to avoid this deadly chasm, so kayaks should give it a very wide birth. Markers give a clue to water levels but only the open-mouthed, flushed faces of fellow paddlers can relay the speed of the Hawaii sur Rhône – expect a velocity that goes right off the scale.

The River Festival is open to both freestyle and 'big air' competitors (120 at the last count), with spectacular aerial moves that see paddlers fly over the water and ramp-propelled several metres into the reaches of the Rhône. Kayakers used to the wave serve up brilliant runs spiced up with donkey flips, big pan-ams and air blunts. Those less au fait with the quirks of the Hawaii sur Rhône just hang around looking dazed. Staged over a weekend in June, the festival also has a programme of rafting and canoeing. Yet it is downtown Lyon's incredible big two-channelled wave that takes centre show – be it long or steep, fluffy, glassy or foamy, it's so loud it positively roars.

BUNGEE JUMPING
NORMANDY

CONTACTS
AJ Hackett Bungy
Tel: +33 231 66 31 66
Fax: +33 231 66 31 67
Email: info@ajhackett.fr
www.ajhackett.fr

Normandy Tourism
Email: info@normandie-tourisme.fr
www.normandie-tourisme.fr

Bungee jumping is certainly not for the faint-hearted, but devotees say 'Why live on the edge, when it's more fun to leap off?' Hurtling towards the ground at speed from a great height attached to a rubber band may seem like the crazed act of a madman – but millions have done it and emerged unscathed. According to the Guinness Book of Records, the highest jump to date is 216 m (708 ft) – no small distance to dangle, upturned with your stomach in your mouth. A reassuring name in death-defying plummets is AJ Hackett, an operator that lends the quest a semblance of sensibility. The world's original bungee firm has been around since 1986, developing a stringent safety framework that is now practised worldwide.

France's AJ Hackett bungee site sits on a historic expanse of land in Normandy and uses part of the dilapidated Souleuvre viaduct built by legendary architect Gustav Eiffel in 1889. Although the railway bridge collapsed many years ago, the structure's robust, moss-covered, 61 m (200 ft) grey stone columns remain gloriously intact. Now connected to a high-tech suspension bridge, the viaduct provides access to a purpose-built jump deck; a statuesque construction high above broccoli-top woodlands and a patchwork of meadows. Would-be jumpers arrive at an upper level flush with the suspension bridge, where registration and safety presentations take place. Anyone in good health can bungee – well almost; weight does play a part. Mega-strong shock cord made from durable latex strands is checked and a harness fitted. Then it's a walk along the bridge, high above an emerald canopy, to the large, rectangular jumping deck. Choose from a standard jump (feet and thighs tethered, harness around the waist); an extreme jump (higher, faster and scarier); or a crazy jump (aboard a pogo stick or monocycle) in either solo or tandem options. Every jump is videoed for posterity – so even queasy jumpers are urged to raise a smile as they plunge.

As soon as a jumper leaps, the cord stretches to absorb the energy of the fall, becoming momentarily taut in resistance, pulling the person upwards as the cord snaps back. This is often the source of an adrenaline rush even greater than that experienced from the anticipation of jumping and the terror of the fall itself. The momentum and power in the cord will cause it to oscillate up and down until all the energy is spent, sending blood pumping to every extreme of the body. The après-jump retrieval team haul jelly-legged jumpers to a ground level recovery platform, as heart rates attempt to return to normal and stomachs settle.

Perfect plunging on an oscillating cord from a disused viaduct.

030 PARACHUTING PAU

GETTING THERE

Lascaveries is 12.5 km (8 miles) from Pau Pyrenees airport. The SNCF station in Pau offers direct services including Bordeaux–Paris, Toulouse–Vintimille and Geneva, Bayonne–Hendaye and Spain, together with access to the Aspe Valley through its service with Oloron-Sainte-Marie.

CONTACTS

Pau Parachutisme Passion
(Aérodrome Lasclaveries)
Tel: +33 559 04 85 89
Fax: +33 559 04 31 45
Email: contact@pau-parachutisme-passion.fr
www.pau-parachutisme-passion.fr

Pau Tourism Board
Tel: +33 (0)5 59 27 27 08
Fax: +33 (0)5 59 27 03 21
Email : omt@pau.fr
www.pau-pyrenees.com

Hold your breath, pull the rip-cord and prepare for a heart-stopping, awesome descent to land.

Few experiences can compare with the excitement of stepping out of an aeroplane while it is still several thousand metres in the air. First there's the eerily silent 60 second freefall that sees our body rush towards the ground. Then there's the moment the ripcord is pulled. The canopy catches air as the skydiver catches their breath. Next, a dizzying five minute glide back down to earth. At landfall, the blood is pumping and the heart racing as pointed trees, barbed-wire fences and brick buildings are safely cleared.

Pau's Lasclaveries skydiving centre has claimed its rightful place amongst the world's top-flight parachuting outfits. As one of France's most popular drop zones it is engulfed by meadows and offers the usual range of corporate team building events and charity fundraisers as well as tandem and solo drops. Around 75 per cent of skydives are tandem drops and Lasclaveries is no exception, flying with larger drogue parachutes to slow the freefall speed of two people to that of a single bodyweight. This lengthens the duration of a tandem dive so that it's not all over in a few seconds, and allows the videographer to capture the moment without a blur. Passenger and instructor (tandem-master) are strapped together for a tandem trip – essentially all the jump responsibilities fall squarely on the shoulders of the professional, with the rookie just tagging along for the ride.

All jumpers receive around an hour of ground prep that includes a safety briefing, such as basic aircraft exit techniques, free-fall tips and landing procedures and positions. At this point, you'll also need to sign a disclaimer, usually with your stomach in your mouth. Being togged out in a jumpsuit, helmet and goggles is part of the 235 euro fee, although the video is an extra 95 euros. After boarding the plane, a nail-biting 15 minute ascent to 4,000 m (13,120 ft) tends to send nerves into a spin. When it's time, the aircraft door is opened to a strong rush of wind and the true adrenaline rush begins. From a crouching position, the divers roll out of the aircraft for a thrilling 190 kph (118 mph) free-fall plummet. Yielding to the wild blue yonder brings with it a floating feeling as the parachute is deployed. An abrupt halt brings this light-as-a-feather dreamlike state to an end all too soon as straps tighten in an ungainly jerk and you are, quite literally, brought back down to earth with a bump.

ITALY

TIME DIFFERENCE GMT +1

TELEPHONE CODE +39

CURRENCY Euro

LANGUAGE Italian

POPULATION 58.1 million

SIZE OF COUNTRY 301,336 sq km
(117,521 sq miles)

CAPITAL Rome

WHEN TO GO Italy's temperate climate has
regional variations but summers are warm and
sunny throughout. Humidity stifles the interior
region in summer, while winter tends to be cold,
damp and foggy. The ski season runs between
December and April and the best time to walk in
the Alps is between June and September, when
coastal Italy's warm waters are at their peak.

TOURIST INFORMATION
Italian Tourist Board
Tel: 020 7408 1254
Fax: 020 7399 3567
Email: italy@italiantouristboard.co.uk
www.italiantouristboard.co.uk

Europe's stylish boot-shaped peninsula dips its toe into the
Mediterranean Sea with two large islands, lava-rich Sicily and
Sardinia – part of its territory, as are the independent nations of San
Marino and Vatican City. Italy is also home to 41 UNESCO World
Heritage Sites, more than any other country on the planet. To the
north, the Alps separate Italy from France, Switzerland, Austria and
Slovenia. To the east, the River Po flows into the Adriatic Sea, while
central Italy's diverse Tuscan landscape contains snow-capped
peaks, sloping hills, sandy beaches and offshore islands. Hilly, broad
grasslands lead to vineyards, olive groves and pine forests with
Puglia, the 'heel of the boot', wild, volcanic, isolated and marshy.
Rome, Italy's capital and largest city, boasts a stunning array of
temple ruins, ornate frescos and marble columns amidst noisy
traffic, tooting horns and pealing bells.

DRIVING BRESCIA

Enzo Ferrari described the Mille Miglia as 'the world's greatest road race' – and in the hearts and minds of Italian rally car aficionados, he was spot on. Few events reflect the sheer passion of cars like that of the Mille Miglia, an ardour that remains even 80 years after its inception. Mix this enthusiasm for fast engines with a zealous pursuit of adventure, excitement and discovery, and the result is an open-road endurance race that epitomizes the Gran Turismo buzz. On 26 March 1927 the first race began with around 75 starters – all Italian, and unlike modern-day rallying, the slower cars set off first. In the early days of the race, most drivers set off before midnight and crossed the finishing line after dusk, if at all. The winner completed the course in around 21 hours 5 minutes – a jaw-dropping time that sparked considerable awe.

The route, from Brescia (Lombardi) to Rome (Lazio) via Firenze (Toscana) and back again, followed in the footsteps of races such as Targo Florio and the Carrera Panamericana to bring Alfa Romeo, Ferrari, Maserati and Porsche worldwide fame. Meaning 'thousand miles', the Mille Miglia took place 24 times from 1927 to 1957 and featured a host of big name sport and touring cars. For the past 30 years or so the event has been run as a retrospective event, after the race was banned in 1957 following a fatal accident. From 1958 to 1961, the event resumed as a rally-like round trip at legal speeds with a few special stages driven at full speed, but this was also discontinued. Today, a showcase of flashy cars continues to draw millions of Italians out onto street corners, although the biggest cheers are reserved for the traditional pre-1957 models. This three day show-stopping event is billed as the Mille Miglia Storica, a parade that includes a 300 SLR from the 1950s and vintage Porsches dating back 40 years.

Several specialized tour companies offer individually created itineraries to recapture the high-octane Mille Miglia thrill. From personally driving the latest model Ferraris and travelling for approximately 1,000 km (620 miles) to accelerating through the steep, winding roads of Tuscany,

packages are tailored to those who are keen to experience their own pedal-to-the-metal adrenaline rush. Most follow the figure-eight shaped course of roughly 1,500 km (930 miles) of the legendary Mille Miglia rally to allow drivers to put their skills to the ultimate test. Choose from a Ferrari 599 GTB Fiorano, a Ferrari 430 Scuderia, a 430 Spider or a Ferrari 612 Scaglietti – expert instructors fully brief each driver on the peculiarities of each engine and give guidance on how to handle the Formula One paddle shift gears. Practice sessions prepare drivers for the power and might of their Ferrari before the route starts in earnest; a sensory at-the-wheel pleasure along an amazing succession of rolling hills and never-ending curves.

CONTACTS
Mille Miglia
Tel: +39 0105 761 799
Email: info@1000miglia.eu
www.1000miglia.eu

Power Service
Tel: +39 0573 33985
Fax: +39 0573 975987
Email: info@powerservicenoleggi.it
www.powerservicenoleggi.com

Classic Car Hire World
Tel: 0845 408 5960 (UK)
Tel: +39 329 292 1615 (Italy)
www.classiccarhireworld.com

High-octane thrills in classic style on the Mille Miglia route.

ROWING FLORENCE

CONTACTS
Canottieri Comunali Firenze
Tel: +39 55 6812151
Fax: +39 55 6812649
Email: info@canottiericomunali
firenze.it
www.canottiericomunalifirenze.it

Florence Tourist Board
Tel: +39 55 23320
Fax: +39 55 234 6286
www.firenzeturismo.it

Even on a rain-soaked, dreary day there'll be a lone oarsman in a single scull on the River Arno, propelling a boat with plough-like momentum across the silvery depths. However, a much more common scene is a flotilla-style swathe of quad sculls, double sculls, straight fours and straight pairs, slicing through the water in a synchronized sequence of strokes. The Arno has been inextricably linked with river boats since the old wooden crafts (*barchetti*) used by city merchants armed with long-reaching wooden sweep-oars in a bygone era. From its source on Mount Falterona the Arno follows a long winding course into Florence before fast-flowing towards Pisa and the sea. Today the River Arno's waters are at the epicentre of Italy's rowing scene, with the thriving riverbank club of the Società Canottieri Comunali Firenze (Florence Rowing Club) the hub.

On the merit of the views alone, it is well worth heading down to the waterside terrace to Florence's prestigious rowing club, as it looks out onto the magnificent Ponte Vecchio. Close by, the non-private Canottieri Comunali opened to all Florentines in the 1970s and offers 100 boats to 600 members aged 9 to 70-plus. The result is a mix of rowers from every fabric from Florentine society, from broad-shouldered Olympic athletes and people just out for a paddle to coxed crews pulling their oars through the water with explosive power at high speed. Some of the most popular rowing routes take in the long, arcaded Uffizi Gallery, one of the oldest and most famous art museums in the world, passing in front of the elevated Vasari Corridor and under the medieval Ponte Vecchio. After skimming the apse of the Church of Saint Jacopo, one can pass under the oft-rebuilt Renaissance-era bridge of Santa Trinita to the elegant grandeur of Palazzo Corsini. In Florence, a rower's seat is an enviable place to be.

Almost every tour operator and concierge will organise a 90 minute rowing session on the River Arno, either on a group or one-to-one basis. Private instruction comes courtesy of a coach from the Canottieri Comunali Firenze, a proud and stalwart bunch who instruct with megaphones in hand. Only skilled, powerful rowers can keep a boat on course in strong currents, and the River Arno is heavy with pull. Expect to pay around 80 euros per person, a price that includes lots of tips on how to get the most from your blades.

Slice through silvery waters admiring the Renaissance grandeur of centuries-old merchant river routes.

CONTACTS
Vesuvio National Park
Tel: +39 81 771 0911
Fax: +39 81 771 8215
Email: protocollo@parconazionale
delvesuvio.it
www.vesuviopark.it

Gnarled lava fields, steamy craters and lunar-like trails are no walk in the park.

HIKING NAPLES

Set around an inlet of the Tyrrhenian Sea, southern Italy's Bay of Naples curves seductively for about 32 km (20 miles). Providing a sharp contrast to the madcap ebullience of the city of Naples itself, the Bay area is a terrain at ease with quiet contemplation. Dotted with archaeological sites from Cape Miseno to Campanella Point, the landscape is ripe with historic drama, from poignant ruins and aged volcanic crusts to fumaroles and craters. Towering above it all, the notorious form of Mount Vesuvius looms large and foreboding, with a well-established footpath for visitors keen to get to know the most dangerous volcano in the world. Be warned, this is not a trek for a Sunday afternoon picnic: your quadriceps and gluteus maximus muscles will soon begin aching as your forehead beads with sweat. Winding up through steep-banked gnarled lava fields to a steam-shrouded crater, the first switchback is steep and the second even steeper. The crater suddenly presents itself at 1,281 m (4,202 ft) as a 500 m- (1,640 ft-) wide gaping chasm, dark and eerie and ringed with silver-grey ash.

According to volcanologists, Mount Vesuvius is likely to erupt again, hence the year-round close monitoring and seven day warning system. Quite apart from its most dramatic outburst in AD 79, Vesuvius has erupted many times – most recently in 1944, shortly after the arrival in Naples of the allied forces. Huge clouds of lava ash spewed out across Naples as two cities were razed to the ground by rivers of molten rock.

The gruelling climb to the summit of Vesuvius rewards visitors with truly priceless views across the Bay of Naples and beyond. Stuck for time? Then take the bus to the highest car park, just a half-hour walk from the crater (7.60 euros). Entrance to the park is 6.50 euros – buy a ticket from the Parco Nazionale de Vesuvio office, open 9am–5.30pm. Surrounding paths wind through lemon and olive groves around the Bay and are still used by mule chains – so are well maintained. Some of the finest views of the Bay of Naples are offered by the Pinto Storey (tel: +39 81 681 260, www.pintostorey.it) in the city – a quaint Art Nouveau hotel that also has excellent guiding contacts, including some dab-hand hikers for whom Vesuvius is merely a stroll in the park.

CONTACTS
Happy Rent
Tel: +39 6 4202 0675
Email: hri@happyrent.com
www.happyrent.com

For a list of Rome's scooter and
Vespa hire companies:
www.tassoni.it/guide/moto-bike-
rent.htm

Rome Tourism
Tel: +39 6 488991
www.romeinfo.com

*Rev up an impossibly
chic Vespa, Italy's
ultra-cool runabout.*

SCOOTER RIDING ROME

Noisy and impractical yet stylish and cool, few Italian modes of transport are as classically elegant as the Vespa. Thrust into the limelight by the 1950s cinematic hit *Roman Holiday*, in which the publicity poster featured an impossibly chic Audrey Hepburn riding side-saddle, the Vespa became a fast-selling brand across the globe. Yet the world's nippiest scooter was born out of humble desires in the wake of post-World War II Italy. A crippled road system necessitated an alternative to cars, so designer Enrico Piaggio set to work addressing Italy's urgent need for a modern and affordable mode of transportation for the masses. Simple, sturdy, economical and ingeniously designed to keep the clothes of the rider spotlessly clean, the Vespa had it all, including a three speed gear change and a top speed of 50 kph (30 mph).

Today, the Vespa continues to epitomize Italian chic; an easy-to-ride two-wheeler of timeless design that boasts legendary style status – and never more so than in Rome. Travelling by scooter allows the freedom to nip and weave along ancient alleyways normally off-limits to vehicles. Negotiating cobbled streets, traversing backstreets and joining heavy traffic on unfamiliar roads can be daunting, but automatic transmission and a push-button start

ensure that even the most nervous of drivers can get to grips with a Vespa. Whizz around Piazza Della Republica before nipping by the Piazza Santa Maria Maggiore to Via Merulana and heading to the Piazza San Giovanni for a cappuccino stop. Then on to Via Santissimi Quattro before speeding around the Colosseum ahead of a full throttle burst into the Parco Del Celio. At the Testaccio enjoy views of the Monte dei Cocci before scooting along Lungotevere Aventino to the Isola Tiberina for a gelato. Next, the Jewish Quarter, before zooming along the Via Arenula to Corso Vittorio Emanuele II and magnificent St Peter's Square. On the dot of noon, swerve to halt at the Passeggiata del Gianicolo to await the daily firing of the cannon. Then weave through the crowds along Via Garibaldi and Piazza Venezia to the palatial grandeur of the Via del Quirinale, where the prancing horses of the obelisk denote the journey's end.

Riders anxious about the Vespa's mechanical quirks should be reassured by a good reliability record. Speed bumps can be taken with confidence – just lift your rear end out of the saddle. So that just leaves one conundrum: where to find a pair of super-cool sunglasses that fit an open face helmet, the Vespa riders' only style dilemma.

MOTORCYCLING PISA

The Ducati family started tinkering about in a garage in the mid 1920s and in the 1960s broke all records to produce the fastest road bike on the planet. Ducati has since chalked up almost five decades and has designed dozens of super-bike models. Gone are the bicycle-like, low-displacement designs of Ducati's post-war era, as Italy's leading high performance motorbike maker continues to push the boundaries of speed and cutting-edge design. Capable, trusted and with a unique sense of aesthetics, Ducati has a clearly defined style that combines the guiding principles of expert handling with power, speed and dynamics – and looking good. On the wide, open roads of the Italian provinces, the smoothness and the power of a Ducati is evident with every confident road-holding on every twist and turn. Surprisingly light to handle yet with the power you'd expect from a dream-bike stable, the Ducati is alive with raw power and torque to provide journeying at an optimum level.

A number of Italian-based tour operators offer Ducati rental from around 175 euros per day plus a deposit of around 3,000 euros as bond. Generally riders need to be over 25 and possess a clean licence. Payments are taken in full by credit card with extra biker gear, such as helmets, boots, gloves and jackets, available for hire. Most offer maps of areas best suited to a Ducati that highlight non-surfaced, bending, narrow country lanes, immaculate motorways and every combination in between. The meaty 160 hp 1098 model is popular for touring as it copes well with varied terrain.

Tuscany is a great region for engine-powered two-wheel exploration, with its quiet roads and leafy lanes, offering the undulating vine-flanked slopes of its wine country and the crazed chaos of Pisa and its leaning tower. In the beautiful setting of the Era Valley, just 25 km (15.5 miles) from the city, age-old family-run wineries grow merlot, cabernet sauvignon, chardonnay, sauvignon blanc and trebbiano grapes in gently rolling formation. Wide, empty, asphalted stretches allow plenty of opportunities for some free-breathing revving with enough power at the top end to generate a serious rush. Yet a comfortable seat, good mirrors and easy low-speed handling make cruising along a breeze. Newcomers to Ducati will discover plenty of little quirks (such as the very un-Japanese style throttle-clutch-gear shifting sequence). They should also factor in extra time for 'bike chat' wherever they stop, as excited teens and grease monkeys alike are lured by a Ducati's magnetic pull.

GETTING THERE
Pisa's Galileo Galilei Airport is 10 minutes from the city centre by bus on the Linea ad Alta Mobilità (LAM) Rossa line. There is also a train.

CONTACTS
Ducati Tours
Tel: +39 340 7677364
Fax: +39 583 050718
Email: info@ducatitours.com
www.ducatitours.com

Pisa Tourist Board
Tel: +39 50 830253
Fax: +39 50 830243
Email: info@pisae.it
www.pisae.it

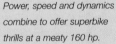

Power, speed and dynamics combine to offer superbike thrills at a meaty 160 hp.

036

HIKING GENOA

GETTING THERE

Cinque Terre is accessible by train (or car, although a first-rate train service makes this unnecessary). From the south take the train to La Spezia, where you change to a regional train that makes all the local stops in the Cinque Terre. From the north, take the train to Levanto (you may have to change at Genoa). Change at Levanto to a regional train that makes all the local stops. Visit www.fs-on-line.com for train information

CONTACTS

Cinque Terre
Tel: +39 187 760 000
Email: info@cinqueterreonline.com
www.cinqueterreonline.com

Genoa Tourist Board
Tel: +39 10 576 791
Fax: +39 10 581 408
Email: aptgenova@apt.genova.it

The Cinque Terre coastal paths, a zigzag of 100-year-old trails.

Just the name Seniero Azzuro ('Sky Blue Path') conjures up a heavenly image of a ribbon-like trail up amongst the clouds. In fact a knitted mesh of trails connects the five villages of the Cinque Terre ('five lands'), but the Seniero Azzuro is the most defined and serves as a core route for hikers who tend to filter off along lesser-known diversions along the way. Arrive in summer and the weather is sunny and hot from early morning, making first-light starts essential in order to avoid the stifling midday highs. Even so, this rugged coastal path is steep in parts and requires a brisk, steady pace. Don't be put off by a rather unpromising initial stretch of ugly paving – the Seniero Azzuro is a treat further on with truly incredible sea views. Flat, blue waters in sheltered coves become thrashing waves, breaking mightily over breakwaters on rocky headlands where pirates once ranged the coast.

In all, the 11 km (7 mile) Azzuro takes around five hours, offering a total elevation difference of 500 m (1,640 ft) between the highest and lowest points. Strung out along the Costa Ligure of Levante, the villages from south to north are

Riomaggiore, Manarola, Corniglia, Vernazza and Monterosso al Mare. You don't have to hike between all five villages in one go – the route is easily split into chunks. To make things easier for tourists, a Cinque Terre card has been introduced. Not only does this pave the way for access to all the services of the National Park of the Cinque Terre, but it also allows unlimited travel in second class on the trains between Levanto and La Spezia – a useful backup when legs are tired, bellies are empty or the weather takes a turn for the worse. Line stops serve each village, while ferries go regularly to La Spezia, Lerici, Portovenere and Sestri Levante. Although the pass stipulates '24 hours', it actually expires at midnight. Keep it safe – you may be asked to present it en route – and you'll also need to write your name it on and get it stamped. Part of the deal is a map of the walking paths (double format A4, with walking times and distances of the paths), a railway timetable and ferry schedule. Pick out the blue trail marked 'Seniero no. 2' – that's the rather clinical-sounding official name for the Seniero Azzuro.

The entire Cinque Terre zone is protected by

UNESCO, a landscape characterized by dramatic vine-cloaked slopes that tumble seawards amidst vertical cliffs and trickling creeks. Paths lead through Mediterranean bush squeezed between the sky and sea – hence the name the Sky Blue Path. The initial south-to-north Riomaggiore to Manarola stretch, a 20 minute shoreline path known as the Via dell'Amore (Path of Love) is the most uninspiring: tiled like a suburban garden, which is truly disconcerting for anyone keen to feel dirt under their boots. Don't worry, things improve significantly within half an hour: the trail from Manarola to Corniglia (1 hour, 15 minutes) is much more interesting underfoot with loose stones and small, aged boulders. An open stretch of pathway skirts just above sea level to hover atop pretty villages and a strip of beach hut-lined shingle.

A zigzagging flight of steps leads up to the town of Corniglia on a steep promontory, with two exclusive small beaches at its sides; a climbing stomp that provides a decent cardiovascular challenge up to a drinking-water fountain. A handful of schizophrenic signposts eventually point the way to Vernazza (1 hour, 30 minutes) on an ancient dry-stone walled trail packed with text-book beauty. Well-worn, hard-packed soil and battered stones wind past streams, olive groves and woodlands as calves and leg muscles get some serious exercise. A series of steep inclines traverse gorgeous valleys in a wriggle-shaped hiking endurance test that deposits the weary and sweat-soaked at a conveniently located family-run café. With thirst quenched, the shaded wood-shrouded descent to Vernazza is glorious – and very welcome. A harbour-side resting point offers pleasant nautical views, while Vernazza'a train connections link to local towns. Monterosso al Mare, the westernmost Cinque Terre settlement, is reached via the most tricky part of the Sentiero Azzuro, a two hour blood-pumping slog through vineyards that may make you wish you'd chosen to travel by locomotive means. This old maritime village is divided into two parts from San Cristoforo hill and the ancient core, protected by a jagged rock spur.

The warm-hued houses in the charming narrow streets and tiny squares of Vernazza, Manorolo, and Riomaggiore are blessed by an almost total absence of traffic. Stroll past a cliff-like face of shuttered windows and flower-filled balconies. Monterosso al Mare is a fitting final stop as it is a bastion of locally produced wine – the delicate dry white Cinque Terre, and the honey-sweet Sciacchetrà – two very good reasons not to walk the Seniero Azzuro north to south.

Warm-hued buildings and traffic-free streets make the Cinque Terre towns a relaxing stop en route.

ORIENTEERING PUGLIA

Tangled woods and boulder-strewn routes require precision use of a map and compass.

Puglia's lack of infrastructure may be an annoyance to car drivers keen to criss-cross the region on asphalt, but it makes the southeastern tip of the Italian peninsula an orienteering Shangri-La. Spanning over 19,357 sq km (7,549 sq miles) of broad plains and low-lying forested hills, Puglia's dry, dusty terrain is nourished by just a handful of torrential rivers at the mountainous tableland of the Gargano promontory. Elsewhere, rainwater permeates the limestone bedrock to form underground watercourses that bubble up in caves and potholes near the coast. What rain there is falls in the winter months, but this is a sprinkling of no more than 500 mm (19.5 in) per annum. With some 800 km (496 miles) of coastline stretching down the Adriatic into the Ionian Sea and the Gulf

of Taranto, all this adds up to the perfect orienteering destination. Sparsely populated hinterlands are dotted with *trulli*, the capped-roofed, cone-shaped stone dwellings so characteristic of the high grassy plateaux. As the 'heel' of the Italian boot, Puglia is an untamed jumble of wilderness and seashores, pockmarked with ruins and prehistoric sites – an area crying out to be explored.

Puglia's orienteering academy is situated in Castellaneta Marina in the Taranto province, on a large stretch of sandy coastline bordered by the cities of Taranto and Metaponto. Set amongst pine trees, the Orienteering Academy Catalano is at the forefront of Puglia's orienteering scene and the first permanent centre in the Mediterranean. It utilizes a 150 km (93 mile) spread of terrain across Bari, Lecce and Taranto and has an ambitious mapping plan for Puglia's raw, off the beaten track expanses. As the host of the prestigious three day Mediterranean Orienteering Championships in March each year, along with numerous camp events and a one day Grand Prix, the academy offers many excellent packages that include accommodation (at the nearby Villaggio de Catalano), breakfast and all entry fees (if applicable) as well as maps and guides. Many of its 'sport of the woods' events attract 500 athletes from 30 countries who, armed with maps and a compass, run the gamut of Puglia's mixed terrain. From remote ditch-flanked wooded trails and seaside paths, to the riddle of alleyways in Taranto's old city, the region is synonymous with the world's greatest 'Foot O' challenges – as an elite field of world champions will testify. Routes run from white (shorter, less demanding) to blue (more technically and physically testing). Runners need to be able to navigate with precision at speed to stand a chance of triumph, using specially marked maps at a scale of 1:15,000 drawn to the magnetic north.

CONTACTS
Venetian Tourist Board
Tel: +39 4152 98711
Fax: +39 4152 30399
Email: info@turismovenezia.it
www.turismovenezia.it

Chioggia Tourism
Email: info@chioggiatourism.it
www.chioggiatourism.it

*The salty waters of the vast
Lagoon are home to myriad
fish, seafood and sea birds.*

CYCLING VENICE

If reclining in a gondola in Venice while someone else does all the legwork just isn't your style, then the rewards of sightseeing the Venetian Lagoon on a bike may be the way to go. Away from one of the world's most urban conurbations, Venice's ecologically blessed crescent-shaped body of water begs to be explored. Set within the clasp-like grip of three grabs of land – Litorale Pellestrina, Litorale di Lido, and Litorale del Cavallino – the Laguna Véneta's 45 km (28 mile) expanse comprises weed-fringed, marshy, river-fed lowlands flushed by the saline waters of the Adriatic. Slow-moving tidal flows and mysterious currents wash past shifting sandbanks and deep basins in salt water pastures rich in crab, shrimp, mussels, limpets, octopus and squid. Nesting gulls, heron, spoonbills, swans, snipe and ducks hide amongst vegetation-cloaked shallows, and even mullet and sea bass thrive around the islands in the lagoon.

Protected by the Lidos of Venice and Pellestrina, the Venetian Lagoon's cycle paths hug these natural levées to allow bikes to work their way south. The route snakes along flat roads and involves some stretches by ferry to Chioggia, at the lagoon's southern tip, passing old sea walls and waters dotted with ramshackle fishermen's huts on stilts among mussel farms. The walls extend for miles in a robust piece of engineering completed in the dying days of the Venetian Republic. Chioggia is a miniature Venice filled with cobblestone streets, canals and a well-known fish market. Take the snaking loop to the Po delta and back to clock up about 54 km (33 miles) in total from the city centre, a scenic and exhilarating journey that's do-able in around six hours.

A specially equipped waterbus service links San Giuliano, the Venice Lido and Punta Sabbioni to the island of Sant' Erasmo, where gentle cycling allows for a meander through some spectacular flower-filled countryside. The waterbus has enough space for 60 bikes, so pre-booking and pre-paying is advisable at any of Venice's many Vela ticket offices. The service runs on weekends and public holidays only, with return tickets costing 9.30 euros, including passenger and bike. A room in one of Chioggia's decent handful of hotels along the seaside Sottomarina Lido provides a restful overnight stop.

039

CONTACTS
Parco Nazionale d'Abruzzo
Tel: +39 863 91131
Fax: +39 863 912132
Email: info@parcoabruzzo.it
www.parcoabruzzo.it/fauna.
schede.php

Tourism Abruzzo
Tel: +39 857 671
Fax +39 857 672 067
Email: turismo@profesnet.it
www.regione.abruzzo.it

Marsican bears roam free in the wild Parco Nazionale L'Aquila.

BEAR-SPOTTING L'AQUILA

It is hard to imagine that a flora-filled feral wonderland lies at the end of an hour's drive along the A24 autostrada from Rome. Yet just 75 km (47 miles) from the capital's fast-paced urgency, the 130 ha (321 acre) wilderness of the resplendent Parco Nazionale d'Abruzzo begs to be discovered. Spanning the L'Aquila, Frosinone and Isernia regions, this untroubled haven for wildlife is crossed by just a single paved road. Over 60 per cent of the park is covered in vast forests of beech, pine, fir, oak, yew, ash and maple that are home to some of Europe's most enthralling wildlife species. A centuries-old tradition still sees shepherds practice the custom of 'transhumance', moving swaths of sheep in autumn from chillier upper meadows to warmer pastures, and back in spring. Since 1923, this state-funded park in the northern part of southern Italy has played an essential role in the preservation of some of the most important species of Italian fauna, especially the Marsican brown bear. This critically endangered subspecies of brown bear is indigenous to the region. Total numbers in the park reach three-dozen at best, with the beech wood thickets at 800–1,700 m (2,624–5,576 ft) the bear's natural habitat. Moving out of this habitat in search of food to high altitude grasslands and lower altitude oak woods and orchards, the Marsican brown bear is a territorial species with a low reproductive rate.

Although classified as carnivorous, it has a wide food spectrum, comprising a large amount of vegetal components (mushrooms, fruit, plants, roots and vegetables) as well as honey, insects, eggs and mammals. An average male will weigh up to 200 kg (442 lbs) to reach a standing height of around 1.9 m (6.2 ft), with distinctive dark brown colouring that can lighten to mid-gold. Rounded ears and a squat tail are other characteristics of this reclusive species. Each occupies a wide territory of several-dozen square kilometres. Females typically deliver one or two cubs of around 400–500 g (16–20 oz) from December to January and the young are then dependent on the mother for around two to three years. Hibernation takes place in winter until the following spring, although this period isn't unbroken. On sunny, warm winter days, bears often wake to find food before resuming their hibernation. In perfect conditions, bears can live for up to 25 years.

Catching a glimpse of the Parco Nazionale d'Abruzzo's legendary endemic bear is far from easy, but not impossible. Several specialist tours offer hikes dedicated to this beloved beast of the central Apennines. Many others combine a bear-spotting trip with some delving into the region's fascinating array of birds and butterflies. Serious hikes offer genuine exposure to the wilds of Italy, with treks through tangled, bloom-filled alpine forests and lowland meadows abuzz with insect life. An abundance of age-old *tratturi* (trails) loop around mountains and wooded thickets where discovering recent bear activity, such as faeces, partially-eaten berries, scratches on tree trunks and unmistakable fresh prints, is an important first step to discovering the animal itself. Bears often skin the carcasses of dead animals and the remaining scrap of skin (the shepherds call it *straccio*, meaning 'rag') is a sure sign that a Marsican brown bear has been around. Trails lead up sloping peaks and cross numerous rivers, streams and creeks where waters bubble up from underground springs to form sparkling gullies. Two lake basins include Vivo Lake, a natural depression of tectonic origin that is part spring-fed and part filled by melting snow. Features of the upper slopes range from caves, crags, calcareous outcrops and dolomite rock, and picturesque waterfalls and water pools – the natural habitat for Abruzzi chamois, wolf, deer, wild boar, fox, mountain goat and Apennine lynx.

Today the Parco Nazionale d'Abruzzo has a recorded inventory of 60 species of mammals, 300 birds, and 40 reptiles and amphibians, as well as an abundance of insects and fish. Maps of the park help to highlight what is found where, with many trails clearly marked with numbers on the ground, and about 150 wildlife intineraries of varying length and difficulty.

Forest rangers hope to raise bear numbers to around a hundred by boosting the variety of plant species in the forests, to make sure that they have enough food year-round. More than 20 different species of fruit tree and bush have been planted in the 1,600 sq km (624 sq mile) area the Marsican bear roams around. Ironically for an endangered species, the Marsican is one of the most people-friendly bears in existence: a non-aggressive, placid animal renowned for its lazy good nature. However, they avoid human beings and are unsettled by invasive activities, so observation is undertaken at a respectful distance to minimize any disturbance. Soft footsteps, low voices and keen eyesight are essential, as are a good set of binoculars. Choose a quiet camera with a telephoto lens, and leave strong perfume and luminous yellow jackets at home.

Age-old trails loop around lakes and mountains and through wooded thickets.

WINDSURFING SARDINIA

CONTACTS
Windsurf Village (Baia dei Dephini)
Tel: +39 789 704 075
Fax: +39 789 704 066
Email: info@windsurfvillage.it
www.windsurfclub.it

Planet Windsurf (travel specialists)
Tel: +44 1273 298 811
Fax: +44 870 746 1267
Email: info@planetwindsurf.com
www.planetwindsurf.com

Sardinian Regional Tourist Board
Tel: +39 70 6067005
Fax: +39 70 6067255
Email: sardegnaturismo@regione.
sardegna.it
www.sardegnaturismo.it

Strong propelling gusts of up to force seven carry you across the bays.

Sardinia's sun-blessed 2,000 km (1,240 mile) coastline is fanned by winds from every direction, with gusty squalls characteristic of the island's northern stretch. Windsurfers across the world rave about Sardinia's exhilarating wind and wave conditions, with Porto Pollo (also known as Porto Puddu) Sardinia's windiest spot. Here, windswept waters are without a doubt the finest in the area, spawning a steady stream of windsurfing schools and hire outlets. Visiting surfers will find a range of equipment and rental paraphernalia that befits one of the premiere windsurfing destinations in Europe. Another lure is Porto Pollo's expansive white sandy beaches, where beach bums and surfer dudes enjoy a mellow, laid back vibe.

Two partially enclosed scenic bays are divided by the Isola dei Gabbiani (or 'gull island'), a sandy limb that forms a bulbous peninsula about the size of a large car park, attached to the mainland by a tiny land bridge. Choppy waves are common on the upwind side, with glass-like conditions on the downwind side of the jut. A vast camping ground provides a focal point for gathering windsurfers and is the epicentre of all the action, where tips are shared

and tales swapped over crackling camp fires. Four small windsurfing schools edge the promontory (private lessons cost around 50 euros an hour) with windsurfing boards for hire at around 20–25 euros for a two hour period (hire for up to seven days) and places that offer board storage. A cluster of cool hangouts are popular with a mixed-age beer-supping windsurf crew from every corner of the globe.

At the end of the sand-spit, the strongest propelling gales blast a trail towards the Magdalena Archipelago, with mast-and-a-half-tall crests fuelled by a funnel effect that carries wind at up to force seven across the bays. Wide swags of sand provide ample space for windsurfers to launch and relaunch unhindered. The result is a windblown seascape scattered with bright-coloured sails, gliding over glistening waters as crosswinds (mistral, poniente, tramontana and sirocco) battle it out 188 days per year. Choose from 4.5 m (15 ft) and 6.7 m (22 ft) sails, pack both wave and freestyle boards and prepare for squalls of up to 35 knots – perfect for trick-loving freestyle hotshots and slalom blasters, as there is only a slither of wind shadow by the shore.

CONTACTS
Via Ferrata Foundation
Email: 123@ferrata.org
www.viaferrata.org

Perilous scrambles and death-defying drops characterize the iron way's challenges.

VIA FERRATA VERONA

Ascending a via ferrata (or 'iron way') near Verona requires swapping a city of love for a place of conflict, yet there is something thrilling about leaving Verona – city of Romeo and Juliet – behind to head to the site of WWI trenches. For it is here that the fixed steel cables and metal ladders of via ferratas open up the most rugged trails of the Dolomite Mountains – those that only roped climbing parties would normally be able to climb. Robust railings and cast-iron bridges offer greater protection on a via ferrata's exposed, scenic, steep cliff edges, acting as safeguards from slips or falls and meaning that any trekker in decent shape can explore this dramatic terrain. With the soaring limestone peaks and spires bordering Austria to the north and Switzerland to the west, the first via ferratas were built in the Dolomites during the First World War, to aid mountain infantry manoeuvres during ferocious hostilities with the Austrians. Both sides tried to gain control of the peaks to site observation posts and field guns,and to help troops to move about at high altitude in very difficult conditions, permanent steel ropes and hawsers were fixed to rock faces and ladders were installed. Today, trenches, dugouts and other wartime relics can be found alongside many of Italy's sixty or so via ferratas. Hikes are graded according to how demanding they are: grade I is little more than an assisted walk, while grade V is an ultra-perilous scramble complete with death-defying plunges. Pick up a copy of *Via Ferratas of the Italian Dolomites*, by J Smith and G Fletcher (published by Cicerone) for an insiders' lowdown and lots of practical tips.

For any route other than the easiest via ferrata, the wearing of a self-belay kit is advisable. Tour operators will provide all the gear required, from climbing harnesses and tethers to karabiners and a helmet. A certified guide who has the full measure of the route is essential on the titanic peaks and crags of the Dolomites and their slithering trails. High-drama scrambles and climbs are part of the nailbiting theatre as, clipped onto the hawser, with a stretch of rope and a climbing harness, you find yourself clinging to a skinny rock ledge with a drop of several hundred metres beneath your feet. A good head for heights and some healthy respect is essential on these high mountain vertigo-inducing ascents and descents. Classic routes include the Via Possnecker (the first via ferrata to be constructed in the Dolomites in the early 1900s), the Via Pisciadu and the Via del Trincees ('the way of the trenches') – all simple to follow and jam-packed with adventure, not to mention jaw-dropping views.

FOUR WHEEL DRIVING
SICILY

CONTACTS
Parco Regionale dell'Etna
Tel: +39 95 914588
Fax: +39 95 914738
Email: ufficiostampa@parcoetna.it
www.parcoetna.ct.it

Sicilian Regional Tourist Board
www.regione.sicilia.it

In 2001, the local Sicilian population prayed for divine intervention as lava flowed down Mount Etna's slopes amidst spluttering ash and soaring smoke plumes. Since it first starting venting steam in 1500 BC, man has failed to tame Europe's largest volcano, spawning deep-rooted faith, superstition, myth and legend. Today brooding layers of rock-formed molten lava are testament to this 3,500 m (11,480 ft) peak's fire-spewing past. Ancient dark, basaltic crags extend outwards from Etna's summit craters. Sprouting shoots of green add colour to fertile craterous soils on older lava flows and mysterious fissures on the lower flanks of the volcano's slopes. Cone-shaped spurts and twisted spouts flank subsurface magma chambers while tangled grape vines dating back to ancient civilisations thrive in the nutrient-rich foothills.

Mount Etna (also known locally as Mongibeddu in Sicilian, and Mongibello in Italian) is the highest mountain in Italy south of the Alps, reaching triple the height of Mount Vesuvius. Despite being in an almost constant state of eruption, Mount Etna is deemed safe to explore, and is easily reached at 29 km (18 miles) from Catania. Several conical towers and ragged summits make up the large volcanic peak, with around 260 smaller craters towards the base. A vast 1,200 m (3,936 ft) gully (Valle del Bove) characterizes Etna's southeastern flank, a gaping cleft created around 3,500 years ago by the collapse of an ancient caldera. The slopes of Etna form three distinct zones. The lower zone, extending up to about 1,190 m (3,903 ft) is scattered with houses and planted with lemon trees, vineyards, olives, figs and almonds. A heavily wooded middle zone stretches to around 2,100 m (6,888 ft). A volcanic wasteland constitutes the top of the mountain, a bleak expanse of solidified lava and crusted, volcanic ash dotted with a few hardy shrubs and covered by snow for much of the year.

Sicily's greatest natural attraction, Etna offers some breathtaking summer trails past mystical caverns, mist-cloaked blow holes and forests of oak, pine, birch and beech. Wind-blown brooms and tufted scrub cling to the lunar-like upper slopes. Trickling streams are home to frogs, toads and turtles, while various species of snake, lizards, foxes, squirrels, weasels, hares, hedgehogs, porcupines and wild cats consider Etna's hidden crevices their domain. Owls, falcons, partridges and the occasional golden eagle also have their homes here, along with herons, ducks and some migratory birds.

At least three-dozen tour operators offer itineraries to reach Etna's formidable summit, including trail-bashing 4x4 ascents priced from 85 euros apiece. After a rollicking journey, the jeep

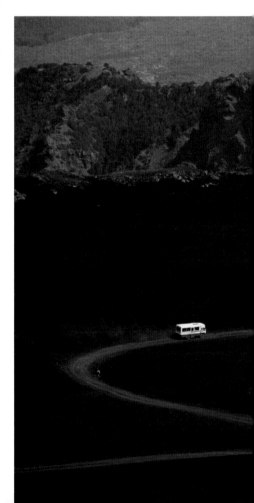

deposits its passengers on the basalt-ridden slopes at 1,200 m (3,936 ft), allowing uphill treks across Etna's middle and upper sections to the top. Each route is graded, although signage is best described as 'patchy', so engaging a guide makes good sense even in fair weather summer months. Depending on the trail, some added equipment may be necessary, such as safety helmets and a torch for exploring gloomy caves and lava tunnels. Sturdy boots are essential for delving into Etna's largest eruptive fractures, while waterproofs may be advisable when crossing some flooded streams. Generally speaking, the going is tough but not mega-arduous, with Etna's ever-changing alien landscape a constant companion during the climb.

Take the western slope from the clearing on the slope of Mount Gallo to reach the lofty Galvarina forest refuge (3 hours) or hike from Casa Pirao to Monte Spagnolo to Cisternazza for a 5 hour stomp up the beach wood paths of the northern slope. Another option is the Monte Nero Degli Zappini Nature Trail, which winds from Piano Vetore to offer stunning views out across bird-filled woodlands. Perhaps even more breathtaking, the Mount Zoccolaro Nature Trail affords spectacular panoramas of the Calanna Valley and the Valle del Bove, climbing a steep aspen-hemmed pathway flanked by a heart-stopping precipice.

At the summit, prepare to be wowed by an ethereal moonscape where Tolkienesque ravines emit vaporous ribbons in silver hues and the reddish tinge of oxidized molten rock provides a stark contrast to scattered yellow blooms. Plunging fissures and giant gaps dominate an inhospitable rugged crater, and bat-filled grottos lie undiscovered behind a shroud of wafting smoke under moist puffs of cloud. Arrive during a mini-eruption to experience Etna's resplendent crimson-gold glow firsthand.

Few off-road terrains are as mysterious as Mount Etna's magma-rich basaltic crags.

CONTACTS
Zero Problem Flying Team
Free Flight School
Tel: +39 75 917 7042
Email: luca.fugnamesi@libero.it

Perugia Tourism Office
Tel: +39 75 573 6458
http://tourism.comune.perugia.it

*Spirited winds ensure
unpredictable flight zones
over the massif, across
dizzying plateaux.*

HANG GLIDING PERUGIA

As a venue for the World Hang Gliding Championships, Sigillo's grand Monte Cucco is one of Europe's most thrilling backdrops. Numerous flying schools and qualified federal instructors run residential and weekend courses here, and it is also one of Europe's hang glider epicentres where more than 1,000 wings are manufactured each year. Favourable weather conditions and strong Atlantic and Balkan thermal currents ensure Monte Cucco's free flights launch with ease. A lack of serious obstacles across the massif means dozens of popular free flight zones, from Pian di Monte and Sella del Culumeo (Val di Ranco) to La Pianaccia. Experts can enjoy Monte Cucco's highly technical challenges, while total beginners can enjoy the freedom from several less arduous take-off points. A wall-mounted 3-D relief map at the hang gliding complex at the Monte Cucco di Tobia offers plenty of tips on how to catch a breeze as it moves up from the Adriatic – and also serves a mean cappuccino.

Gusts race between the windmills at Fosato di Vicco before heading for the peaks, where it funnels into a convergence bubble above the ridges to the east of the Massif before bouncing around the Cucco by mid-afternoon. Distinctive cloud base levels also make Monte Cucco memorable, with moisture-draped mountains and lower shrouding on the eastern slopes. Shifting winds offer spirited unpredictability, with changeable switches in direction that can put newbie gliders in a spin. Gusts from Lago Trasimeno to the west of Perugia can also threaten to blow up in the early morning, although launch sites – both north and south – are untroubled. The south launch offers views across the cities of Sigillo and Costacciaro and is reached via an asphalt road, while the north sits in Fabrianese with coastal views on clear days. Old 'flyer' Alberto Beni is usually on hand to impart words of wisdom to first-timers dizzied by the emerald hues and resplendent panoramas. His whirling hand gestures signal Monte Cucco's thermalling and turbulence, across a cave-riddled rolling terrain rich in fossils, and gasp-inducing plateaux overlooking vineyards and sunflower fields. Smooth, rounded hills offer super-soft landings right next to the take-off point. Tour operators offer tandem flights priced from 50 euros per person – bring your own wings or hire on site.

SWITZERLAND

Lying east of France and north of Italy, Switzerland is primarily a mountainous landscape with the rising peaks of the Alps in the south and the Jura in the northwest. A grassy central plateau of rolling hills, plains and large lakes is popular with waterskiers, walkers, climbers and hang gliders. However, it is snow sports that remain at the heart of this sophisticated Alpine nation, from tobogganing and snowboarding to downhill skiing, ice-skating and cross-country skiing. In the summer, these snow-topped peaks transform into wildflower meadows ideal for hiking. Adventure-lovers will discover that Swiss cities Geneva, Zürich and Bern provide excellent access out to the thrills of the wild, via a transport network that runs like clockwork.

TIME DIFFERENCE GMT +1

TELEPHONE CODE +41

CURRENCY Swiss Franc

LANGUAGE Schwitzerdütsch (Swiss German), French, Italian and Romansh

POPULATION 7.5 million

SIZE OF COUNTRY 41,295 sq km (16,105 sq miles)

CAPITAL Bern

WHEN TO GO Although renowned for its snowy, cold ski regions, Switzerland is blessed with over 290 days of sunshine and boasts warm summers when temperatures can rise to around 30°C (86°F). Even in the mountains the sun is hot, while winters rarely become cold enough to drop below -5°C (23°F), apart from on higher ground.

TOURIST INFORMATION
Swiss National Tourist Office
Tel: +41 800 100 200 30
Fax: +41 800 100 200 31
Email: info.uk@myswitzerland.com
www.myswitzerland.com

044

MOUNTAIN BIKING BERN

GETTING THERE

To get there by public transport, take tram 9 from the train station to Gurtenbahn in the suburb of Wabern, and walk 100 m (328 ft) along Dorfstrasse to the funicular (daily every 20 minutes, May–Sept 8am–10pm, Oct–April 8am–6.30pm).

CONTACT

Bern Tourist Office
Tel: +41 31 328 12 12
Fax: +41 31 328 12 77
Email: info@berninfo.com
www.berninfo.com

Gurten – Park im Grünen
Tel: +41 31 970 33 33
Fax: +41 31 970 33 44
Email: info@gurtenpark.ch
www.gurtenpark.ch

Few days on a mountain bike are as perfect as those on scenic, long, challenging downhill stretches of rocks, scary ledges, overhangs and jump-offs, all without the nuisance of uphill slogs. Switzerland – a mountain bike (MTB) idyll with its rough terrain and perilous outcrops – requires bags of energy off-road, while rattling, loose-stone mountain trails demand maximum skill and control.

Although townies have tried their best to commandeer mountain biking, it is in the world's most foreboding, jagged, rocky ridges that it can be enjoyed in its purest form. 'The higher the better' has long been the mantra of a hardcore MTB crowd who relish fearsome downhill runs against the odds. Criss-crossing tracks lead to full-tilt plunges across ravines and airborne jumps. Roughly hewn trails carved from the rocks by the elements demand robust durability: wide, knobby tyres, top-notch shock absorption and a sturdy frame make MTB models the weightiest in the cycle world, with every bell and whistle on a downhill bike heavy duty – even a standard model weighs around 15 kg (33 lbs), despite continued efforts to shave off excess mass. Yet these powerful monsters of the mountains cope easily with unrelenting bumps, bashes and wipeouts to withstand full-force impact on potholed back roads, brutal singletracks and trunk-strewn forested trails.

Swiss MTB routes are great for riders who enjoy remoteness and self-reliance far from civilization, where the risk of being stranded many kilometres from help is real. Long, full-day treks combine cross-country, downhill and freeriding – often with some street runs thrown in for good measure. Alpine shrub-covered, razor-sharp crags (often spaced around bike-length apart) provide the ultimate awkward hump and require a skilful pumping of the terrain. Rollers, small ditches, drops and the debris of fallen branches demand precise, well-timed and confident negotiation. Bunny hopping comes into its own when jumping and rattling over troublesome rocky ledges, while weight-fuelled racing-oriented downhill riding covers extremely steep terrain at terrifying speed, often using ski runs in summer. Few rides are as physically demanding and dangerous for mountain bikers, often including jumps of up to 12 m (39 ft) and drops of 3 m (10 ft) or more – a true test of commitment for even the most competent rider, over an intimidating ragged jigsaw of razor-sharp peaks.

A particularly hair-raising trail is located in Bern's Wabern suburb and can be accessed by a 30 minute ride on the Gurtenbahn funicular train – ensuring no tiring uphill slog interferes with your downhill kicks. Buy a day card for the Gurten Park railway and allow an extra fee for the bike (special compartments are designated for storage). At the terminus at the top of the peak, the trail head is located about 50 m (164 ft) down a paved path. A series of braking bumps leads to a short drop into the woods where steeply-banked sections offer a wide variety of jumps, allowing a great opportunity to try out technical moves. Don't take things too fast, as some of the key features are obscured by the bigger lifts. Flatter routes trim the most complex trails, where pro riders will be tempted by a vast jump over a road gap – look out for a warning sign on the right hand side.

Gurten is a favourite Bernese getaway and signature mountain, towering 280 m (918 ft) above the city and 864 m (2,834 ft) above sea level. As the closest MTB trail to the city centre it can get crowded on Sundays, but it's open every day and is often totally isolated off-peak. Ignore the touristy kids' play area and cafés to head to the wide expanses of countryside laced with tracks overlooking the city, out towards the Jura and across the peaks of the Bernese Oberland. Pack a proper set of serious clothing for mountain biking in Switzerland, even on suburban trails. Head protection is essential as falls are commonplace on rough, rocky mountainous trails. Gloves, protective eyewear, rough terrain clothing and full body armour (including under jackets) are all advisable. You'll also need water bottles (or toteable water bags) and a proper tool kit. Riders keen to join the crowds should arrive for the November Gurten Classic, a mixed cycle race that includes a heavily-subscribed 16.8 km (10 mile) MTB event.

Prepare for brutal single tracks and log-cluttered trails on this intimidating hardcore slog.

CONTACTS
Aéroclub de Genève
Tel: +41 22 798 65 08
Fax: +41 22 788 00 06
Email: secretariat@aero-club.ch
www.aero-club.ch

Geneva Tourist Office
Tel: +41 22 909 70 00
Fax: +41 22 909 70 11
www.geneve-tourisme.ch

Powering 800 kg (1,768 lbs) of metal in the air over the Salève Mountains provides a heart-thumping rush in the clouds.

FLYING GENEVA

Anyone with the merest urge to pilot a light aircraft will enjoy the thrill of a taster flight over Geneva. Flights depart the city's Aero Club to climb high above flower-filled green pastures, church spires and the Salève Mountains, allowing rookies a chance to sample the freedom of the skies. A 60 minute induction provides some basic instruction on the fundamentals of aviation and aerodynamics, in a two-part tutorial designed for first-timers. First a 45 minute interactive lesson covering the parts of the plane, the mechanics of taking off and steering – plus a few important safety tips. Then the adrenaline-rush segment, the flying of the plane itself: no theoretical stimulation or computer generated trickery, but a full and proper take-off. The three seater AS202 Bravo is a Swiss-built small civil aircraft that is not just speedy and steady but also capable of aerobatics.

Students fly from the pilot's seat after a reassuring briefing in the plane. After starting up the engine, the pilot helps to guide the aircraft into a taxi down to the runway. Poor steering, swerving and wobbling at this stage just serves to confirm who is at the controls. Then it's time for take-off – a real buzz that prompts a rapid heartbeat as 800 kg (1,768 lbs) of metal becomes airborne. The engine roars as the plane circles the peak of the Salève in order to gain altitude, curving around lush meadows and an orderly suburban sprawl.

The instructor runs through how to turn, fly straight, ascend and descend. The feeling of being in control (even partially) up in thin, low cloud is utterly awesome. You can feel the pull, the speed or the thrust and the experience is so surreal that it is almost dreamlike. After pointing out a few of Geneva's landmark views way down below, the pilot prepares for the approach to the airport and begins to line the plane up with the runway, explaining each step of the process. The student reads the cockpit instruments, guides the plane to the landing strip and breathes a sigh of relief when the landing gear and ground meet. A quick debrief allows time for a few last minute flying questions, such as 'when can I do it again?'.

The Aéroclub de Genève flight school is open Monday to Friday from 9.30am–5.00pm, and prices start at around 150 euros.

BODYFLYING ZÜRICH

Zürich's state of the art bodyflying centre is one of a handful in Europe, a vertical wind tunnel driven by a huge five-blade propeller producing an air stream with a speed of up to 180 kph (112 mph). The wind tunnel is similar to that which assesses the aerodynamics of Formula One racing cars, but when someone had the idea to flip it on its head and leap into the airflow to freefall in a completely safe environment, bodyflying was born; a thrilling air dive without the need to jump out of a plane at 3,000 m (9,840 ft).

Easily strong enough to support a human's bodyweight, the wind tunnel allows a weightless airborne flight. An initial session begins with a safety briefing before a full kitting-out (in specialist flight suit, helmet, goggles and gloves) before revelling in four incredible 60 second bursts – far longer than a 30 second freefall from a plane. Perfecting the X-position is a prime goal as all other moves stem from this position, such as flips, rolls and turns. Three or four day programmes (a 16 session Learn to Fly course) are a popular option and include video briefing and debriefing, with 95 per cent of students able to master starts, landings (up and down), horizontal turns, shifts (four directions) and some freestyle figures by the end of the course. Experienced skydivers are eligible for a high level course that skips all the basics to focus on complex moves. Your instructor will almost certainly whet your appetite in a bid to encourage you to attain this level, with a demonstration of freefall acrobatics using arcing limbs and a flatter posture to lower the centre of gravity to affect fall rate – to dramatic effect.

Anyone who is fit and healthy can bodyfly, as long as they are over eight years old and under 95 kg (210 lbs). Without the constraints of weather conditions the Bodyflying Centre is open year-round, eliminating the frustration of fog-cancelled flights. Prices start at 55 Swiss francs for basic instruction, equipment and briefing, with intensive four day Learn to Fly courses from 685 Swiss francs per person.

GETTING THERE
BodyFlying is on motorway A20, exit Rümlang/Seebach, or 1 km (0.6 miles) from Rümlang railway station. From Zürich main station take train number S5.

CONTACTS
BodyFlying
Tel: +41 44 817 02 09
Fax: +41 44 817 03 84
Email: info@bodyflying.ch
www.bodyflying.ch

Zürich Tourist Office
Tel: +41 44 215 40 00
Fax: +41 44 215 40 80
Email: information@zuerich.com
www.zuerich.com

Aerodynamic freefall flips at 180 kph (112 mph) do much to recreate the skydive thrill.

LUXEMBOURG

TIME DIFFERENCE GMT +1

TELEPHONE CODE +352

CURRENCY Euro

LANGUAGES Luxembourgish, French
and German

POPULATION 480,222

SIZE OF COUNTRY 2,568 sq km
(1,002 sq miles)

CAPITAL Luxembourg City

WHEN TO GO Summers in Luxembourg can be
warm, dry and sunny although showers remain
common year-round. Northern regions are wetter,
with June and September often the best months
for hiking, climbing, cycling and camping.

TOURIST INFORMATION
Luxembourg Tourist Office
Tel: 020 7434 2800
Fax: 020 7734 1205
Email: tourism@luxembourg.co.uk
www.luxembourg.co.uk

Pint-sized Luxembourg is largely overshadowed by its bigger
neighbours, sharing borders with Belgium to the west and north,
France to the south, and Germany to the east. A landlocked tiny
territory, shielded from the sea by Belgium, Luxembourg's cross-
frontier fraternization has nurtured a cosmopolitan, trilingual society
that boasts the highest percentage of foreigners of any EU nation.
The capital, Luxembourg-Ville, has a delightful UNESCO-listed old
centre complete with turrets, towers and spires. Surrounding
countryside expanses are a scenic mix of rolling hills and lush valleys
nestled amongst forests, vineyards and striking sandstone crags.

CONTACTS
Luxembourg Youth Hostel Association
Tel: +352 26 27 66 40
Fax: +352 26 27 66 42
Email: info@youthhostels.lu
www.youthhostels.lu

Luxembourg City Tourist Office
Tel: +352 22 28 09
Fax: +352 46 70 70
Email: touristinfo@lcto.lu
www.lcto.lu

Grande Randonnée Cinq
www.grfive.com

*Luxembourg boasts the
densest network of hiking trails
on the planet.*

HIKING LUXEMBOURG CITY

Luxembourg may be one of the world's most compact countries at around 2,500 sq km (975 sq miles), but this pocket-sized nation is a veritable hiker's paradise. Sandwiched between Belgium, Germany and France, landlocked Luxembourg is bisected from north to south by the GR-5 (Grande Randonnée 5), a 2,576 km (1,600 mile) cross-continental route that runs from Hoek van Holland on the North Sea to the French Mediterranean resort of Nice. Home to the densest network of hiking trails and hostels on the planet, Luxembourg's 210 km (130 mile) stretch of the GR-5 is a popular package deal with visiting hikers, winding through magnificent valleys and forests. The GR-5 enters Luxembourg at Trois Frontières, south of the tiny town of Burg Reuland, and meanders along the German border in a series of rise-and-falls to the pretty towns on the Moselle River. Although the entire Luxembourg route takes a week, a shorter succession of trails offer day hikes for weekenders.

Customized packages from the Youth Hostel Association run at around 75 euros per person, complete with maps and accommodation. Those that go it alone will find a copy of the *GR-5 Du Luxembourg Aux Vosges Cotes de Moselle – Pays de Nancy* (published by Fédération Française de la Randonnée Pidestre in French) is pretty much all that they'll need, with youth hostel B&B priced at around 15.70–18.70 euros per night.

Stuck in the capital and need to stretch your legs? Then follow one of Luxembourg's many urban hiking routes. For a two hour stomp, set off from the Gare Centrale and follow the Avenue de la Liberte into the heart of the city to the 46 m (151 ft) Pont Adolphe Biéck (Adolphe Bridge). Take a right towards the Place de la Constitution and follow the Rue de Chimay two blocks north to the Place d'Armes, a pleasant square-facing plaza dotted with cafés, restaurants and bars. From the Rue du Cure, turn right onto the Rue du Fosse and on to the Place Guillaume II, before heading off to the Grand-Ducal Palace and the Chamber of Deputies and north to the Place du Théâtre. A steady walk south leads to the resplendent 17th-century Notre Dame Cathedral. Cross the valley and continue on the Avenue de la Gare, home of the landmark Hotel Nobilis. A dozen surrounding cafés serving cold Bofferding beer confirm that you're now just a few metres from your starting point – and a much-needed refreshment break.

BELGIUM

TIME DIFFERENCE GMT +1

TELEPHONE CODE +32

CURRENCY Euro

LANGUAGES Flemish and French

POPULATION 10.3 million

SIZE OF COUNTRY 30,528 sq km
(11,906 sq miles)

CAPITAL Brussels

WHEN TO GO Low-lying Belgium is prone to
showers pretty much year-round. April to
September is drier, with July and August the
hottest and sunniest months when rooms are
more expensive and harder to come by. Winters
are generally wet and cold, but not bitterly so.

TOURIST INFORMATION
Visit Flanders-Brussels
Tel: 020 7307 7738
Email: info@visitflanders.co.uk
www.visitflanders.co.uk

Belgian Tourist Office
Tel: 020 7537 1132
Fax: 020 7531 0393
Email: info@belgiumtheplaceto.be
www.belgiumtheplaceto.be

Often described as 'Europe in a nutshell', Belgium's multicultural and
multilingual flatland is punctuated with needle-thin canals, castles and
cities – not to mention 350 different homespun beers. Northern
agricultural regions are dominated by farmland pastures while the
central regions are largely urban, with wooded plateaux in the south.
Flanders, the upper Dutch-speaking provinces, is proud of its fine art
cities, while French-speaking Wallonia, in the south, is characterized
by the rolling hills of the Ardennes. As one of the Europe's most
cosmopolitan cities, Brussels is over overlooked as a bureaucratic
bastion of red tape. Yet despite being home to the European Union,
NATO and numerous giants of international trade, the city has a
sophisticated cultural and gastronomic scene.

TREKKING BRUSSELS

Expiratory pilgrimages from all over the world have placed the Ardennes on the map in a nation famously described by Flemish songwriter Jacques Brel as *'le plat pays qui est le mien'* ('the flat country that is mine'). More than 1,000 km (620 miles) of waymarked walking trails and a host of medium and long distance walkers' paths squiggle across the region, taking in flower-filled plains and stream-hemmed mountain routes. Stretching to the south and east of Brussels, the Ardennes' rolling hills and wooded valleys may not rise in crested peaks like the Alps, but don't let an absence of fearsome heights dampen your enthusiasm. It is no less scenic, with gently sloping forested hills, meadows and grasslands dotted with villages that provide relief from the monotony of the Flanders lowlands, with a swirl of sign-posted walking trails across the boggy marshlands of the Hautes Fagnes to the resin-scented woodland thickets. Local tourist maps and specialist travel guides provide plenty of half-day and full-day options. *Walking in the Ardennes* (published by Cicerone) details 53 circular paths, from a 4 km (2.5 mile) meander to more gruelling hikes. Each route allows plenty of time for sightseeing, even on the breathless stretches, with many founded by Belgium's former monarch King Albert I, a world-class mountaineer who pioneered a host of new routes in the Ardennes.

Today, highlights include a 22 km (13.6 mile) trek out on a steep path from La Roche-en-Ardenne on a forest climb up from a valley. After reaching level ground, the landscape opens up to a meadow out to Roumont before winding into woodland stretches to Sprimont. At around 23 km (14.3 mile), the route from the small town of St Hubert involves plenty of ups and downs through silent beech and oak forests teeming with wild deer. Leafy paths nudge along the rivers of Palogne, Masblette and Diglette to the historic town of Nassogne. Other favourite full-day hikes trail the Ardennes' limestone clifftops, criss-crossing the fertile rivers of the Amblève and Lienne, the Aisne, Semois, Ourthe and Lesse. In wetter months, paths crash through gushing streams and bubbling weirs and cross moss-covered boulders. If wanted, longer hikes can be combined with stretches on horseback to allow greater distances to be covered across the massifs.

GETTING THERE

Most scheduled airlines fly into Brussels Airport which is situated 14 km (7 miles) from Brussels city centre, to which it is connected by a train service that leaves every 20 minutes. Some airlines from the UK also use Charleroi Brussels South Airport, which lies 46 km (29 miles) south of Brussels.

CONTACTS

Russell Hafter Holidays
Tel: 01946 861652
Email: enquire@walking-in-belgium.co.uk
www.walking-in-belgium.co.uk

La Roche Tourisme
Tel: +32 84 36 77 36
Fax: +32 84 36 78 36
Email: info@la-roche-tourisme.com
www.la-roche-tourisme.com

Bubbling weirs, river trails and gently sloping forests offer 1,000 km (620 miles) of waymarked trails that were pioneered by royalty.

049

GETTING THERE
The Flemish coastline stretches 67 km (42 miles) and is served by a coastal tramline. To get to De Panne, the best way to travel is either by rail from Brussels or by car. Alternatively you can travel to any Flemish coastal city and catch the coastal tram, which starts in De Panne and has regular services during the day.

CONTACTS
Flemish Land Yacht Federation
Tel: +32 5841 5747
Email: info@lazef.be
www.lazef.be

De Panne Tourism
Tel: +32 5842 1818
Fax: +32 5842 1617
Email: toerisme@depanne.be
www.depanne.be

Wide, empty, open sands ensure obstacle-free racing conditions ad record speeds.

LAND YACHTING BRUGES

For a chance to ride three times faster than the wind, head to West Flanders, the birthplace of land yachting (also known as parakarting, kite buggying, speed sailing and sand sailing) and a landscape of gently contoured rolling sand. With neighbouring Oostduinkerke (meaning 'Church of the Eastern Dunes'), the beach resort of De Panne is inextricably linked with the racing land yachts crafted by the brothers Dumont. A vast 20 km (12 mile) carpet of sand (the widest expanse on the Flemish coastline) is free from obstacles, interruptions and breakwaters. A blueprint for land yachting, West Flanders offers a model for the rest of the world to follow, with world-class craft and stiff sea breezes hemmed by extraordinary waves that allow you to clock up record speeds.

Rather bizarrely, land yachting can be traced back to Pharaonic Egypt, when wind-powered carts built for leisure were used on desert sands. Today's Dumont-inspired sails are based on those of contemporary Nile boats, while the trend of three-wheeled fibreglass and metal carts with wing-masts and full-batten sails began to gather popularity in the 1960s. Modern designs are rigid, aerodynamic designs capable of reaching a

velocity of 120 kph (74 mph) – with 188 kph (116 mph) the current record breaking top whack. Even at very low winds, the sleekest land yachts ride at up to three times the speed of wind to pip 70 kph (43 mph) in around five seconds.

In simple terms, land yachts are divided in four classes that are primarily dependent on size and design. In Europe, the bigger class three and class two yachts are by far the most dominant model, boasting a lightweight fibreglass hull and wing-shaped mast and wooden rear axle. Expect an average class two craft to measure around 5.25 m (17.2 ft) long, 4.2 m (13.8 ft) wide and 7.25 m (23.8 ft) high at the mast tip. Sails can be as large as 10 m (33 ft), with easily manipulated aeroplane wing-shaped masts used to improve airflow and accelerate pace and dynamics, allowing powerful rides at sharp angles against the wind. Yet De Panne's super-sleek sands aren't just for speed junkies – plenty of land yachters enjoy a more leisurely experience, sand sailing for fun with passengers in two-seater yachts. Drivers (pilots) sit so low to the ground that they are almost lying down, using a foot pedal to steer the front wheel, often with a handle bar and no brakes.

NETHERLANDS

The low-lying Netherlands mixes its trademark national icons –
windmills, clogs and tulips – with some less obvious Dutch
treasures, including some world-class active pursuits. Reclaimed
polders and river deltas sit mainly below sea level, while an extensive
network of coastal dunes and levées runs along the coast. Gentle
slopes constitute the Netherlands' upper ground in the foothills of the
Ardennes, while the lush, green forest of Arnhem and the grassland
landscape's criss-crossing rivers and canals offer excellent hiking,
trail running and fishing. Airborne adventures run from ballooning and
parasailing to hang gliding and microlights, while the Netherlands'
cities offer a gamut of urban pursuits, from cycling and bungee
jumping to abseiling.

TIME DIFFERENCE GMT + 1

TELEPHONE CODE +31

CURRENCY Euro

LANGUAGE Dutch

POPULATION 16.3 million

SIZE OF COUNTRY 41,864 sq km
(16,327 sq miles)

CAPITAL Amsterdam

WHEN TO GO Springtime brings a rush of colour
to Holland as tulips reach full bloom. Summers are
generally dry, with sunshine peppered with rainy
days, while autumn turns cool and winter is wetter,
with cold and icy spells.

TOURIST INFORMATION
Netherlands Board of Tourism
Email: hollandinfo-uk@nbt.nl
www.holland.com

050

CYCLING AMSTERDAM

CONTACTS

Amsterdam Tourist Office
Tel: +31 20 551 25 25
Email: info@atcb.nl
www.amsterdamtourist.nl

Bikes NL (Amsterdam Rental)
www.bikes.nl

Dutch Cycle Union (KNWU)
www.knwu.nl

Rightly known as the 'City of Bikes', Amsterdam and cycling have long been synonymous, with more than 40 per cent of rush-hour traffic the two-wheeled, man-powered mode. Some 800,000 cycles weave, wobble, race and screech throughout Amsterdam's confusing maze of canal paths, cobblestone streets and bridges. In the Netherlands, bikes are not only practical, efficient, economic and environmentally-friendly – they are positively endorsed as Kings of the Road. In a nation of 16.4 million, bike ownership runs at more than 17 million – 1.1 per person – with over 3.4 million choosing to do their daily commute in the saddle. Refreshingly, function is overwhelmingly valued over style. Battered old rust-laden bone-shakers far outnumber the city's sleek, streamlined gleaming machines. Amsterdam's beloved single gear Oma boasts solid handlebars, thick tyres and a pair of industrial-sized locks, one for the frame and one for the back wheel. Rules of the road appear forgotten by all riders, but speed is compulsory, especially when the distinctive clanging of a tram bell tolls.

Every hotel and B&B in Amsterdam offers bike hire and tours. Rental booths can be found in train stations across the city, while Damstraat, Holland Rent-a-Bike and MacBike do a roaring trade. Expect to pay about 20 euros a week (or 5–8 euros per day) for Amsterdam's trademark black municipal model. Grab a bike path map (Amsterdam *op de fiets*, meaning 'Amsterdam on the Bike', 4 euros) from the VVV tourist information office outside Central Station for a standard urban meander. However, for the ultimate thrill off the metropolis's beaten track, ask at MacBike for a few hot tips – but be sure to hire a lightweight, high velocity machine.

Navigating Amsterdam's 400 km (248 mile) muddle of cycle paths (*fietspaden*) is confused by the Netherlands' perplexing right of way rules, a theoretical framework that is open to loose interpretation. In theory, traffic coming from your left should give you the right of way, but it pays to err on the side of caution. Cycle paths are well maintained, to say the least – regular caretaking schedules involve sprucing-up, power washing, de-icing and sweeping. A round blue sign with a white bicycle indicates a dedicated bike lane – although, rather

bafflingly, mopeds are allowed to use the route too. City maps denote areas closed to cyclists, bike repair shops and flat tyre specialists en route.

As a city poorly equipped for cars, the narrow streets and skinny canal paths of Amsterdam's 17th century inner core make it a good place to cycle. The city is flat and compact, with a maximum distance across the centre of around 7 km (4 miles), an ideal distance to settle into the saddle. All manner of cycle-friendly initiatives make bike travel a breeze, from umpteen bike parking facilities to the inauguration of a 'green wave' on the Raadhuisstraat, where cyclists travelling at a constant speed of 15–18 kph (9–11 mph) catch every green light, thanks to a synchronized timing system. Amsterdam's frenzied flow of traffic even has its very own expert bicycle co-ordinator to manage the day-to-day needs of cyclists.

One of Amsterdam's most adventurous urban cycle routes starts at the Haarlemmerplein by the 1840 triumphal arch. Zoom under the six-track rail viaduct to the speed-gathering Houtmanstraat. Cross bridges in the Zoutkeetsgracht to the old quayside of Houtmankade and the frenetic pace of traffic on busy Van Diemenstraat. Fly by west Amsterdam's prime canal shipment passage, lurch along chaotic Tasmanstraat, past dykes, timber docks and re-excavation projects and slums slated for gentrification. Pump the pedals along the history-packed sea dyke route towards Haarlem, then nip along two-way cycle paths on the Nieuwe Hemweg to race past grain docks, railway tracks, freight depots, cooling towers and the North Sea Canal. Push on before bumping down the path towards the former national Artillery Establishment (Staatsbedrijf der Artillerie-Inrichtingen). Whizz around Zaandam and Westzaan, passing medieval sea dykes, estuaries, stepped alleys, pumping stations, farm buildings, open pasture and Jewish cemeteries. The road back into the city centre allows a chance to weave in and out of the urban melée towards Zaanstraat, sprinting along a rat-run cycle path under a rail bridge before making a triumphant return into Haarlemmerplein at speed – just remember to pedal backwards to brake to a halt, a quirk of the Dutch cycle.

Over 400 km (248 miles) of cycle paths riddle Amsterdam's core, from leafy canal routes to gritty urban rat-runs.

ABSEILING ROTTERDAM

CONTACTS
Euromast
Tel: +31 10 436 4811
Email: info@euromast.nl
www.euromast.nl

Rotterdam Tourist Board
Tel: +31 10 205 15 00
Fax: +31 10 205 15 99
Email: contact@rotterdam-
marketing.nl
www.vvv.rotterdam.nl

Urban abseiling has fast become a modern extreme sport phenomenon immortalized in a zillion jaw-dropping YouTube clips. Capturing the hearts and minds of adventurers keen to explore the most challenging concrete jungles on the planet, abseiling a cityscape of sleek, smooth towers offers a unique array of Metropolitan hazards from steam-spewing vents to dive-bombing pigeons. Towering monolithic skyscrapers sit high atop the blaring horns, while engines rev in gridlocked streets a death-defying drop below. Simply lean back, respectful of the 100 m (328 ft) plunge, brace yourself and pull on the ropes. Feed your inner fears, exhale and stay focused. It's time to abseil inner-city style.

Rotterdam's tallest tower is also Europe's highest abseiling challenge and a gathering point for thrill-seekers keen to experience the ultimate sight-seeing kick. Just a glimpse of the Euromast soaring towards the heavens prompts an involuntary stomach-lurch of excitement. It's not beautiful, far from it – but there is definitely something awesome about its robustly built reinforced concrete stature. Spanning 9 m (30 ft) in diameter with 30 cm (12 in) thick walls, Euromast's 130-plus piles support almost 2 million kg (4.4 million lbs), including a steel crow's nest that alone weighs in at a staggering 240,000 kg (530,400 lbs). In fitting style, an elevator transports visitors to the top at a breakneck speed –

a white knuckle ride at 4 m (13 ft) per second. From the top the view alone is breathtaking, extending 30 km (19 miles) out to Belgium on a clear day. Looking down, a blur of bag-laden shoppers and city folk form a distant kaleidoscopic mass on the urban landscape, rather like a sea of jellybeans. So far, more than 6 million people have braved the tower to enjoy the vertigo-inducing panorama, though only the very brave have opted for a rope.

Every descent is carefully guided by Euromast's dedicated team of so-called Height Specialists. Each provides tuition in safety basics before pointing out landmarks on Rotterdam's magnificent urban horizon. The key to abseiling, they assure you, is confidence. It is this, they continue, that will help you to step off a ledge into thin air and dangle high above the traffic. Once fully trussed-up in a harness it is time to head for terra firma, the hard way. Breathe in, exhale and after a reassuring 'thumbs up' – you're off. Weight distribution and rope friction controls the travel speed, but most abseillers get from top to bottom within about 40 minutes, including prep talk. When the Euromast was under construction in 1960, townsfolk cheered workmen on with chants of "Ram, ram those 130 piles!" Today, waving bystanders offer similar levels of vocal encouragement to abseiling tourists, and with such beguiling distractions, unconquered fear doesn't stand a chance.

Take a rope-tied plunge down Rotterdam's tallest monolithic tower to abseil inner-city-style.

DENMARK

The Jutland peninsula, and its 400 surrounding lush, green, windswept islands, form one of Europe's smallest countries: a nation that links the rest of Scandinavia with continental Europe. Home to fine, modern cities and fairytale castles, Denmark has its roots buried deeply in the riches of the sea. Quaint fishing villages, boatyards and maritime harbours spawn yachts, sailboats and fishing vessels amidst waters that were once a Viking domain. Nowhere in Denmark is farther from the coast than 52 km (32 miles) – a close land-to-ocean connection that permeates Danish food, folklore and lifestyle pursuits. Some 7,300 km (4,526 miles) of coastline, 10,000 km (6,200 miles) of cycle paths and 100 bird sanctuaries offer plenty for lovers of the great outdoors.

TIME DIFFERENCE GMT +1

TELEPHONE CODE +45

CURRENCY Danish Krone (DKK)

LANGUAGE Danish

POPULATION 5.4 million

SIZE OF COUNTRY 43,094 sq km (16,807 sq miles)

CAPITAL Copenhagen

WHEN TO GO Denmark has a temperate climate with very little fluctuation between day and night. February is the coldest month at 0°C (32°F) while warm, sunny summers can see highs in the low 20s (68°F-plus).

TOURIST INFORMATION
Visit Denmark
Tel: 020 7259 5959
Email: london@visitdenmark.com
www.visitdenmark.com

CYCLING ODENSE

GETTING THERE
Odense is served by Billund Airport.
There is no direct link – catch a bus
to Vejle and take the train from there.

CONTACTS
Odense Tourist Bureau, Funen
Tel: +45 6612 7520
Email: otb@odenseturist.dk
www.odenseturist.dk

Visit Funen (Fyn)
Email: info@fyntour.dk
www.visitfyn.com

Fairytale Funen's green flats.

Even an enchanting land of fairytale make-believe has its monsters, but in Denmark's Hans Christian Andersen country the demons are a composition of nature. For amongst the magical fields of flowers, castles and windmills of Funen (Fyn) that provided the inspiration for the storyteller's tales of fairies and princesses, lie some fiendish unpaved cycle tracks. Criss-crossing manicured asphalt roads, these rugged tyre-worn trails lead across the hop-filled meadows of the South Fyn Archipelago. Cycling along this picture-book narrative is to journey through a legend-steeped chapter of moat-ringed towers and spires. Denmark's circular 'Garden Island' sits in the centre of country, forming a convenient 2,985 sq km (1,164 sq mile) stepping-stone to bridge the channel between Jutland and Zealand.

As befitting a 'cycle-friendly' nation, Denmark publishes a map of its several hundred cycle routes, over 100 of which run through Funen. Published by the Danish Cycling Association, the *Cykleguide* is available from tourist offices nationwide (priced at 119 Danish Kroner). A popular 55 km (34 mile) route connects the tiny market town of Bogense with Odense via the beaches of Hasmark Strand, and offers a mix of paved and unmade tracks on a full day's ride. As Denmark's second-largest island Funen is nourished by a year-round maritime climate, so it's wet in winter, dry in summer and sea-sprayed in between. Narrow roads weave through fishing villages of half-timbered houses still home to sea-legged mariners poised for combat with sand eel, herring and cod.

Cyclists keen for adventure without excessive fatigue will enjoy Funen's gently undulating countryside. Only a couple of intimidating hills invoke any huffing and puffing, with off-road trails providing exhilaration in short, manageable bursts. Unorthodox views of this fabled terrain are best absorbed along the hidden back roads, passing shimmering lakes, dragonflies, windmills and jumping fish. From the medieval gatehouses of Gyldensten a tougher road leads to the woodlands of Sandagergård Manor, before winding down to the unspoiled shores and dykes of Hasmark Strand – the perfect spot for a cooling dip.

Odense Fjord is an important resting place for Denmark's migratory bird species and a breeding ground for gulls, terns, herons and swans. Nip across expanses of moorland vegetation, such as juniper, ling, heather and crowberry, carefully avoiding adders, grass snakes and sand lizards. Then race parallel with a narrow strip of pebble beach bordered by salt plains and reed swamps, close to tumbledown cottages in vibrant Barbie-pink hues – a happy ever after to this unforgettable two-wheeled adventure.

GERMANY

As Europe's largest economy and most populous nation, Germany is an industrial heavyweight that ranks amongst the world's most technologically advanced. Design-led luxury brands boast world-class style and functionality, from Bosch and Boss to Porsche, BMW, Audi, Wolfgang and Joop. Germany lies wedged between Holland and Poland to the south of Denmark on the Baltic and North Sea. As Europe's sixth largest nation, it extends to the Alps in the south while the northern plains are riddled by northward-flowing watercourses with bird-filled wetlands. On the French border, the Black Forest divides the Rhine from the Danube's headwaters. Glacier-formed lakes date to the last ice age in the northeast, while central uplands soar and the coast offers more than 1,000 km (620 miles) of beach.

TIME DIFFERENCE GMT +1

TELEPHONE CODE +49

CURRENCY Euro

LANGUAGE German

POPULATION 82.5 million

SIZE OF COUNTRY 349,223 sq km (136,197 sq miles)

CAPITAL Berlin

WHEN TO GO Germany's climate is almost as varied as its country, but extreme temperature highs and lows are rare. Summers average between 20 and 30°C (68–86°F), although frequent showers can be unpredictable. Winters are generally cold.

TOURIST INFORMATION
German National Tourist Office in London
Tel: 020 7317 0908
Fax: 020 7317 0917
Email: gntolon@d-z-t.com
www.germany-tourism.de

053

CONTACTS
Trabi Experience
Tel: +49 30 7020 9494
www.trabi-x.de

Trabi Safari
Tel: +49 30 2759 2273
www.trabi-safari.de

It may be low on comfort and high on noise, but the low-tech, trundling Trabi is a gear-handling delight.

DRIVING BERLIN

Following the tearing down of the Berlin Wall in 1989, only a handful of East Germany's tinny, low-tech Trabant cars survived. They now live on in an inverted one-upmanship among Westerners, who enjoy filling Karl Marx Allee with engine splutter and thick, blue smoke. Trabants, or Trabis for short, were produced for more than three decades in the German Democratic Republic. Today, with post-Wall cult status fully established, tourists pay good euros to fold themselves into a Trabi and splutter around Berlin. A sluggish two cylinder cross between a golf cart and a Sri Lankan tuk tuk, the Trabi was actually planned as a three-wheeled motorcycle, not a car – something the low, squashed seating and a top speed of 30 kph (20 mph) betrays.

At just under 360 cm (140 in) long, 150 cm (59 in) wide and 146 cm (57 in) tall, the Trabant is low on comfort and high on engine noise; a trundling gear-crashing tin can strangely inspired by the Russian satellite Sputnik. The name Trabant means 'fellow traveller' or 'satellite', and in 1957 televised ads by Sachsenring Automobile Works praised the Trabi for being 'agile', 'fast' and 'robust' – prompting demand that caused waiting lists of up to 15 years. Around 3.7 million cars were churned out and today about 58,000 are still in use in Germany, of which around 85 per cent are in the former East. A Trabant spews out five times as much carbon monoxide as most other cars in western Europe but, in its defence, fuel consumption is a modest 7 litres per 100 km (41 miles to the gallon).

Berlin's fleet of 60 tourist-ready Trabis benefit from the support of a team of on-call mechanics armed with wrenches and mallets. Sightseeing in a spluttering curb crawler will set you back 33 euros per person for a 180 minute, self-drive option through the Trabi Experience, or from 25 euros per person for an hour-long chauffeured jaunt with Trabi Safari Tours. Self-drivers will need to swot up on some of the basics of the German highway code to avoid the wrath of horn-tooting, Mercedes-driving sophisticates. They'll also need to be prepared for some unsolicited humour from passersby, including 'Why does the Trabi have a heated rear window? It keeps your hands warm while you push it'. Strong arms are actually essential – turning the steering wheel is like rolling a 4 tonne boulder – while the brakes require heavy footwork to bring the car to any sort of pre-planned halt. As for the gear lever, well – it seems to be for ornamental purposes only.

The Wild East Tour incorporates Berlin's more traditional tourist spots, such as Norman Foster's Reichstag, and also passes all the Communist-era landmarks, from Checkpoint Charlie and Red Town Hall to the Brandenburg Gate, pausing for thought at the Holocaust Memorial. The long, sleek drag of Strasse des 17 June is the only pedal-to-the-metal stretch, causing the engine to hit a deafening peak. Day tours run from 10am–6pm daily, with tours after dark available on request.

CYCLING MÜNSTER

In Münster – Germany's 'Bicycle Capital' – children are tutored in cycling from the age of three, such is the city's enthusiasm. Bikes outnumber residents by almost 2:1, while Münster's extensive cycle path network boasts a 4.5 km (3 mile) Bicycle Promenade used by 1,200 cyclists per hour. Even the city's car-strewn one-way system has been adapted to accommodate two-way cycle traffic. Residents spend an average of 15.6 minutes per day on two wheels, with 40.5 per cent of all inner city journeys made by bicycle. In November, a six day cycle race brings the city to a virtual standstill, as the Olympiahalle stadium heaves with lean, two-wheeled warriors of the road – a state of excitement matched only by the eruption of city-wide fervour when the Giro d'Italia bike race sprinted into town in 2002.

Italy's most important cycle race paid a visit to Germany as part of the PR machine to plug the euro, calling at Belgium, Luxembourg and Strasbourg, too, before whizzing off to its native Turin. Münster was awarded the honour of hosting the first stage of the 85th Giro d'Italia in 2002, a fitting accolade for a city so slavishly devoted to

two-wheeled pursuits. The cavalcade clocked up record speeds as it raced over the German border, cutting through central and lower Emsland across a ripple of hedge-ringed meadows, whipping Münster up into a frenzy to further forge its bond with cycling. Münster has since built a flourishing tourist trade on the back of its Giro d'Italia pedigree, encouraging visitors to follow the first stage of the route by bike.

A map details the 218 km (135 mile) route (in reverse) from Münster to Groningen (Netherlands), a small slice of the race's total 3,334 km (2,067 mile) slog but a full, hard day in the saddle nonetheless. To date, hundreds of would-be pace lines have followed in the footsteps of stage winner Mario Cipollini, pounding the pedals at incredible speeds in true pink jersey style. For a nippy route closer to the city, speed off around 4,000 km (2,480 miles) of bicycle paths, meshed together in honeycomb fashion to allow cyclists to dip in and out. Need a map? Then pick up a pocket PC with satellite navigation, directing cyclists to the most fearsome hill-climbs en route – and pinpointing decent recovery spots.

CONTACTS
Munster Tourist Office
Tel: +49 2514 922 726
Fax: +49 2514 927 759
Email: tourismus@stadt-muenster.de
www.muenster.de

Join this cycle-mad community to pound the pedals of a two-wheeled sprint around town.

055

SNOWSHOE TREKKING
BADEN-BADEN

GETTING THERE
The train station at Baden-Baden is a stop for ICE/EC/IC/IR trains as well as all other regional trains.

CONTACTS
Schwarzwaldverein e.V.
Tel: +49 761 380 530
Fax: +49 761 380 5320
Email: verkauf@schwarzwaldverein.de
www.schwarzwaldverein.de

Schwarzwald Tourismus
Tel: +49 761 2962 271
Fax: +49 761 2962 270
Email: mail@schwarzwald-tourist-info.de
www.schwarzwald-tourismus.info

Deep-drift snowshoeing across Baden-Baden's uneven forest trails soon works up a sweat.

Snowshoeing in the Black Forest is an age-old tradition in a region that founded Germany's first 'snowshoe club' in the late 1800s. More than 23,000 km (14,260 miles) of criss-crossing country trails riddle an emerald-green coniferous landscape – a network of paths that if laid end-to-end would encircle half the globe. The Black Forest's most famous hike is a long-distance slog, across 280 km (174 miles) from Pforzheim to Basle. However, winter walkers with just a weekend to spare will find plenty of hardcore hikes other than Westweg, through untouched pine forests and boggy lakes to deep rocky valleys and verdant mountain ridges. Climb up from marshy lowlands across steep, plant-filled slopes to the pretty, flora-rich spa town of Baden-Baden, a scenic base for Black Forest exploration that former US president Bill Clinton described as "so nice they had to name it twice."

The 60 km (37 mile) Black Forest High Road trail makes an excellent three day option for experienced hikers, stretching from Baden-Baden along a scenic path to Freudenstadt on a level between 600–1,000 m (1,968–3,280 ft). Walkers who have followed this trail in summer will find that snowshoeing makes it an entirely different experience. Even familiar forests are transformed into something new, strange and wonderful in midwinter. In the Black Forest, deep snow makes obstacles more easily bypassed, such as large boulders and fallen logs. Snowshoeing also expands the potential for exercise on a snow-covered landscape. Trail runners will find a light pair of snowshoes invaluable when attempting to cross-country after snowfall, enabling sprints and hurdling (using tree trunks, stiles and ditches). Black Forest skiers often combine cross-country with a snowshoe trek on a less skiable section, often to a mountain summit on uneven terrain. Maps of the upland trails around Freudenstadt, Dobel, Baiersbronn, Triberg, Furtwangen, Neustadt-Titisee, Lenzkirch and the Kniebis Plateau are freely available from tourist offices and the Black Forest Association.

Known as 'webs', snowshoes are designed to distribute body weight over a larger area, thus preventing you from sinking into the snow. Not only does this 'flotation' technique enable hikers to make lighter work of ultra-deep powder, but it also offers a serious cardio workout, burning twice as much energy as a standard hike at around 600 calories an hour. Snowshoeing in deep drifts or light, fluffy snowfall requires a light tread and a steady pace. Settle on an intensity and momentum that allows your stride to stay natural – don't try to modify or exaggerate your gait, simply allow the terrain to dictate your steps. The steeper and deeper it gets, the more challenging the tempo, and a rhythmic pace – be it running or walking – will soon work up a serious sweat.

CONTACTS
Munich Tourism
Tel: +49 89 2300 180
Fax: +49 89 2300 181 11
Email: tourismus@muenchen.de
www.muenchen.de

Surging crests and powerful riverine currents test surfers to the max on the Eisbach.

CANAL SURFING MUNICH

You could be mistaken for wondering what natural comparisons can be drawn between Munich and Malibu Beach, given that Germany's landlocked Bavarian city offers very little sun and no beach. Yet a rather surprising fact about Munich is that is has a cult-status surfing scene, thanks to a tributary of the mighty River Isar. So, although German surfing may sound about as plausible as snowboarding in the Sahara, surfers have been heading here since the 1970s after three rows of concrete blocks were laid along the canal bottom to reduce the flow of water surging up from underground. Today, this underwater ridge has been enhanced with some wooden boards wedged into the canal by local surfers. The result is a fast but surfable standing wave of wildly gushing rapids that has created a year-round surf spot, German-style.

Munich's river-surf Mecca is located on the Eisbach (or 'Ice Creek') immediately outside the Haus der Kunst museum, where two underground canals meet and emerge under the 19th century Prinzregentenstrasse Bridge. Although the crashing surf may lack the sun-drenched glamour of California or Hawaii, the clear water surges in spectacular fashion, emitting a not unpleasant freshwater smell. Neoprene aromas intermingle with riverine spray on a churning crest that offers a powerful perpetual motion, with waves at waist-height. At around 15 m (49 ft) wide the Eisbach has its limitations, requiring a wait in queues along each bank. Once in the water a complex curl is tricky to master, as all the energy is at the front. A powerful oncoming current pushes backwards much like a wind tunnel on turbo, threatening the humiliation of being dumped downwater. In the early days, Munich's surfing pioneers tied ropes to the bridge or trees in a bid to understand its foibles. Today, balance is a key focus on the Eisbach, as is avoiding injury from the concrete blocks.

Despite not being officially sanctioned or controlled, surfing the canal is tolerated by the local authorities. In the peak of summer, more than 300 surfer dudes descend on the Eisbach with their boards under their arms, while neighbouring Flosslände – a canal 8 km (5 miles) south – hosts the annual Munich Surf Open. Easier waters rear up into a metre-high (3 ft) curl, offering tricksters plenty of scope to try out 360s, off-the-lips, floaters and little hopping aerials – all without a shark in sight.

057

GETTING THERE
Sylt is connected to the rest of
Germany on the Westerland route, a
fast service.

CONTACTS
Surf Schule Westerland
Tel: +49 4651 27172

Westerland Tourist Centre
Tel: +49 180 500 9980
Fax: +49 4651 998 6000
Email: info@westerland.de
www.westerland.de

*Crashing beach breaks and
year-round gusts lure surfers to
these remote North Sea dunes.*

SURFING SYLT

In summer, the jutting sandbar of Sylt
(pronounced 'zult') heaves with tourists jostling
for a spot on the beach. Winter is a much more
mellow affair, when the water turns icy grey under
a dark, brooding sky as a bracing breeze whips
up a heavy surf. Although commonly referred to
as an island, Sylt is tenuously attached to the
mainland, jutting out over 35 km (22 miles) into
Germany's northwest coast and reaching up to
13 km (8 miles) wide. On the eastern side, the
dunes and rugged cliffs are less windblown and
more tranquil. The North Sea location of Sylt
means that winds are strong all year long on the
western side, which receives swell with crashing
beach-breaks. The first German native to surf on
home waters is said to have been Uwe Drath, a
lifeguard on Sylt, in 1952. Today it plays host to
the Surf World Cup – the most prestigious
competition of the Professional Windsurfers
Association (PWA) World Tour – attracting
190,000 surfing pilgrims and 100-plus
competitors from over 27 nations to a remote
spot just a stone's throw from Denmark.

Sylt's finest surfing hotspots are tucked
beyond the rolling dunes of Westerland, where
fierce winter swells on a sandy bottom appeal to
hardened boarders not easily dispirited by the
chill. Be prepared to don a thermal 5/4 wetsuit,
hood, booties and gloves to survive water
temperatures of less than 5°C (41°F). A handful of
cafés offer plenty of warming food to keep the
inner furnace burning – nothing stops the cringing
before a duck dive into a freezing cold wave like a
bowl of steaming pea and sausage broth
(*Erbsensuppe mit Würstchen*). Sylt also lays claim
to bracing sea air that is rich in iodine, a
therapeutic tonic said to aid convalescence and
winter blues. Head-high waves will soon get the
blood pumping – Sylt is renowned for surfers with
grace as well as aggression, and watching the
local guys bash the churning water is a thrilling
spectator sport. Kicks, carves and slides lead to
perfect 360s, and even in the gustiest winds the
regulars manage to stay up for five minutes,
trimming back and forth in place and making it
look a synch. Newcomers should head on down
to Surf Schule, an iconic surfer hangout that offers
lessons and rental gear – and plenty of hints and
tips. Just ask anyone with a surfboard tucked
under their arm to point you in the right direction.

DRIVING NÜRBURG

As joint host of Germany's thrilling Formula One schedule, the Nürburgring is synonymous with 360 kph (225 mph) auto racing with up to five G pull. Attracting the *crème de la crème* of the motor world's cutting-edge design and world-class electronics, aerodynamics, suspension and tyres, the Nürburgring's podium boasts a star-studded winners list. Jackie Stewart, Stirling Moss, James Hunt and Niki Lauda are just a few of the stadium's alumni in a country renowned as the birth-nation of Porsche and BMW, two of the most prestigious high-performance models in the world. In recent years, Germany's racing heritage has been bolstered by Michael Schumacher, who holds the record for having won the most Drivers' Championships (seven). As the first German winner, it is Schumacher who is credited as the dynamo behind the popularization of the sport in his homeland. Motor racing is now so popular Germany-wide that the Nürburgring offers diehard fans the ultimate thrill – to speed around the Grand Prix circuit in a zillion white-knuckle laps from pole position.

The Nürburgring's special packages for speed-freaks are loaded with added extras, from circuit and stadium tours to autograph sessions. However, those seeking a co-pilot's view should opt for the BMW circuit; an acceleration-heavy high velocity lap on the Nordschleife at Grand Prix speeds. While racing through the so-called 'Green Hell' (as Jackie Stewart so succinctly put it) along a lightening stretch in the latest BMW M5, it is hard to believe that the Nürburgring is a public toll road. It's also a testing centre for major German automobile manufacturers. Yet the most amazing thing about this breakneck strip of asphalt is that ordinary people fresh off the street can drive a 20.8 km (13 mile) lap at the Nürburgring, in their very own vehicle, for a mere 15 euros. Completed in 1927, this track is widely regarded as the toughest and most dangerous in the world, testing driving skills under demanding conditions that include blind curves, treacherous crests and steep grades. Ever-changing surface conditions and friction require nerve, sensitivity and focus on a route that is fortunately free of opposing traffic. It's a daredevil run and a dizzying experience – forget the podium; avoiding a tailspin is the prime goal on this circuit, an amazing feat of showmanship deserving of pole position.

GETTING THERE
The Nürburgring is situated 90 km (56 miles) southwest of Cologne and 60 km (37 miles) northwest of Koblenz. The closest airports are Köln-Bonn (80 km/50 miles) and Düsseldorf (120 km/74 miles).

CONTACTS
Nürburgring
Tel: +49 2691 3020
Fax: +49 2691 302 155
www.nuerburgring.de

Nürburg Tourist Information Service
Tel: +49 2691 302610
Fax: +49 2691 302650

Enjoy pole position on white-knuckle laps of this exhilarating F1 circuit, a fiendish track of blind curves and treacherous tailspins.

AUSTRIA

TIME DIFFERENCE GMT +2

TELEPHONE CODE +43

CURRENCY Euro

LANGUAGE German

POPULATION 8.19 million

SIZE OF COUNTRY 83,858 sq km
(32,705 sq miles)

CAPITAL Vienna

WHEN TO GO Two distinct seasons affect rural tourism. Mountain resorts, for example, have a winter sports calendar and a season for summer hikers. In between times, many tourist facilities are closed. Urban centres are popular year-round, with tourist numbers swelling during peak holidays and annual festivals. Visit during May–August for the best of the warm weather, while snow is pretty much guaranteed November until early April.

TOURIST INFORMATION
Austrian Tourist Office
Tel: 0845 101 1818
Fax: 0845 101 1819
Email: holiday@austria.info
www.austria.info

Breathtaking mountain scenery and magnificent rivers characterize Austria's natural riches, from the Alps in the west to the Danube basin in the east. Snow-topped peaks and gingerbread-style Alpine chalets typify the country's picture-postcard ski regions, while Austria's bustling cities mix historical splendour with world-class museums, opera houses and galleries, from ornate capital Vienna and Salzburg, Mozart's birthplace, to Innsbruck's dramatic backdrop as the gateway to the Austrian Alps. Landlocked Austria shares its borders with eight countries – Switzerland, Liechtenstein, Germany, the Czech Republic, Slovakia, Hungary, Slovenia and Italy. An enduring reputation for music, literature and the arts is peppered with influences from neighbouring cultures – both classical and contemporary – yet Austria's classic sparsely Alpine landscape remains seemingly untouched by time.

CONTACTS
Donauturm
Tel: +43 1263 3572
Fax: +43 1263 3572 39
Email: info@donauturm.at
www.donauturm.at

Vienna Tourist Board
Tel: +43 124 555
Fax: +43 124 555 666
Email: info@wien.info
www.wien.info

A stomach-churning leap from this sky-high city spire can turn legs to jelly at 152 m (499 ft).

BUNGEE JUMPING VIENNA

A genteel way to enjoy Vienna's soaring 325 m (1,066 ft) city spire is to allow the super-speedy elevator to deliver you effortlessly to the top. Here, a gently rotating restaurant serves fine pastries on an ever-changing panorama of eye-popping city views. Affectionately dubbed the 'concrete needle' by the Viennese, the Danube Tower was erected in a record breaking 20 months in 1964. Adding a more daredevil aspect to this elegant, pencil-thin shaft was considerably less rapid than its construction. However, within four decades, Vienna's lofty landmark building adopted the (unofficial) motto 'the higher the climb, the prettier the fall', adding a launch pad at 152 m (499 ft). Today it ranks among the highest urban bungee jumping venues in the world, offering a stomach-churning 100 kph (62 mph) drop that gives a whole new meaning to the term 'Viennese whirl'.

Bungee fans in Vienna will enjoy 80 km (50 mile) views from the Danube Tower before they leap. A weekend programme runs from mid-June to early October, weather permitting. Expect to pay around 139 euros for the bungee, with an extra charge for a video memento of the plunge itself. In 2001, world-record bungee champion Jochen Schweizer of Germany plummeted from the Danube Tower in a televised inaugural jump. Several thousand jumpers have followed suit, with over 15.6 million visitors opting to survey the views without the danger of a free-fall dangle. Those that opt to jump 'Vienna's Eiffel' will almost certainly need to queue if they've not pre-booked, especially if a stag party is in town. By far the easiest way to secure a slot is to pre-pay online. After a safety briefing and harness check, a multi-coloured super-strength cord is attached. It's then time to edge out on to an 8 m (26 ft) ramp to wonder at the awesome views and gaze across the clouds. At over 17,000 tonnes, the 12 m (39 ft) diameter tower was the creation of Austrian architect Prof Hannes Lintl, who incorporated almost 800 ultra-steep stairs into his design – another good reason to jump. Those keen to try their hand at a stair-dash should aim for 3 minutes, 19 seconds – the current record. This is no mean feat, especially with legs like jelly, a stomach full of butterflies and a 152 m (499 ft) death-dive in sight.

060

CONTACTS
Tourismusverband Fuschl am See
Tel: +43 6226 8250
Fax: +43 6226 8650
www.fuschlseeregion.com

Famously captured in the 1965 film *The Sound of Music*, the snow-topped peaks and bloom-filled grasslands of Salzkammergut's Fuschl am See are every bit the Alpine wonderland. Set within the lush, green Salzkammergut Lake District in the foothills of the mountains, the region's numerous old salt mines date back as far as the iron age and give Salzkammergut its name (*salz* = salt). Today, Fuschl am See is blessed with one of the Lake District's most beautiful expanses of water, Lake Fuschl. This 4 km by 1 km (2.5 by 0.6 mile) stretch is sheltered by pine-clad hills and offers secluded bays and shingle beaches, wrapped in over 900 km (558 miles) of invigorating hiking trails in the midst of a Nature Reserve.

Choosing where to explore on foot around Fuschl am See isn't easy, as the local maps will testify. Dozens of trails lead out to Lake Wolfgang, 6 km (4 miles) away, while hundreds of others sprawl out across the mountains in an orderly jumble of well-signed paths. Several maps detail local hiking routes at different scales, and can be picked up from the tourist office and major hotels. Free guided walks are run throughout the year by the local tourist authorities and serve as excellent 'tasters' for a full-on all-day mountain slog. The topography of the region pulls in all manner of amblers, ramblers, trail runners, Nordic walkers and trekkers, from those seeking a leisurely meander by clean, crisp waters to those keen to achieve the optimum respiratory rate of 70 breaths a minute. Imbibing the fresh air is part of the lung-busting tonic of Fuschl am See, looking out to rolling hills, thick, green forests and meadows tumbling into the lake. Only electric-powered craft are allowed to sail the waters, so the mood is mellow, with the sound of birdsong uninterrupted by the noise of spluttering engines. Plentiful stocks of trout attract a steady flow of shoreline anglers, while birders trek the marshland trails in search of wagtails, coots, great crested grebes, mute swans, mallards, tufted ducks and pochards.

For a blood-pumping first excursion, take the trail from the lakeside promenade to pass Ebner's Waldhof Hotel before bearing off to the right. Climb up through the forest to the Waldhof Alm and Forsthaus Wartenfels on a steep path that leads to the Wartenfels ruins. Then follow the signs to the Frauenkopf summit and the Schober Mountain to complete a pretty challenging trio in around two and a half hours. Handrails and pull-cables offer good support up to the Schober summit – a trek that is worth the exertion for the views alone.

Looking for a gentler option? Don't be fooled by the rather cozy sounding lake stroll 'Fuschlseeweg' (Trail 1). Not only does it snake for almost 12 km (7 miles) to reach 180 m (590 ft), but some pretty demanding conditions underfoot make the circuit no walk in the park. Wear proper walking boots and pack plenty of grit and determination for this trail – it may look innocuous but the path deteriorates from gravel to mud, plus every stage in between. Much of the trail hugs the shore, until at Schloss Fuschl it veers away to the mouth of the Fuschler Ache stream a few hundred metres along a small road before curving back through woods. Leave at least three hours for this scenic stomp – or a good four hours-plus if the ground is wet.

For a four to five hour circuit, try the 20 km (12 mile) Trail 13 from Eibensee to Ellmaustein, a scenic round-trip through conifers out on the Wolfgangseebundesstrasse. A perfectly maintained signpost denotes the turn-off through wild moors, meadows and forests, along the Eibensee stream to the mountain lake Eibensee. A forest track winds to the Ellmau Valley road, where the mountain path connects with the Ellmausteinpeak – and a truly memorable mountain panorama complete with wispy clouds and a blue-green haze.

Trail 22 provides a pleasant 6 km (4 mile) forest romp that should take around one and a half hours at a steady stomp. Follow the signs to Mühlreitweg from the underpass on the main road by the church. This connects with a small road first, then to a trail from which a path to Bambichl can be picked up. Pass a deer enclosure to the Old Ruming Mill before the Bambichl Farm, and then loop back into the woods for the return loop to town. Trail runners enjoy tackling this route with a stopwatch, clocking up times of under 60 minutes – and laying down the gauntlet to all like-minded visitors passing through.

'The hills are alive' in Salzkammergut's Alpine wonderland, thanks to hundreds of invigorating trails.

SKIING INNSBRUCK

GETTING THERE
The Stubai Glacier is 30 minutes from Innsbruck by car and 50 minutes by train and bus. There are over a dozen departures daily, from about 7am to 4pm.

CONTACTS
Innsbruck Tourism Office
www.innsbruck-tourism.at

Dependable snow and supercharged descents lure adrenaline niuts to Stubai's 3,000 m (9,840 ft) heights.

Guaranteeing snow is a bold move for any ski resort, yet the Stubai Glacier's year-round skiable runs are deserving of brash claims, assuring skiing 65 days per year. Austria's largest glacial ski zone boasts around 150 km (93 miles) of piste at an altitude of 3,200 m (10,496 ft) along with 4.5 km (3 miles) of cross-country ski trails, 44 chairlifts and a maze of hiking paths. Located 20 km (12 miles) south of Innsbruck, the Stubai Valley ranks among Austria's most beautiful ski centres, edged by five picturesque villages – Schoenberg, Telfes, Mieders, Fulpmes and Neustift. A network of 25 high-speed lifts transports 36,000 people per hour up to the peaks. Views are expansive, with facilities that include a 20 m (66 ft) artificial ice climbing tower and permanent race course. Access to the slopes involves a 20 minute cable car ride, but once up, skiers are presented with an exquisite selection of runs. Novice, intermediate and expert skiing are all well catered for, but if it's a heart-pounding double black diamond run you're after, you'll need to be an intermediate-plus hotshot at least.

With a highest lifted point of 3,333 m (10,932 ft), the Stubai Glacier's plenitude of snow is at its most reliable October to June. Sitting well above the tree line, off-piste lines are easy to scope, with jagged granite slabs forming a striking contrast to alpine foliage on snow-capped peaks. Catch the free half-hourly shuttle bus, then ridge to the Stubai Glacier ski area lifts for a short downhill on the piste from 3,000 m (9,840 ft) – a guaranteed adrenaline-surging descent. A Stubai-Superski lift pass covers all resorts, from the intermediate trails above the village of Neustift to the extensive slopes of Fulpmes and Telfes. Backcountry fans will have plenty of scope for off-piste and skiing into the crud to look for steeper fare.

Just one word of advice: avoid Stubai over public holiday weekends, as Germany empties at the region's expense. A sea of gleaming black Audis, BMWs and Mercedes snake into the car park of this usually orderly resort complex. Queues form and patience is tested, so stick to mid-week or off-peak.

CZECH REPUBLIC

Split into two distinct geographical and cultural portions, the
Czech Republic is characterized by the spa towns of Bohemia and
the wine-growing villages of Moravia, along with over a hundred
castles, fortresses and fine chateaux. Almost 1,000 km (620 miles)
of waymarked trails provide a major draw for hikers, cyclists and
cross-country skiers. Sun-blessed in summer and snow-covered
in winter, the Czech Republic's mountain ranges peak at 1,602 m
(5,255 ft) while low hills roll into basin plains and rivers stretch out
across borders towards the sea. The country is also home to one
of the most beautiful cities in Europe, Prague: a dazzling architectural
collection of Art Nouveau, Baroque and Neo-Classical splendour on
Central Bohemia's River Vltava.

TIME DIFFERENCE GMT +1

TELEPHONE CODE +420

CURRENCY Czech crown

LANGUAGE Czech

POPULATION 10.2 million

SIZE OF COUNTRY 78,866 sq km
(30,758 sq miles)

CAPITAL Prague

WHEN TO GO The Czech Republic is situated
in a temperate zone and boasts four distinct
seasons of equal length. Winters are relatively
mild (at around -2°C/28°F) and summers rarely
exceed 22°C (72°F).

TOURIST INFORMATION
Czech Republic Tourist Office
Tel: 020 7631 0427
Fax: 020 7631 0419
Email: info-uk@czechtourism.com
www.czechtourism.com

062

WHITEWATER RAFTING
PRAGUE

HOW TO GET THERE
Prague Airport is approximately 15 km (9 miles) from the city centre. Taxis cost around £20, or buses operate every 10 minutes from the front of the airport building. Bus number 119 will take you to the nearest underground station, Dejvicka. From there take the green line.

CONTACTS
Inge Tour Canoe & Kayak Rentals
Tel: +420 380 746 139
Fax: +420 380 746 953
Email: info@ingetour.cz
www.ingetour.cz

The sweeping twists and turns of the Vltava River on the rural outskirts of the capital boast a rafting tradition that dates back to the early 12th century. In that era, vessels were wooden-slatted constructions, bound by rope and sealed with resin. Today, Vltava's waterborne crafts are inflatable, self-bailing speed tubes, manufactured using high-tech gadgetry to ensure the ultimate in endurance rafting. Dubbed the Czech Republic's 'rafting epicentre', the Vltava River's prime whitewater rapids are at their wildest from April to October. Host of the World Rafting Competition, the river also contains a purpose-built trial canal, a real boon for those keen to ease in gently. Otherwise the water is fast and furious, with characteristic gushing torrents and plenty of chop. After a test ride, rafters in tour groups warm up with competitive slalom and parallel head-to-head races to get the feel of the craft. Then it's time for a full dose of adrenaline out on the wild water river, negotiating the riffles, swirls, tight turns and rapids with the guidance of an English speaking instructor.

Rafting on Vltava River delivers year-round grade IV conditions along a run that draws a buoyed-up crowd from all over the world. Each is hell-bent on achieving maximum thrills even on the thigh-high stretches. A friendly rivalry exists between rafters and canoeists on the Vltava, so don't be fooled by the friendly *ahojs*. Grounded on a rock? Then brace yourself for some good natured jibes, pounding paddles and cat-calls. On less troublesome stretches, soak up some pleasant riverbank views across wildflower meadows as circling falcons scrutinize the rolling grasslands.

Highlights include the run by Vssyí Brod where an old paper mill at Vetmí denotes a wider, deeper stretch requiring greater effort from lazy paddlers. Thirsty rafters will enjoy the downstream stretch towards Ceské Budejovice, where a succession of lively riverbank pubs serve ice-cold jugs of Staropramen. Gusty winds can make this journey a battleground in poor weather, so keep an eye on the colour of the river; an oily black surface means rain is on the way. Flips happen, so it also pays to be especially vigilant around the partially submerged rocks and strong undercurrents of the upper section. Pack lots of drinking water, suncream, swimming gear, a towel and a change of clothing.

Fast and furious grade IV white water draws a buoyed-up crowd to the Vltava River.

CONTACTS
Brno Tourist Information Centre
Tel: +420 542 210 762
Fax: +420 542 423 963
Email: info@ticbrno.cz
www.brno.cz

With the Czech-Moravian highlands beyond, Brno's hiking trails rise and fall along riverbanks and forests.

MOUNTAIN BIKING BRNO

Having long tired of unfavourable comparisons to the prettier capital, the Czech Republic's oft-overlooked second city Brno has carved out a niche of its own. As a hub for cycling fanatics, Brno is the Republic's bike-friendly city; a destination woven with cycle paths and trails. It may not have Prague's pastel-coloured aged architecture and handsome, picture-postcard streets, but Brno forms the very heart of the Czech Republic's sporting country, bounded by the striking Bohemian massif and leafy lowlands of southern Moravia, with the Svratka and Svitava rivers as a frame. Brno will never be the new Prague, but then it doesn't want to be: a comfortable assurance that is as pleasing as its vast swathes of tree-clad sloping hills.

Cyclists keen to get acquainted with Brno should check out the city's cracking 60 km (37 mile) round route to Pernstejn, one of the most finely preserved Gothic fort towns on the planet. A favourite ride with Brno cycling fans racing into the stunning Czech-Moravian highlands, through both urban and rural terrain, the route comprises an exhilarating mix of cycle paths, small streets, riverside trails and unmade tracks. A flurry of ups and downs ups the ante between Tisnov and Doubravník through Lomnice, but the journey is light on traffic apart from the section that connects Doubravník with Nedvedice and a breakneck stretch at Zouvalka opposite Veven Castle.

Begin at Brno's FC Sparta stadium along the signposted routes of one, four and five until you join the manicured cycle trails along the Svitava and Svratka rivers. This is where mountain bikers and road racers compete in the Brno Lake Challenge each May on tracks that range from 100 km (62 miles) for road racers, 55 km (34 miles) for mountain bikers and a flat 30 km (19 mile) route for hobbyists. Follow the signs for Pernstejn via Hrad Veven, Veverská Bítysk, Cebín and Lomnice – a picturesque little town situated 7 km (4 miles) north of Tisnov reached through the Besének valley. Next, the riverside town of Doubravník leads to a fast-paced road into Nedvedice before a more leisurely, winding uphill slog to the castle of Pernstejn atop a rocky ledge. This beautifully fairytale setting dates back to the 13th century and is a much-used film location for period dramas. Cyclists keen not to experience their own mini-drama should watch out for razor-like rock chippings in and around the castle – it's wise to keep a couple of reliable puncture kits to hand.

SLOVAKIA

TIME DIFFERENCE GMT +1

TELEPHONE CODE +421

CURRENCY Slovak Koruna

LANGUAGE Slovak

POPULATION 5,423,567

SIZE OF COUNTRY 48,845 sq km
(19,050 sq miles)

CAPITAL Bratislava

WHEN TO GO Bloom-filled April and May brings
zest and vigour to Slovakia after what are typically
cold, dark, cloudy winters. Bright, cool and breezy
summers are ideal for outdoor pursuits, with
sunshine that runs well into September and
October.

TOURIST INFORMATION
Slovakian National Tourist Office
Tel: +421 48 413 61 46
Fax: +421 48 413 61 49
Email: sacr@sacr.sk
www.slovakia.travel

Slovakia's resplendent mountains rise in the hills of the Malá Fatra
and run east to the Alpine peaks of the starkly beautiful High Tatras.
Some of the highest peaks are some of Europe's most magnificent,
with plunging valleys, scenic lakes and snow-covered soaring peaks.
A puzzle of downhill ski runs and cross-country tracks weave through
icy crevices and coniferous forests. It is less glamorous than some of
its more cosmopolitan neighbours – Slovakia shares its borders with
Austria, the Czech Republic, Hungary, Poland and Ukraine – but
pretty, flower-filled meadows and simple, traditional villages
characterize the country's off the beaten track retreats. Slovaks
love to camp, fish, ski and mountain bike the rough terrain of the
Tatra Mountains, in which a multi-day trek is arguably the ultimate
physical test.

SNOW RAFTING POPRAD

East central Slovakia is synonymous with the jagged, beautiful peaks of the High Tatras, a breathtaking Alpine ridge that draws over 5 million visitors a year. The High Tatras are part of the 795 sq km (310 sq mile) Tatra National Park, Czechoslovakia's first such area, established in 1949. Rugged trails snake through an awesome series of gorges, rapids and waterfalls, with 25 peaks at more than 2,500 m (8,200 ft) and over 100 lakes. Home to bears, chamois and thousands of summer hikers, the Tatras provide a more peaceful retreat once snow has fallen. As the 1970 host of the World Nordic Skiing Championship and a candidate for the 2014 Winter Olympics, Slovenia is justifiably proud of its Tatras ski trails: a tangle that forms an inverted east–west arc along the Slovak–Polish border, curling to the north as they move east. Yet it is snow rafting that is capturing the imagination of non-skiing winter visitors keen to get a kick from the slopes.

As the latest extreme sport to hit the mountains, snow rafting is much like whitewater rafting – just without the rapids. In simplistic terms, a rubber dinghy is towed up a mountainside by a snowmobile where it is perched on the summit facing downwards. Whilst attached to bungee cords, the raft is propelled catapult-style down the hill, bouncing across a crest of bumps at speed on the descent. Downhill rafts can reach up to 65 kph (40 mph), so paddles (for steering) and safety helmets are essential. All of the most reputable snow rafting operators are registered with Satur tourist agency office, above the train station in Stary Smokovec, the most accommodating (and touristy) of the Tatra villages. Pick up a detailed map (VKÚ's Vysoké Tatry) and wear full cold weather gear even if the sun is shining. A puzzle of pre-defined trails loop a snow-covered route to allow up to a dozen rafters to barrel down the slopes in the ultimate winter joyride. When the raft reaches a smooth flat area, brakes are applied to bring the raft to a pirouetting stop, allowing lungs to slowly re-inflate and the squeals to subside.

GETTING THERE
Flights go directly to Poprad, where numerous taxis offer transfers to the mountains. There's also a frequent train service that runs between the towns and villages in the High Tatras.

CONTACTS
Slovak Adventures
Tel: 08444 128 890
Email: info@slovakventures.co.uk
www.slovakadventures.co.uk

Bounce at speed down a snow-crusted mountain slope propelled by a catapult-style bungee.

POLAND

TIME DIFFERENCE GMT +1

TELEPHONE CODE +48

CURRENCY Zloty

LANGUAGE Polish

POPULATION 35.8 million

SIZE OF COUNTRY 312,684 sq km
(121,947 sq miles)

CAPITAL Warsaw

WHEN TO GO Poland's weather is unpredictable,
with winters that vary dramatically in intensity from
mild to bitterly cold. However, summers are
generally warm and the most pleasant time to visit,
with July the hottest month. September turns cool
as October approaches, with colder weather
increasing until December when the temperature
drops below zero – sometimes to -20°C (-4°F).

TOURIST INFORMATION
Polish National Tourist Office
Tel: 08700 675 012
Fax: 08700 675 011
www.poland.travel

Poland's 500 km (310 miles) of coastline trims the Baltic Sea to the
north in an unbroken rolling stretch, while the Carpathian Mountains
dominate the south. Bordered by seven countries – Germany,
Russia, Lithuania, Belarus and the Ukraine to the north and the
Czech Republic and Slovakia to the south – Poland's varied mix of
climates is greatly influenced by its neighbours. Cool polar breezes
bring chilly blasts from Russia and Scandinavia, while warmer gusts
come up from the south. Off-roaders, hikers, kayakers and boaters
have large expanses of pasture and fast-flowing rivers at their
disposal, while mountain trails and hill tracks are ideal for mountain
biking, trail running and orienteering – all just a stone's throw from
major cities.

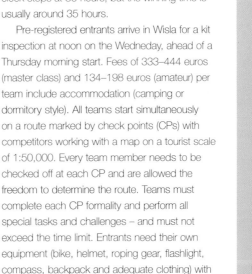

GETTING THERE
Krakow is easily accessible by train, including an InterCity service from Warsaw that takes 2.5 hours.

CONTACTS
Zamberlan Adventure Trophy
Tel: +48 126 261 436
Email: krzysztof.rapala@adventure trophy.pl
www.adventuretrophy.pl

Wisla Tourist Board
Tel: +48 338 552 425
Fax: +48 338 552 995
Email: um@wisla.pl
www.wisla.pl

ADVENTURE KRAKOW

In May each year, Poland's gruelling three day Zamberlan Adventure Trophy brings the mad, bad and dangerous to Wisla, a small southern town on the border with the Czech Republic. Set in the ski run-riddled Silesian Beskids Mountains at the River Wisla's source, the town is surrounded by beautiful thick woodlands, deep gorges and crashing waterfalls. Umpteen well-marked paths run through the city and around it along relatively flat mountain ridges, through rocky fissures and rolling pasture. Over 75 per cent of Wisla's 110 sq km (43 sq mile) spatial limits is densely forested, while surrounding peaks contain ski lifts, jumps and downhill runs at the core of a full-on winter sports scene. When the Zamberlan Adventure Trophy comes to town, Wisla plays host to Poland's most demanding physical challenge: a multi-disciplined event that combines mountain biking, trekking, trail running, rope-work, zip wiring, river kayaking and inline skating over 350 km (217 miles).

Teams of four people enter male-only, mixed and veteran categories in either the master class or amateur class – the latter is shorter at 225 km (140 miles) and is for two-person teams, regardless of sex. With a time limit of 80 hours, the 350 km (217 mile) course includes 220 km (136 miles) of mountain biking, 95 km (59 miles) of trekking, 25 km (16 miles) of river kayaking and 20 km (12 miles) of inline skating. Winning times come in at under 54 hours – no mean feat. In the amateur class, the breakdown runs to 155 km (96 miles) of mountain biking, 60 km (37 miles) of trekking and 10 km (6 miles) of river kayaking. The clock stops at 80 hours, but the winning time is usually around 35 hours.

Pre-registered entrants arrive in Wisla for a kit inspection at noon on the Wednesday, ahead of a Thursday morning start. Fees of 333–444 euros (master class) and 134–198 euros (amateur) per team include accommodation (camping or dormitory style). All teams start simultaneously on a route marked by check points (CPs) with competitors working with a map on a tourist scale of 1:50,000. Every team member needs to be checked off at each CP and are allowed the freedom to determine the route. Teams must complete each CP formality and perform all special tasks and challenges – and must not exceed the time limit. Entrants need their own equipment (bike, helmet, roping gear, flashlight, compass, backpack and adequate clothing) with maps, kayaks and lifejackets supplied. Each team member must carry photo ID and each team needs at least one mobile phone.

Wisla's 80-hour, multi-discipline endurance test pushes stamina and grit to the max.

GETTING THERE

Torun's nearest airport is Bydgoszcz, a 30 minute drive away. It also has direct railway connections with all large cities in Poland. Bear's Gorge is near the small town of Steklin, but the easiest transfer option is the shuttle offered from Bydgoszcz airport to the riding centre (£50) – a 93 km (58 mile) journey that is also served by the PKS regional bus system. Taxis and car rental are both available from the airport.

CONTACTS

Torun Trips
Tel: +48 5662 10406
Email: info@toruntrips.co.uk

Visit Torun
Tel/fax: +48 5662 10422
Email: info@turystyka.torun.pl
www.visittorun.pl

Saddle up in Torun for leisurely rides through wild, bucolic splendour on bridle paths and unmarked hill trails.

HORSE RIDING TORUN

Experienced riders frustrated by the tooting horns and exhaust fumes of road hogs will revel in the sleepy peacefulness of the unspoilt wilds of Torun. A beautiful swaddle of green countryside wraps this (as yet) largely undiscovered medieval city with untamed meadows peppered with gushing creeks and wooded thickets. Even in Torun itself, smells of pine needles and gingerbread predominate throughout a fine UNESCO-listed old quarter of Baroque façades, Gothic turrets and Renaissance gables. Straddling both banks of the Vistula River, Torun is an ancient trading hub with an 800 year commercial history. Set within the centre of the Kuiavia–Pomerania region and bordered by three contrasting provinces, Torun is blessed by surrounding rural expanses that offer a getaway just a short drive from the heart of the city.

Torun's most relaxed horseback escapes are found at Bear's Gorge, a 30 minute drive from the city and a fast-emerging ecotourism destination popular with campers, hikers and birders alike. Raw, untamed countryside overlooks the waters of Lake Steklin looped by bridle paths, riverside trails and winding hedgerows. Ranch-based riding and trail riding are offered guided and unguided to riders, with customized trips tailormade. A range of

handpicked horses ensure a choice of temperament and size, usually up to 16.2 hands. All rides set off from Bear's Gorge Ranch, but a range of trails offer plenty of variation, from all-out gallops and day-long hacks to more sedate treks. Ditches, streams and gates allow thrilling jumps in a bucolic wonderland, where a tufted wilderness of ponies and traps seems stuck in time and you can tear across sodden pasture and shallow rivers and climb through leafy hillside trails. Summer is predominantly warm, with highs of 35–40°C (95–104°F), but plentiful sunshine is interlaced with heavy rainfall, especially in July. Autumn is warm and usually sunny but turns cold, damp and foggy in November. Mid-May and early October are popular with active holidaymakers as the weather is crisp, cool and sunny but not sticky.

Costs are competitive compared to Europe's more established horse riding destinations. Budget for around £47 a day, including accommodation, food, three hours' riding and transfers from Torun, although riders should bring their own riding gear. Those that feel constrained by fixed itineraries will enjoy the flexible per-day payment system offered. Not only does it provide the flexibility to extend a stay, but it also allows weekenders stuck for time to piece together a short trip that fits.

SAILING GDANSK

The history-rich city of Gdansk has long been tied the Baltic Sea and shipping due to its location at the mouth of the River Vistula, once an ancient seaport at the centre of Poland's sea trade. Shipbuilders and cargo magnates both held sway here thanks to a waterway system that linked the city to the national capital. Today, Gdansk continues to welcome sailors from across the globe to its historical quarter, as host of many Olympic-class regattas on the Bay of Gdansk. Dozens of sailing clubs, marinas and yachting associations have their headquarters in the city; a popular launch point for visitors keen to undertake the Radunia Loop (*Kolko Radunskie*) – a 40 km (25 mile) scenic circuit that leads out along the River Radunia to half a dozen picturesque lakes just outside Gdansk's urban sprawl.

Stretching 105 km (65 miles) as a tributary to the River Motlawa, the Radunia flows on the Pojezierze Kaszubskie, a magnificent chain of postglacial lakes in a river basin in the Upper Radunia region. This complex network of 16 natural water reservoirs spans over 20 sq km (8 sq miles). Most boaters stock up on supplies in Gdansk, organize a skipper or a hire boat (expect to pay around 50 euros per day for a yacht for up to 12 people) and pick up a detailed map of the Radunia Loop from the Gdansk tourist information office in the centre of town.

What makes this lake-filled region special is the way that the river flows through a narrow forest valley, forming numerous bends and carving out distinctive shapes and curvatures on a leafy terrain. Riverbanks, gorges, rocks and meadows are sprinkled with wild flowers on a landscape blessed with over 500 species of vascular plants. Beavers, voles, weasels and polecats each have a home here, as do dozens of species of nesting birds. Marshy river banks are dotted with butterflies, while sediment-filled waters are rich in freshwater fish. Pack a kayak for the skinny channels, and delve into boggy pools and shallow creeks along fine woodland-trimmed waterways. It may be impossible to pick up speed along the Rudunia Loop, but that doesn't diminish the thrill.

CONTACTS
Gdansk Tourist Board
www.gdansk.pl

A rich natural history and a river system of waterways and post-glacial lakes offers boaters a buzz.

SNOWBOARDING WROCLAW

GETTING THERE
From Wroclaw, the Sudeten Mountains' main resort of Karpacz is 150 km (93 miles) away.

CONTACTS
Karkonosze Tourist Board
Tel: +48 601 882 771
Email: akcept@wczasy.net.pl
www.karkonosze.pl

Wroclaw's elongated runs.

Despite being smaller than the Alpine massifs, Poland's Sudeten Mountains still offer a host of sporty challenges, providing excellent skiing and snowboarding on some thrilling terrain. Located in the southwest of the country, the Sudeten also benefit from a well-organized tourism infrastructure across a mosaic of divergent landscapes. The expansive Karkonosze and the cloud-shrouded Góry Stolowe ('Table Mountains') provide some striking scenic contrasts with the low, broad slopes of the Izerskie, Bialskie and Zlote ranges, which hide cascading waterfalls, woodlands and postglacial rocky crags. Shaggy-haired wild sheep (*mouflons*) graze on scrubland renowned for precious minerals and gem stones, with crystal, agate, amethyst, jasper, garnet, topaz, and nephrite still evident amongst the shrub. During the winter snowfall, the Sudeten Mountains take on an otherworldly guise, as deep drifts add curves and softer edges to the serrated skyline of this spiky ridge.

Skiers and snowboarders start descending on the slopes from December until mid-April, many choosing the cable car-served Mount Szrenica and its diversified trails on the northwest flank. Deep glacial cirques sit snugly just beneath the rim of the summit, in a region blessed by 100 days of snow. Avalanche risk is real, with crampons essential on the ice-packed upper slopes, while snowboarders around the hotspot of Karkonosze should also keep one eye on the clouds. Elongated runs, well-signed routes and illuminated paths host various winter sport championships, including the Snowboard National Cup. Winter sports enthusiasts enjoy the freestyle possibilities at Mala Kopa Mountain as well as the trails of Liczyrzepa, Wilcza and Zlotowka. For ease, several organized tours will shuttle you and your board to giant slalom courses and take-offs. Conditions are good, offering some gently contoured stretches for newbies keen to stay within their comfort zone. Some white-knuckle descents won't clock world records, but who needs speeds of 200 kph (124 mph) when you can tear up a course in single carve? Beginners will find that rolling down the window (being caught off balance, prompting a wild rotation of the arms in the air) is an occupational hazard. Locals swear by slamming snow on the bare skin of their neck to get pumped up ahead of getting to the bottom the fastest. But be warned, hauling downhill on these well-groomed, lunatic slopes can get scary when you catch an edge.

LITHUANIA

A land of lakes, castles and forests, Lithuania is located on the eastern Baltic coast, sharing borders with Belarus, Latvia, Poland and Russia. Lithuania's 100 km (62 miles) of coastline boasts tree-fringed beaches popular with summer picnickers, while the frozen shallows of the Curonian Lagoon are a major ice fishing draw. Set within the 18 ha (44 acre) Kursiu Nerija National Park, the non-tidal stretch runs along the Baltic coast to straddle the Lithuania–Russia border. Pike, perch, bream, smelt, bass, whitefish and roach are fished on the lagoon, with Lithuania's hot, dry summers offering great potential for camping, hiking, cycling and swimming. Vilnius is situated in the southeast of the country, and is the least known and visited of the three Baltic state capitals, despite its superbly preserved and beautiful historic core.

TIME DIFFERENCE GMT +2

TELEPHONE CODE +370

CURRENCY Litas

LANGUAGE Lithuanian

POPULATION 3,575,439

SIZE OF COUNTRY 65,300 sq km (25,467 sq miles)

CAPITAL Vilnius

WHEN TO GO Summer and spring (May through to September) are warm and sunny, although the midsummer holiday (June) sees crowds swell. July and August draw international visitors while many locals are on holiday. Winter (November to March) brings snowfall and only a few hours of daylight each day.

TOURIST INFORMATION
Lithuanian National Tourism Office
Tel: 020 7034 1222
Fax: 020 7935 4661
Email: info@lithuaniatourism.co.uk
www.lithuaniatourism.co.uk

ICE FISHING VILNIUS

On a bright, clear, winter's day in Lithuania, the trees dangle with spear-shaped icicles as rolling pasture groans under the weight of thick snow. Ice-encrusted hedgerows dazzle like cut-glass crystal on the frozen shores of the Curonian Lagoon, a non-tidal shallow stretch that runs along the Baltic coast. Spanning over 1,580 sq km (616 sq miles), the almost freshwater lagoon has an average depth of around 4 m (13 ft) and straddles the Lithuania–Russia border. As the largest Baltic Sea lagoon, the Curonian Lagoon is fed by the fertile waters of the River Nemunas, ensuring an inflow of a wide variety of fish. Pike, perch, bream, smelt, bass, roach, vimba and whitefish are found in plentiful abundance, as well as burbot – an elongated eel-like freshwater cod species (also known as dogfish) now extinct in the UK.

Lithuania's hot, dry summers offer lots of untapped fishing potential, but it is the bitterly cold winters for which the Curionian Lagoon is world-renowned. As the temperatures plummet, the lake's surrounding pine forests take on a magical, frosted aura as wild boar, elk and deer snuggle away in snowed-in comfort. Succulent fish smoked to an old Curonian recipe provide sustenance for any fishermen plucky enough to brave -20°C (-4°F) temperatures around the shore. Vodka is another source of warmth for those who are patient enough to ice fish, especially after dark. Each person is allowed a catch of up to 5 kg (11 lbs) of fish per day, so snagging a fully-grown burbot at a whopping 20 kg (44 lbs) can cause a conundrum – unless your four fishing buddies draw a blank.

Solid preparation is crucial to ice fishing in sub-zero temperatures, as is the guidance of a seasoned pro. Wear as much cold-weather clothing as you can (layering is everything) and swaddle up penguin-style in a bevy of thermal undergarments to protect against the elements. Night fishing often involves a long, cold wait in a biting wind that can freeze nostrils at forty paces. Most ice anglers perch on a stool or chair, but some simply squat on their haunches, making sure the ice is at least 10 cm (4 in) thick. A few may choose to set up an ice shanty as a form of protective windbreak. Unlike Finland, where solitary and contemplative isolation is often the object of the pastime, Lithuanian ice fishing is a social affair. The oft-frozen waters of the Curonian Lagoon draw ice fishing diehards between late December and early March, when holes are bored in the ice with makeshift ice chisels and baited hooks are dropped into the icy depths. It's an ad hoc affair, so don't worry about swanky fishing gear – simply wander out onto the ice with a bottle of vodka and ask a thirsty local if it's OK to share their ice hole. Then, dangle a line teased with live maggots – and wait for something to take a bite.

The Curonian Lagoon's ruddy-cheeked hook and bobber crowd use a skimmer to keep the hole clear of ice and slush to ensure an unobstructed view. In tougher ice, an easy way to bore a hole is to drill into the dent of an old hole. Use a pole to work away at the surface, then wrap a line around the stick. A hook, a small weight and a bobber is all that is required as terms of tackle. Move around to change position and alter depths and holes a few times, but as far as technique goes, that's about it. Those keen for greater know-how can pick the brains of the ice fishing trainers at Vilnius' Fishermen's Club, about a 20 km (12 mile) drive from the lake.

Even in the chilliest winter, the adrenaline of a fishing bite can warm an ice fisherman up, or at least divert their attention from the cold for a while. Another buzz is the anticipation in awaiting that first strike, not knowing if it is a potential trophy fish or a wriggler barely worthy of a cheer. However, when the 'Big One' is landed, prepare for plenty of back-slapping camaraderie washed down with a few decent swigs. The fun doesn't stop after the fish have stopped biting, either, as there are few things more pleasing to a Lithuanian than a plate of freshly-caught fish on the ice. Grilled over an open wood fire, dining on snow is another great plus-point of the Curonian Lagoon's freezing temperatures – not only is there an absence of flies, but storing the fish is easy in hard-carved 'freezers' by the shore.

In ice-encrusted Lithuania it's not just the sub-zero temperatures that are biting; simply bore a hole in the frozen lake and cast a line...

LATVIA

TIME DIFFERENCE GMT +2

TELEPHONE CODE +371

CURRENCY Lats

LANGUAGE Latvian

POPULATION 2.5 million

SIZE OF COUNTRY 64,589 sq km
(25,190 sq miles)

CAPITAL Riga

WHEN TO GO Latvia's prime tourist season runs
from April to September, with July and August the
most crowded months. From October to March,
Riga's streets are reclaimed by the locals.
Midsummer is highly popular with domestic
tourists, so accommodation needs to be
booked in advance.

TOURIST INFORMATION
www.latviatourism.lv

Latvia's extraordinary biodiversity is determined by its geographical
position in the western part of the east European plain. Set on the
eastern coast of the Baltic Sea, Estonia's mixed forests and brackish
waters enrich the serene Gulf of Riga with numerous surrounding
fertile bogs and fens. This wildlife-rich terrain is home to nesting
birds, flowering plants and ferns in a beautiful countryside setting
studded with sparkling lakes. 900 year old capital city Riga – once
revered across Europe as the 'Paris of the North' – balances a
handsome maze of cobbles and spired architecture with easy
access to a jumble of country walking trails, cycle routes and
seaside jaunts.

ENDURANCE TEST RIGA

Only a contest demanding considerable grit from its competitors would kick off at 11pm, but that's when the starter's pistol fires for the ultra physical Riga Challenge. It is fitting, as somehow a comfortable starting time would be at odds with this gruelling mixed discipline event. The Riga Challenge tests its participants with not just one, but eight competitive components – not to mention an untold number of secret physical tasks. Part endurance and part test of skill, this annual competition promises a trial of body, spirit and morals. From its starting point in Riga's Old Quarter at the *Ratslaukums* (town hall), smack bang in the middle of the city on the banks of the Daugava River, the Riga Challenge covers between 70 and 250 km (43–155 miles), depending on the class of entry. It attracts many of Europe's toughest elite to the Latvian capital for a weekend of orienteering, biking, kayaking, trekking, swimming, coasteering, climbing and abseiling – and more.

The Riga Challenge's trio of entry classes offer three distinct contests in the Elite, Sport and Mass divisions. A restricted field allows a total of 120 teams, with 30 in the Elite class, 40 in the Sport class and 50 in the Mass class. Both the Elite and Sport divisions impose a pre-competition test of ability, assessing skills in some of the specific disciplines a couple of hours before the race is scheduled to start. Each four person team must represent both sexes, although the exact gender split isn't specified in the rules. However, on the basis of strength and endurance, a 3:1 male-to-female split is the norm. Dense forests, the icy Baltic Sea, glacial pools, rough country terrain, slippery crags and urban trails form the basis of the Riga Challenge route. Duration and distances differ between classes, with 250+ km (155+ miles) for Elite, 150+ km (93+ miles) for Sport and 70+ km (43+ miles) for Mass – all against a ticking stopwatch. The clock is stopped at a maximum of 48 hours, 36 hours and 24 hours respectively, although on this unsupported non-stop test of stamina and strength, about a quarter of participants – however tough and wily – fail to make the finish.

CONTACTS
Riga Challenge
Tel: +371 2912 1166
Email: info@adventurerace.lv
www.adventurerace.lv

Riga Tourism Office
Tel: +371 6702 6072
Fax: +371 6702 6068
Email: tourinfo@riga.lv
www.rigatourism.lv

Gruelling physical challenges and secret tasks await competitors in the Riga Challenge.

ESTONIA

TIME DIFFERENCE GMT +2

TELEPHONE CODE +372

CURRENCY Estonian Kroon

LANGUAGE Estonian

POPULATION 1.3 million

SIZE OF COUNTRY 45,226 sq km
(17,638 sq miles)

CAPITAL Tallinn

WHEN TO GO Estonia's temperate climate is
characterized by warm summers and fairly
severe winters, with year-round breezes from
the Baltic Sea. Summer temperatures average
21°C (70°F) with July the hottest month. Winters
can be severe with temperatures of -8°C (18°F)
on average, although drops to -23°C (-9°F)
aren't uncommon.

TOURIST INFORMATION
Estonia Tourism c/o Estonian Embassy
Tel: 020 7589 3428
www.visitestonia.com

Located on the eastern shores of the Baltic Sea, Estonia is the most
northerly of the three former Soviet Baltic republics. Low, flat and
partially forested, Estonia has a shallow 1,393 km (864 mile)
coastline dotted with 1,520 outlying islands. The country's highest
point, *Suur Munamägi* ('Egg Mountain') reaches 318 m (1,043 ft)
above sea level in Estonia's hill-covered southeast. Rolling, tufted
meadows are home to over 8,500 lakes, pools and rivers that feed
large wetland expanses. Tallinn, Estonia's largest centre and capital
city, packs a powerful cultural punch: its UNESCO-listed old quarter
is already gearing up as the 2011 'Capital of Culture'.

CONTACTS

Tallinn Tourist Information Centre
Tel: +372 645 7777
Fax: +372 645 7778
Email: turismiinfo@tallinnlv.ee
www.tourism.tallinn.ee

Travel Estonia
Tel: +372 562 61160
Email: info@travelestonia.ee
www.travelestonia.ee

Mud-filled ruts and plunging ravines face adventurers in Estonia's 4x4 country.

OFF-ROAD 4X4 TALLINN

Daredevil Estonia is increasingly billed as Eastern Europe's extreme sport adventure playground, especially with the team-building crowd. On Tallinn's rural outer fringes, a host of purpose-built off-road centres offer full-day and half-day 4x4 packages that combine undulating, rugged terrain, plunging ravines and muddy pools. Sludgy slopes on a forested backdrop ensure a rigorous off-road challenge through Estonia's gateway from the city to the countryside beyond. Interchanging between woodlands and open plains, 4x4 driving demands skill and speed from drivers of all levels and experience. Using gears and clutch control to power across mud-filled ruts can truly test a driver's skills and nerve. Tours run all year round (even in a drenching downpour) so prepare for a mud-splattered soaking – and pack a change of clothes.

Most operators provide all the gear necessary for a day of 4x4 driving, such as helmets, gloves and overalls. Given the locality, few rules or restrictions are applied other than those that impact safety, allowing drivers the freedom to carve up the countryside to their heart's content. Sessions begin with a briefing on technique and four wheel drive systems followed by a demonstration drive complete with tips – then it's time for the off. Much of the region was once used by the Soviet army, and a number of ghost-like ruins hide among the rounded contours of the rolling, untapped trails. Cleared meadows have been replanted in widespread regeneration projects that add extra trickery to the natural layout. Using large tyres for extra ground clearance, most of the off-road vehicles in use in Tallinn are non-adapted, regular traction-controlled 4x4s. Vast drop-offs typify Tallinn's all-weather valley routes edged by steep forested ascents, gullies and fallen trees. Coffee-coloured rivers provide troublesome water hazards prone to flooding in winter, while skidding slopes can cause the blood to really pump. The reward for balancing on a bog-ridden precipice in 1.5 tonnes of metal is a commemorative photo and certificate; a memento of a highly-charged engine-revving battle with the ups and downs of the Estonian terrain.

RUSSIA

TIME DIFFERENCE GMT +2/GMT +3

TELEPHONE CODE +7

CURRENCY Ruble

LANGUAGE Russian

POPULATION 142 million

SIZE OF COUNTRY 17,075,200 sq km
(6,659,328 sq miles)

CAPITAL Moscow

WHEN TO GO Russia's humid continental
European climate turns subarctic in Siberia and to
tundra in the polar north. Summers vary from hot,
dry and sunny to cool and breezy along the Arctic
coast, with sticky city micro-climates and
windblown rural expanses.

TOURIST INFORMATION
Russian National Tourist Office
Tel: 020 7495 7570
Fax: 020 7495 8555
Email: info@visitrussia.org.uk
www.visitrussia.org.uk

As the world's largest country, Russia has a very diverse geography
with most of the country nearer to the North Pole than the Equator.
At around double the size of the United States, Russia encompasses
around an eighth of all the inhabited land on the planet. The route
north to south spans a inhospitable expanse across 4,500 km
(2,790 miles) from the northern tip of the Arctic isles to the Republic
of Dagestan's southern nub. Some 14 countries share Russia's
57,790 km (35,830 mile) border – the world's longest – from Europe
through Asia to North Korea, China and Mongolia. Thousands of
lakes, a dozen seas, a part of three oceans, vast tundra, forests and
grasslands border Russia's mountains, towns and cities, including
the capital Moscow, almost a country within itself.

FLYING MOSCOW

While only a few highly skilled elite are likely to achieve the elevated kudos of fighter pilot status, the dream of flying the world's most exciting Cold War spy jet can become a reality. Incredible speeds ensure a natural high on the edge of outer space, in the ultimate airborne adrenaline junkie fix. Numerous operators offer MiG-15 fighter jet packages for an unforgettable weekend experience, flying over former Eastern Bloc military haunts. Would-be Kremlin secret agents on the frontline can enjoy the force of a kerosene-guzzling four-tonne turbine engine, delivering 6,000 pounds of thrust and achieving over 1,000 kph (620 mph) – and sky-high G's.

The legendary MiG-15 first hit the skies shortly after World War II, when the Soviet Union invested huge sums of money into developing a world-beating high altitude craft. Agile and exceedingly fast, the MiG is adept at using short and rough landing strips, exploiting vast amounts of power to reach heights of 24,800 m (80,000 ft) at three times the speed of sound. Each trip over Moscow is custom-designed to suit individual flying preferences and satisfy any flight of fancy, from Cold War espionage incursions to gut-warping rolls. Diehard MiG nuts favour three of the world's most modern supersonic fighters, the MiG-29,

Sukhoi-27 and the classic MiG-21. Today, these symbols of 1960s Soviet air power and military interceptors appeal to jet junkies from all over the globe. Each completes a brief pre-flight medical, with nerves the major cause of high blood pressure. Then it's into the G-suits, flight suits, helmets and rubber oxygen masks – the ultimate in aviation apparel. Once settled in the ejection seat, the twin exhausts flame orange as the MiG's afterburners kick in, fuelling a phenomenal climb rate of 3,660 m (12,000 ft) per minute – enough to pin a grown man to the ground.

Flying at such high altitudes (twice that of a commercial jet), the atmosphere above the MiG is eerily black, requiring skilful control to manoeuvre the aircraft over Moscow's landmark Red Square. Once piloted exclusively by the Soviet Union's most trusted wings, Russia's MiGs are today flown by an oddball assortment of capitalists and adventurers. Powering a supersonic Kremlin war bird while the Mach metre reads .85 at 13,500 m (45,000 ft) – and rising – sends everyone aboard the jet into a Wild East frenzy of yee-haws. Only the bullwhip crack of sonic boom can eclipse the elation of this heart-stopping journey behind the Iron Curtain: a tailormade surveillance reconnaissance packed with supersonic thrust.

CONTACTS
Moscow Tourist Information Centre
Tel: +7 232 5657
Email: info@moscow-city.ru
www.moscow-city.ru

Wildwings UK
Tel: 0117 9658 333
Email: wildinfo@wildwings.co.uk
www.wildwings.co.uk

Taking a high-velocity Cold War spy jet provides the ultimate airborne adrenaline fix for espionage junkies.

HUNGARY

TIME DIFFERENCE GMT +1

TELEPHONE CODE +36

CURRENCY Forint

LANGUAGE Hungarian

POPULATION 9.9 million

SIZE OF COUNTRY 92,340 sq km
(36,013 sq miles)

CAPITAL Budapest

WHEN TO GO Hungary is characterized by warm,
dry summers and fairly cold winters, with January
the coldest month. May to September is mild and
pleasant, with cool nights and comfortable
daytime temperatures. October to December is
chilly and wet and sometimes snowy. January and
February are usually subject to snowfall, especially
in the mountainous regions.

TOURIST INFORMATION
Hungarian Tourist Board
Tel: 020 7823 0412
Email: info@gotohungary.co.uk
www.gotohungary.co.uk

A complex fusion of Balkan and Slavic influences add to the
Hungarian national mix – a historic melting pot of Finno-Ugric and
Turkish invasion and shared borders with Slovakia, Ukraine, Romania,
Croatia, Serbia, Austria and Slovenia. Hungary's thousands of acres
of vineyards and orchards, plus 11 national parks and hundreds of
protected areas, are complemented by some stunning stretches of
water, such as fish-filled Lake Balaton. Much of Hungary's landscape
bubbles with hot thermal subterranean springs, the source of dozens
of medicinal baths and curative spas. Lively Budapest – situated on
a beautiful stretch of the Danube dotted with floating restaurants and
pleasure craft – boasts a buzzing literary and arts scene.

CONTACTS
All Weather Toboggan Run Visegrád
Tel: +36 626 397 397

Budapest Tourist Office
Tel: +36 1266 0479
Fax: +36 1266 7477
www.budapestinfo.hu

*Hurtling down a custom-made
sled run at 50 kph (31 mph)
tests nerve and focus.*

BOBSLEIGHING BUDAPEST

Budapest's extreme sports scene may lag a little behind Prague and Riga in blood and guts, but bobsleighing has ensured the city has retained its place on the adventure map. Not that Hungary has a lengthy bobsleighing tradition – far from it. Although the sport has been in Olympic competition since the first winter games in 1924, Hungary's national team was formed as recently as 1992. That it is new to Hungary matters not, for this bobsleigh bug is no passing fad. Vast investment has ensured a decent handful of facilities around the capital, offering thrill-seekers an expeditious gravity-powered white-knuckled descent.

Budapest's bobsleigh tracks are based around 40 km (25 miles) from the centre of the city, so tours run at around four hours. Facilities include computer-driven magnetic brake systems on lightning-fast 700 m (2,296 ft) runs. Sleds hurl along the track at speeds of around 50 kph (31 mph) at an all-weather toboggan course that hurtles from the base of Nagyvillám Hill. Some 11 serpentine runs have been custom-made for maximum blood rush from the height of an 11 storey building. Jolting bends lead into a succession of super-fast chicanes that plummet 35 m (115 ft) along a dry track. Single manned

bobsleighs offer little room for error, with just 25 mm (1 in) of clearance between the rider's backside and the track.

Budapest's snow-free runs are completed on a wheeled model, with five timed heats deciding the winning streak. Narrow, banked tracks with a curvature have the manoeuverability of a rat run and the feel of an icy road. Unlike bobsleighing in snow, there is some friction between the wheels and track surface, so a certain amount of steering is possible. Upping the physical forces that help acceleration and minimizing the forces that slow it down is the key to beating the time trial – as long as you keep your nerve and focus. Any sudden moves can send the sled into an uncontrolled semi-spin, so exploiting drag, friction and momentum is as important as speed. Drivers are encouraged to adopt an aerodynamic hunched body position, and a good push-off is crucial in optimizing velocity from a standing start. Race times are measured in hundredths of seconds, so any error can have a significant impact on the final result. Only a couple of Hungary's bobsleigh tracks are open during winter, mainly because wet weather renders the brakes useless at speed – a perilous extra most can do without.

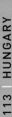

SLOVENIA

TIME DIFFERENCE GMT +1

TELEPHONE CODE +386

CURRENCY Euro

LANGUAGE Slovene

POPULATION 2 million

SIZE OF COUNTRY 20,273 sq km
(7,906 sq miles)

CAPITAL Ljubljana

WHEN TO GO Slovenia's varied climate includes
a continental weather pattern in the northeast, a
harsh Alpine climate in the mountains and a sub-
Mediterranean climate on the coast. For walkers
and hikers, April–June offers a colourful wildflower
landscape as well as inexpensive prices. Both are
gone by the time a dry, hot summer arrives, while
pleasant autumns can often bring fog and snow
by mid-October.

TOURIST INFORMATION
Embassy of the Republic of Slovenia
Tel: 020 7222 5400
Fax: 020 7222 5277
Email: vlo@gov.si
www.slovenia.info

Slovenia sits tucked between Italy, Austria, Hungary and Croatia
in a small pocket of heavily wooded terrain looped by meadows,
lakes, rivers and historic towns. A limestone region of subterranean
streams, gorges and caves occupies the stretch between Ljubljana,
the capital, and the Adriatic coast. Likened to a mini-Prague without
the tourist crowds, Ljubljana offers easy access out to Triglav
National Park – a playground for climbers and hikers; a vast
mountainous expanse that spans the major part of the Julian Alps
and Slovenia's highest peak, Mount Triglav at 2,864 m (9,394 ft).
Towards the borders with Croatia and Hungary, the landscape is
essentially flat – a sharp contrast to the rest of Slovenia where hills
and mountains dominate.

BACKPACKING BOHINJ

The Julian Alps' dramatic limestone crest dominates Slovenia's northwest to peak at soaring Mount Triglav at 2,864 m (9,394 ft). Preserved as part of the 84,000 ha (207,480 acre) Triglav National Park, the region transforms into a snow-covered wonderland each winter. In summer, it is a landscape of soaring peaks, deep valleys and crystal-clear rivers looped by meadows of wildflowers. Cascading waterfalls and tumbling streams spill into caves and gullies. Larch, spruce, beach and pine forests cover the lower slopes below around 1,600 m (5,248 ft), while alpine scrub tops the upper flanks. Quite different from the Western Alps, the Julian's beige-white peaks are home to edelweiss and jet-black salamanders. Hikers keen to rise to a multi-day challenge will find a dense network of mountain cabins for overnight stops, with numerous fine treks through the mountains hut-to-hut.

A popular starting point is the eastern shores of Lake Bohinj, where traditional settlements include the villages of Ribcev Laz and Stara Fuzina. Approaching the Julian Alps on this route allows a foray into marmot-inhabited forests via trails that typically climb around 600 m (1,968 ft) in 15 km (9 miles) on good, established paths. A scenic path from Ribcev Laz up to the Vodnikov hut (1,817 m/5,960 ft) requires a steady climb, with a further uphill trek to Dom Planika (2,401 m/7,875 ft) on Triglav's upper slopes. Keep a pair of binoculars at the ready for some jaw-dropping unfolding views that stretch out to the Karavanke and Kamnik-Savinja ranges in good weather. A complex and engaging cross-country trail winds its way up to 2,151 m (7,055 ft) across tricky rocky sections. Arriving at the vast limestone Hribarice plateau at 2,358 m (7,734 ft) is a genuine high point after an exhilarating day-long climb, before descending to the sparkling Triglav Lakes Valley. At 1,922 m (6,304 ft), the peak of Vogel is an add-on for those with plenty of stamina. The route winds back to Bohinj via deeply cut river gorges and atmospheric karst past ancient sacral sites, and offers a fast-paced stomp for those keen to up the ante. Energy-expending stamina-busters will also find that pleasant temperatures July to October provide ideal conditions in which to trail run 'boot camp style' on the Alps' mid and lower slopes.

GETTING THERE
Ljubljana airport is 60 km (37 miles) away from Bohinj Lake – take a taxi, hire car, bus or train to Bled or Bohinjska Bistrica. Buses from Ljubljana are very frequent and take 1 hour, 20 minutes to Bled, or 1 hour, 52 minutes to Bohinjska Bistrica.

CONTACTS
Secret Slovenia
Tel: 01736 799910
Email: enquiries@secret-slovenia.co.uk
www.secret-slovenia.co.uk

Climb to 2,401 m (7,875 ft) on a hut-to-hut trek in the soaring Julian Alps.

CROATIA

TIME DIFFERENCE GMT +1

TELEPHONE CODE +385

CURRENCY Kuna

LANGUAGE Croatian

POPULATION 4.49 million

SIZE OF COUNTRY 56,542 sq km
(22,051 sq miles)

CAPITAL Zagreb

WHEN TO GO Pleasant, mild temperatures in April and September are spared the humidity of Croatia's oppressive summer highs. May and June boast long, sunny days. By October, the weather is too cool for camping but still suitable for outdoor pursuits. By early November the cold has set in – as has the wind and rain.

TOURIST INFORMATION
Croatian National Tourist Office
Tel: 020 8563 7979
Fax: 020 8563 2616
Email: info@croatia-london.co.uk
www.croatia.hr

Sitting adjacent to Italy across the Adriatic in the northern Mediterranean, Croatia boasts nearly 2,000 km (1,240 miles) of rocky, indented shoreline sprinkled with over a thousand islands – one of Europe's most dramatic coastal stretches. Numerous off the beaten track sleepy coves and stone-built fishing villages remain unspoilt by modern development, with red-roofed coastal cities packed with historical Mediterranean culture and ancient remains. Lakes, mountains and bird-rich marshlands offer vast scope for hikers, walkers and cyclists, while idyllic wind-funnelled sailing waters lap forested islets. Sun-drenched curved bays snake around jagged white cliffs, and sheltered pools offer scuba and snorkelling sites dotted with caves and wrecks.

RIDING
DUBROVNIK

Do not let talk of unexploded landmines dent your enthusiasm for Mount Srdj, as Dubrovnik's rugged ascent offers views that induce an involuntary gasp of breath. Hemming the city to one side, the mountain is the highest point in Dubrovnik, dominating with an omnipresent gravitas and gazing out on open sea. Ancient old mule trails wind up from the foothills, allowing visitors the opportunity to rove by donkey. Just follow the roughly-hewn path above Sipcine as it winds its way circuitously to the summit to enjoy a jaw-dropping panorama of outlying Adriatic islands all the way to Italy on a clear day.

Srdj Mountain is dotted with the remnants of old mule shacks (*kucica*) amidst scatterings of wild rosemary, pine, cedar and dry, arid scrub. Gangly cows nibble on sun-baked hillocks while a parched breeze catches the acrid saltiness of the red stone harbour-side waters below. Although war ravaged the mountain, destroying large expanses of ancient forest, Srdj's rocky slopes still boast fruit-laden fig, pomegranate and kiwi trees. Fragrant dried ferns, thistles and grasses flank each zigzagging mule trail, connecting earth to heaven according to the locals. Segments of the route show signs of the battles of the early 1990s, with tumbledown bunkers, old ramparts and a bombed chairlift.

Dubrovnik's donkeys seem well rehearsed in ascending Srdj Mountain, making light work of navigating the awkward, crumbling limestone underfoot. Each brown-hide donkey is tacked up with a cloth and leather saddle, reins, a harness and saddle bags. Some have more energy than others, but only a few are gloomily reluctant. Eroded soil and loose footings don't seem to faze these steadfast beasts one iota. On level stretches, they break out into a mini stampede, jostling for position and braying loudly at the freedom to pick up speed. Riders will find that the bumps, lumps and lurches add to the rustic charm of exploring the slopes of Srdj on the back of a pack animal. After earning the confidence of

its charge, Croatian donkeys make companionable and dependable partners. At the top of the hill, a final scramble delivers each human cargo to a shady glade in a dusty cloud.

On the downward trek, donkeys often peel off along other tracks to descend the mountain, so no two return trips are the same. But don't hurry: views from the airy summit at 500 m (1,640 ft) are well worth lingering over, offering a heady mix of colours in the seascape alone. Riders with the foresight to load up with a goat wineskin of Croatian wine can quench their thirst with a drop of Dingac, under a canopy of wind-blown leaves.

GETTING THERE
Buses meet flights at Dubrovnik Airport for the 30 minute shuttle into the city. There are also lots of taxis and plenty of car hire options.

CONTACTS
Dubrovnik Tourism Board
Tel: +385 20 323 887
Email: info@tzdubrovnik.hr
www.tzdubrovnik.hr

Dubrovnik Private Tours
Tel: +385 959 06 06 06
Email: dubrovniktours@gmail.com
www.dubrovnik-tours.info

Ascend Mount Srdj's rough-hewn paths on mule-back for stunning cityscape views.

ISLAND HOPPING SPLIT

GETTING THERE

Buses from Split Airport serve the city's downtown areas. Taxis are in plentiful supply (the journey takes around 30 minutes) and there are lots of local car hire options. Ferries depart regularly from Split and Dubrovnik to the islands – see www.jadrolinija.hr for details.

CONTACTS

ACI Marina
Tel: +385 12 325 234
Fax: +385 12 325 237
Email: charter@euromarine.hr
www.aci-club.hr

Split Tourism Office
Tel: +385 21 345 606
Fax: +385 21 339 898
Email: tic-split@st.t-com.hr
www.visitsplit.com

Explore hidden caves, curvaceous bays and sandy beaches on the island-scattered Dalmatian coast.

Croatia's Dalmatian coast has been dubbed the Croat d'Azure by the media, an island-flecked shoreline of striking natural beauty. Largely on the periphery of the travel mainstream, Croatia's Adriatic coast dazzles just enough to attract the hyper-trendy whilst retaining sufficient obscurity to appeal to those on the fringe. Visitors are drawn to the Dalmatian coast's hidden coves, limpid bays and gorgeous beaches, edged by vineyards, olive groves and forests of cypress and pine. Pockmarked ancient settlements hold well-preserved Roman, Greek, Venetian and Slavic architecture, while a sailing scene rivals the finest in the world. Umpteen harbours, ports and marinas and countless natural inlets are scattered over a thousand islands. Million dollar luxury yachts rub shoulders with dinghies and micro-engine run-arounds, as royals, bluebloods, film stars and regular tourists enjoy what astronauts say is the bluest water on the planet.

Numerous charter boats, captains and craft for hire operate in the coastal town of Split, serving the southern Dalmatian coast and the islands of Dugi Otok, Ugljan, Pasman, Brac, Hvar, Korcula, Vis, Lastovo and Mljet. Split's main marina, located north of the Sustipan Peninsula, has 360 berths, top-notch facilities and is open year-round. A frequent ferry service also links Split to the archipelago's main islands, so an alternative is to use this and pick up a boat locally. Of the Dalmatian coast's 1,185 islands just 67 are inhabited, with many smaller forested islets less than a football pitch in size. Easily accessible by boat, and offering an ever-changing passing landscape, the Adriatic's cruising and island hopping possibilities are endless. Do it in style aboard a grand, rigged vintage ship or top-range schooner, or simply pack a pair of shorts, a couple of t-shirts and a swimsuit to chug around the Dalmatian coast at a lazy pace. Placid, pearly waters ensure mill pond conditions for swimming and diving around rock-bound coves, craggy bluffs and outcrops teeming with a rainbow of fish.

After a thorough exploration of Split's UNESCO-listed Diocletian's Palace, which dates from AD 295, it pays to stock up on nautical supplies and gear in the city's many specialist shops. Next, grab an island hopping map from the tourist booth on Split's busy port-side. Additional sailing information is available during the coastline's regatta season from October to January each year, such as amateur dinghy competitions and yachting soirées. Then determine an itinerary, allowing a good half-day for even the most straightforward route. Realistically, a weekend allows for a decent jaunt out to the three or four outlying islands, with most visitors opting to stay overnight in or around Hvar, with the most adventurous choosing lesser-known Vis.

As the birthplace of Marco Polo, pine-scented Korcula is immersed in tales and legends, while noble Hvar's charming riddle of climbing, narrow streets and lavender fields intermingle with lively seafront bars and cafés. Vendors sell dried herbs, seashells, olives, sarongs, and coral necklaces in the backstreets, while shaded pathways stretch up to wooded hills above. More than a dozen snorkelling spots are within a quick jaunt from Hvar's main promenade, out to the Paklinski Islands' flora-rich underwater caves. Brac offers one of Dalmatia's most fabled beaches, the Zlatni Rat ('Golden Cape'), a shimmering shale headland constantly redefined by the contouring might of wind and waves. Choose from the main settlement of Bol on the south side of the island facing Hvar, or head to the resorts of Supetar, Postira, Milna or Sumartin, where dozens of local boatmen offer a variety of vessels for hire. Vis is as insular as Hvar is glamorous; a hardscrabble landscape of scrub and herbs dotted with fishing huts, caves and drying nets. Unforgiving hills offer dizzying trails through aromatic rosemary and sage, wild asparagus, garlic, carob trees and a tangle of vines. Weigh anchor here to explore gin-clear waters. Take a dinghy to explore the mysterious depths and extraordinary marine life in the Blue Cave. Swim amongst 360 vivid species of fish, algae and sponges while seabirds soar overhead and crickets thrum in the trees. Dive from creamy white rocks into green-blue depths to spot lobsters, sunken shipwrecks and red and yellow gorgonia. Or throw a line overboard for the dusk-time thrill of grilling freshly caught fish (mackerel is plentiful), shrimp and octopus up on deck, revelling in the sea-carried scents of jasmine and the views of distant yachts dropping anchor on the horizon.

ROMANIA

TIME DIFFERENCE GMT +2

TELEPHONE CODE +40

CURRENCY Leu

LANGUAGE Romanian

POPULATION 22.2 million

SIZE OF COUNTRY 238,391 sq km
(92,972 sq miles)

CAPITAL Bucharest

WHEN TO GO Scorching summer highs form a
sharp contrast with cold snowy winters from mid-
December until the end of March. June, July and
August are hottest near the Black Sea coast,
where average temperatures reach 24–30°C
(75–86°F). In summer there are frequent showers
and thunderstorms in the mountains. Pleasant
autumn days keep the sunshine going until mid-
October, but Transylvania and the Carpathian
Mountains can be wet year-round.

TOURIST INFORMATION
Romania National Tourist Office
Tel: 020 7224 3692
Email: romaniatravel@btconnect.com
www.romaniatourism.com

Over a third of Romania's fish-shaped landmass is shrouded in thick
forest, with the Carpathian Mountains to the southwest peaking with
Mount Moldoveanu at 2,544 m (8,344 ft). 10,000 year old glacial
lakes, volcanic rocks and boggy marshes are dominant landscape
features, with orchards and vineyards in the foothills. The Danube
delta's reed bed sediment provides rich nourishment to fish-filled
rivers, while remote, wildlife-rich expanses lead to medieval towns,
castles and white sandy beaches. Folkloric Transylvania – home to
Bran Castle of Dracula fame – is one of Romania's most beautiful
regions; an adventurer's paradise riddled by fine hiking trails and
rustic mountain tracks.

HIKING TRANSYLVANIA

As part of the Alpine–Carpathian–Himalayan system of mountains, the Romanian Carpathians boast an extraordinary range of peaks in an impressive and spectacular scenic expanse rising from glacial lakes. With crests that soar to over 2,500 m (8,200 ft), the mountains are renowned for their snow-shrouded ski resorts. Yet visit the Carpathians from April to September and a stunning array of flora-scattered meadows, alpine forests and secluded valleys boast a plenitude of colour. At its heart sits the region of Transylvania, by far the most romantic and inspiring of Romania's provinces, where dense woodlands and sparkling streams lie steeped in the legend of Transylvanian fortress Bran Castle.

Transylvania occupies the central part of Romania, surrounded by the Carpathians' far-reaching rocky ridges. One of the main cities, Cluj-Napoca, stands on the plateau, while Brasov and Sibiu sit in the foothills of the southern Carpathians. Hiking maniacs keen to push themselves to the max should follow the rugged hiking paths leading upwards to the tree-covered gullies and high plateaux of the Bucegi Mountains, where megaliths rain-carved into human forms adorn a dramatic landscape. Equally as challenging are the Fagaras Mountains

in the southern Carpathians, a wild and imposing ridge that is home to Romania's highest peak, at 2,544 m (8,344 ft). Trails are tough, rough and far-reaching, requiring a steady marching pace for six to nine hours. Paths along Romania's most difficult winter mountaineering route – the Albota–Arpasel ridge and then 'Dragon Window' – eclipse all others. Yet it is the country's highest peak, Moldoveanu, that provides the most rewarding views and also allows a stunning descent into the Sambetei Valley, a serenely beautiful picnic spot. Almost a third of Romania is clad in mountains of great natural beauty, but this is where hikers lie back with bellies full of smoked cheese and giant tomatoes and reflect on just how lucky they are, amidst a kaleidoscope of wildflowers.

Trails around Bran Castle, a magnificent red-turreted fairytale tower built around 1377, can be busy in summer due to the myth of Dracula. Today the castle is synonymous with B-movie horror born out of vampire tales. Now a museum, the building is open to garlic-wielding tourists (it is closed on Mondays) but if the weather is good and the paths of the Bucegi Mountains crowd-free, you may prefer to give it a miss and tackle another exhilarating hill climb instead.

CONTACTS

Hiking in Transylvania
www.visit-transylvania.co.uk/
hikingtours

Bran Castle
Tel: +40 268 238 333
Fax: +40 268 238 335
Email: info@brancastlemuseum.ro
www.brancastlemuseum.ro

Cluj-Napoca Online
www.clujonline.com

Delve into dark forest trails and blood-pumping hill tracks near Dracula's lair in Romania's Carpathian Mountains.

BULGARIA

TIME DIFFERENCE GMT +2

TELEPHONE CODE +359

CURRENCY Lev

LANGUAGE Bulgarian

POPULATION 7.3 million

SIZE OF COUNTRY 110,910 sq km
(43,255 sq miles)

CAPITAL Sofia

WHEN TO GO Northern Bulgaria has a moderate
continental climate, while southern Bulgaria is
distinctly Mediterranean. Summers are hot, winters
cool and crisp, while spring and autumn can be
pleasantly mild. Half a dozen mountain ranges play
a significant part in determining regional variances,
with cold temperatures in the peaks and on the
maritime Black Sea coast.

TOURIST INFORMATION
Bulgarian National Tourist Board
Tel: +359 2933 5845
Fax: +359 2989 6939
Email: info@bulgariatravel.org
www.bulgariatravel.org

Occupying the southeastern segment of the Balkan Peninsular,
Bulgaria was founded in 681, making it Europe's most elderly state.
Home to an impressive array of ornate mosques, rustic villages and
flamboyantly decorated churches, Bulgaria boasts a rich folkloric
tradition and a varied, beautiful and rugged terrain. Fertile valleys give
way to the rolling plains of the Danube, and large mountainous areas
give way to coastal lowlands along the Black Sea. Aged fishing
settlements remain much as they have done for centuries, just a
stone's throw from the vibrant capital Sofia, still home to a number of
ancient Roman and Byzantine buildings and a UNESCO-protected
World Heritage site.

CONTACTS
Bulgarian Waterski Federation
Tel: +359 288 0261
Email: bulwsf@satline.net

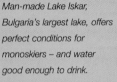

Man-made Lake Iskar,
Bulgaria's largest lake, offers
perfect conditions for
monoskiers – and water
good enough to drink.

WATERSKIING SOFIA

As the largest manmade lake in Bulgaria, Lake Iskar is renowned throughout the nation as the favoured watery get-away for Sofia's weekending city slickers keen to kick back far from the daily grind. Dubbed the 'Sea of Sofia', Lake Iskar sits amid the slopes of the Lozenska Mountain, adjoining the southwestern flanks of the highlands of Ihtiman at an altitude of around 1,150 m (3,772 ft). At 16 km (10 miles) long by 6 km (4 miles) wide, the lake is actually a dammed reservoir that spills out into five large, beautiful creeks edged by oak, beech and fir trees. Shrub-tufted hills and mountains shield the water from prevailing 30 knot winds, ensuring mill pond-calm conditions for waterskiing from May to October. Flat rails, ramped rails, fun boxes and 1–1.5 m (3–5 ft) kickers offer plenty of challenges to total beginners and those keen to polish up on their slaloming in blue, sparkling waters clear enough to drink.

In recent years, Bulgaria's surging tourist industry has attracted large numbers of waterski instructors from the traditional resorts of France, Switzerland and even North America. Many signed up out of curiosity, others to be a part of Europe's next big thing. The result is a skilled pool of English-speaking guides and experts who have 'done the rounds' elsewhere and know what works well – and what to give a miss. Prices in Bulgaria compare well with many other European waterski destinations in their infancy, but are rising fast. Lake Iskar's popularity with an upwardly mobile Bulgarian middle class means that cafés, bars and waterskiing schools have sprouted up around the shoreline against a backdrop of tree-clad mountains. Dramatic peaks, ragged foothills and evergreen forests seem to almost topple into the waters of the lake; a tranquil location just a 40 minute drive from Sofia's central hubbub.

Waterskiers heading to Lake Iskar will find opportunities to mono-ski, jump, kneeboard and slalom, with lots of space for trick skiing – however gymnastic the move. Spellbinding jump events showcase an array of daredevil antics, from multiple trick skiing involving backflips, frontflips and helis to mindblowing freestyle solo stunts. To pre-book, contact any tour operator in Sofia or simply head to the watersports complex at Lake Iskar. Although you can pretty much hire everything you need there, be sure to pack a towel and some sunscreen – and take along plenty of water, if loosening up with the local liquor (*rakia*) isn't your thing.

GREECE

TIME DIFFERENCE GMT +2

TELEPHONE CODE +30

CURRENCY Euro

LANGUAGE Greek

POPULATION 10.7 million

SIZE OF COUNTRY 131,945 sq km
(51,459 sq miles)

CAPITAL Athens

WHEN TO GO A Mediterranean climate boasts
plenty of sunshine and a limited amount of rainfall.
Dry, hot days in summer are cooled by seasonal
winds (*meltemi*) but can still be stifling. Winters are
generally mild in lowland areas, with a minimum
amount of snow and ice.

TOURIST INFORMATION
Greek National Tourist Office
Tel: 020 7495 9300
Fax: 020 7495 4057
Email: info@gnto.co.uk
www.gnto.co.uk

As the birthplace of European civilization, Greece remains a hotbed
of magnificent architecture, sculpture, drama, philosophy and
literature, and boasts an extraordinary history rich in battles for
supremacy. Telltale mementoes of a golden era provide a captivating
historical narrative, from ancient temples and magnificent
amphitheatres to civilizations dating back thousands of years. A
rugged, dry, dusty interior is home to whitewashed rustic villages,
pebbled alleys, olive groves and citrus trees. Edged by the Aegean
Sea, a seemingly endless lacework of coastline is scattered with
wave-lapped isles. Capital city Athens remains a centre of learning,
while Thessaloniki in the north has a Byzantine feel. As Greece's
home to the gods of Greek mythology, snow-frosted Mount Olympus
is the country's highest point at 2,197 m (7,206 ft).

SAILING MYKONOS

Greek island sailing epitomizes windswept, sun-drenched freedom well away from the stuffy flotilla crowds. Free from the nautical pomp and swank of Europe's glitzy yachting centres, the Greek Islands are the domain of adventurous salty old dogs of the sea. These 2,000 or so rugged, wave-gnarled rocky mounds rise from clichéd turquoise waters as emerald-green depths meet aquamarine shallows on an iris blue horizon. Curved bays and bubble-shaped coves hide amongst bare hills and dramatic shorelines dotted with traditional whitewashed settlements. Dusty, dry terrain is home to terraced olive groves, vineyards and crumbling dry stone walls, with red-topped cottages clinging to scrubby slopes. It is little wonder sailors have been exploring these sea-scattered isles for centuries, aided by clear waters and strong prevailing winds.

Greece's Cyclades island region lies to the east of the Peloponnese and southeast of the coast of Attica, stretching as far as Samos and Ikaria to the east and bounded to the south by the Cretan Sea. Summer winds of between 7 and 35 knots have long tempted visiting seafarers. Today, numerous family-run boat companies offer skippered charters and bareback sailing that encompasses every gamut of waterborne craft.

Options range from a 10 m (33 ft) two-person cruiser with fore-peak cabin and a shallow draft that allows anchor close to the beach; a 13 m (43 ft) yacht with four cabins, two hot-water bathrooms and a high-tech kitchen; and a spacious 15 m (49 ft) vessel with expansive galley and all mod cons – including the latest model GPS. If old-fashioned adventure is more your style, check out the captained *Quarantine of Delos*, a classic handcrafted wooden sailing cruiser built by the esteemed boat-building Mavrikos family. Stretching 17 m (56 ft) and powered by twin inboard 175 hp engines, the '*Q of D*', as skipper Captain Panayiotis Faroupos refers to it affectionately, can comfortably sleep up to eight people. Not only is she ideal for Mediterranean cruising, but she also offers levels of comfort rarely seen on charter yachts, in a design that dates back several hundred years.

In Mykonos, dozens of boat hire and yacht charters operate out of Plati Gialos and Agios Gianis beaches. For a bareboat yacht, you'll need a certificate of competence from a sailing club, school, or association (or a motor yacht licence). To hire a skipper budget for around 130 euros per day, and allow anything from 200 euros per day for the boat.

GETTING THERE
Mykonos Airport is situated 4 km (2.5 miles) from the town of Hora and is served by Olympic Airways buses, local buses and taxis. There are two ports near Athens: Pireus and Rafina, both with a regular and high speed ferry service to and from Mykonos.

CONTACTS
Quarantine of Delos
Tel: +30 22890 26462
www.aegean-ventures.com

Mykonos Tourist Office
Tel: +30 22890 23990
Fax: +30 22890 22229

For bygone-era adventure, enjoy seafaring on a classic handcrafted wooden cruiser.

RUNNING ATHENS

CONTACTS
Athens Classic Marathon
Tel: +30 21093 31113
Fax: +30 21093 31152
Email: info@athensclassic
marathon.gr
www.athensclassicmarathon.gr

Athens Tourism
Tel: +30 21032 53123
Fax: +30 21032 16653
Email: info@atedco.gr
www.athenstourism.gr

Just the word 'marathon' is a byword for the ultimate athletic effort, a great feat that places considerable demand on the human body, mind and soul. Designed to test mortal endeavour to the limits, the marathon was borne out of the legend of Pheidippides, a heroic Greek soldier, who ran to Athens from the town of Marathon. After completing the entire 40 km (24.8 mile) distance without stopping to deliver his message, Pheidippides collapsed and died at the Senate. Today, marathons across the world recreate the incredible run that started it all nearly 2,500 years ago, although the Athens Classic Marathon is considered the ultimate. Held in the Athens' historical centre amidst some of the finest ancient architecture on the planet, the 42 km (26 mile, 385 yard) route (the distance was increased slightly following the 1908 Olympic Games) reaches a triumphant finale in the marble grandeur of Panathinaiko Stadium, an area of epic proportions cut into a hillside in 1896. Unlike the arid, dusty unmade road of the original route in 490 BC, today's Athens Marathon is a flawless asphalt swathe, levelled to perfection. Although runners have achieved mind-boggling times close to the two hour mark, a sizeable number of participants enter the event for personal goals, not to break records. To meet the demand, marathon organizers have added in three additional facets: a 10 km (6 mile) run, a 5 km (3 mile) run and a power walking event. Dozens of tour companies have tailor-made packages to incorporate the Classic Marathon, and many offer additional running coaching, motivational sessions, training clinics and sports psychology. However, every participant, whatever level, gets a numbered bib, timing chip and commemorative medal in return for a modest entrance fee (80 euros, 75 euros and 70 euros respectively) – along with free public transport, drinks, a t-shirt and sports bag and top-notch medical support. Unlike the crisp, icy chill of many other winter marathons, Athens in November boasts trademark tepid breezes and sunny skies. However, Athens isn't all good news: the route is riddled with hill climbs; a challenge even for the super-fit and a psychological 'mountain to climb' for anyone with their sights on the finishing line. Although the first 12 km (7 miles) are flat, the middle 19 km (12 miles) is a long succession of hills, a strenuous slow, steady slog that places a drain on energy reserves. At the 39 km (24 mile) mark at Vas, runners can wave goodbye to the route's most arduous ascents at last, passing the US Embassy, the *Megaro Mousikis* ('Music Hall'), the Hilton hotel and the National Gallery on flatter terrain. That the final 11 km (7 miles) are all downhill is some sort of saving grace: a final phase when rhythmic momentum and adrenaline combine with sheer grit to pull your body through to the end.

Non-runners keen to power walk the marathon route depart the start line at 7am sharp for a

stamina-charge requiring dogged determination. Participants in the 10 km Road Race start and finish at the Panathinaiko Stadium, with the initial 5 km run in the opposite direction of the Classic Marathon. The 5 km Road Race begins in front of the Panathinaiko Stadium and runs through the city's historical core. Both the 10 km and the 5 km race begin at 9.30am, half an hour later than the Classic Marathon. In 2007, the 10 km route was won in 32:13 and the 5 km in 16:22. On the Classic Marathon route, a vehicle topped with a huge digital chronometre leads the runners, with another placed at the finish line. However, every participant is given an electronic self-timing chip to enable the retrieval of an intermediate time at key points: 5 km, 10 km, half marathon and 30 km, with 1 km and 3 km

for those running the 5 km Road Race. Apart from the top-flight competitive athletes, the Athens Classic Marathon attracts its fair share of runners simply keen to 'have a go'. Fancy-dressed charity fundraisers jog merrily alongside smiling octogenarians while puffing housewives and hobbling fun-runners capture momentous moments on camera for posterity, posing in front of advertising hoardings for Greece's Marathon beer. Several hundred thousand spectators roar with applause along the route until the clock runs out at six hours – and beyond. It serves as a prelude to the mass eruption from Panathinaiko Stadium's 72,000 capacity cheering crowd, as an exhausted field of runners arrive to elatedly punch the air in triumph, a race in the footsteps of Pheidippides under their belt.

It no longer tests mortal endeavour to the limits, but Athens remains the ultimate place to compete in a marathon.

GETTING THERE
Thessaloniki (Salonica) Airport is 16 km (10 miles) outside the city. Rail services link Salonica with Athens and the towns of Macedonia and Thrace. Coach services are operated by KTEL between Salonica and Athens, Larissa, Volos, Patras and Aedipsos (summer only).

CONTACTS
Olympic Wings (Tours)
Tel/Fax: +30 23520 41741
Email: info@olympicwings.gr
www.olympicwings.gr

An unyielding symbol of divinity, Mount Olympus emphasizes human frailty with an arduous ascent.

TREKKING SALONICA

To follow in the footsteps of the ancient Greek gods to Mount Olympus is to tread a storied path. As the country's highest summit, the mighty peaks of Olympus seem to give emphasis to mortal frailty, a strong and unyielding symbol of divinity just a one hour and 30 minute drive from Salonica. Today, this hallowed haven inspires thousands of visitors to flock here from all over the world to tackle the tough trek to the 2,919 m (9,574 ft) summit. Dark forests of cedar, oak, chestnut, walnut, fig and beech are home to around 1,700 plant species, many unique to Olympus, while mountainside lairs harbour wolves, bears and lynx. Declared Greece's first national park in 1937, Mount Olympus offers a good, old fashioned footslog, beginning with an early morning anointment in Mediterranean waters for a real sea-to-summit ascent.

Setting off on a crisp, clear dawn from the coastal village of Litochoro allows time for some off the beaten track bushwhacking before harder stomping along well-crafted paths. Stuck for time? Then drive up a shingled section to cut five hours or, even better, set off at daybreak so as not to miss the gorgeous leafy glades and sparkling river pools of the Mavrolongos gorge. Solid deciduous woodlands make way for skinny pines at a strategic stop-off at a whitewashed chapel – where it may be prudent to light a candle, as this is where the serious trudge begins.

Since the first ascent in 1913, many thousands have trodden the trail to Mytica. Summiteers are fed and watered by a scattering of wayside pit-stops that not only provide hearty food, but generous words of encouragement to boot. Rusting signposts point to the overnight hut Spilios Agapitos, a convivial gathering point for climbers from all across the globe. Fortified, they leave at sun-up to slog and scramble across rocky limestone gullies described by the Greek poet Homer as "heaven". Super-fit types can dash up and down in a day, but two or three days is the norm. As the seat of Zeus, Mount Olympus is synonymous with lightning flashes and thunderbolts, but summer hikers will find the weather less lively, with hot, dry days, a smattering of cloud cover and snow lurking in shadowed crevices. Only experienced climbers should attempt an ascent outside the months of June to October, but pitch up without a reservation in July or August and you'll almost certainly have difficulty finding a bed.

MOUNTAINBOARDING
CYPRUS

CONTACTS
Kite Ko
Tel: +357 9667 6338
Fax: +357 2582 8118
Email: kiteman@logosnet.cy.net
www.kiteko.com

ExtremeCY
Tel: +357 999 8779
Email: john@extremecy.com
www.extremecy.com

The ExtremeCY sports festival has thrust the island's mountainboarding scene into the spotlight.

Hot, arid weather ensures numerous off-road trails in Cyprus are usable pretty much year-round, a real boon for mountainboarders looking for a buzz 365 days a year. Snaking slopes twist and turn, following the gradients around Parekklisha and Fionikaria where diehard boarders are truly tested on some of Cyprus' most demanding downhill tracks. Similar to skateboarding – its urban cousin – mountainboarding offers an expanded terrain to conquer, with shock absorption and inflatable tyres that can cope with heavy-duty rough stuff. Smaller than the average snowboard, a mountainboard's deck construction determines how much weight the board can support and influences performance on harsher ground. Suspension and composite axels absorb the bumps and flex to get maximum grip from the ground, while composite split rim hubs, with up to 25 cm (10 in) tyres and hydraulic brakes, deal with the rigours of the toughest mountain run.

Mountainboarding in Cyprus was thrust into the limelight when the island staged the World Downhill Championships and European Downhill and Freestyle events in 2006 and 2007, as part of the ExtremeCY extreme sports festival. Today the Limasol region, with its thrilling multi-level slopes and traffic-free tracks, form the hub of island's burgeoning mountainboard scene. As a mountainboarding destination still in its infancy, Cyprus has limited freestyle facilities – although this is sure to change. Ramp jumping and tricks (such as 180 and 360 rotations, backflips and frontflips, board grabs and one foot variations) characterize freestyle riding, while sloping dirt tracks provide ideal downhill runs. The island's huge 7 m (23 ft) competition ramps don't suit rookies, although a scattering of grassier tracks offer slower runs on which balance and control can be safely honed.

At every level, riders should pack plenty of water and sunscreen. Full body armour is advisable (with wrist protectors and knee and elbow pads as a minimum). A helmet and strong footwear are essential, especially for those planning to ride the challenging 3 km (2 mile) downhill European cup track. Looking for top brand gear and instruction? Then check out specialist board shop Kite Ko in Germasogia near Limassol. Owner John Tice stocks NoSno and MBS models for beginners to pros, as well as Trampa custom-built boards to individual specifications. He also offers expert instruction in downhill and kite boarding, with beginner boards available to hire.

TURKEY

TIME DIFFERENCE GMT +2

TELEPHONE CODE +90

CURRENCY New Turkish Lira

LANGUAGE Turkish

POPULATION 71.1 million

SIZE OF COUNTRY 780,580 sq km
(304,426 sq miles)

CAPITAL Ankara

WHEN TO GO Because of Turkey's geographical
location, pinpointing a single climate is tricky as
the weather spans from moderate and temperate
to long, hard winters. A Mediterranean climate in
western Anatolia offers average temperatures of
9°C (48°F) in winter and 29°C (84°F) in summer,
while the snowy plateau regions can reach winter
averages of -2°C (28°F). On the Black Sea coast,
a wet, warm and humid summer climate
(23°C/73°F) and mild winters (7°C/45°F) forms
a sharp contrast to eastern Anatolia where
harsh winters see snow cover from November
until the end of April and temperatures of
around -13°C (9°F).

TOURIST INFORMATION
Turkish Culture & Tourism
Tel: 020 7839 7778
Fax: 020 7925 1388
Email: info@gototurkey.co.uk
www.gototurkey.co.uk

Turkey's rich history can be traced back to Neolithic times. Today,
this southeastern European nation occupies a smaller span of the
northwestern Middle East, bordered to the southeast by Georgia,
Armenia, Iran, Iraq and Syria and to the west by Bulgaria and
Greece. As an 'east meets west' gateway, Turkey links the old world
of Asia, Africa and Europe and has a hybrid culture derived from a
hotchpotch of stimuli, especially in the ultra-cosmopolitan city of
Istanbul. Turkey's rural areas remain deeply traditional and reliant on
the landscape, from the soaring mountains that run parallel to the
coast and the broad plains and plateaux, to the fishing settlements
of the Black Sea region and large tracts of natural forest.

GETTING THERE
The nearest airport to Dalyan is Dalaman, 26 km (16 miles) away – a minibus shuttle departs every 30 minutes to connect with a bus to Koycegiz, a journey of 20 km (12 miles). Alternatively, a taxi for four people is £35, or £25 one way for one to three people. Car hire is available.

CONTACTS
Kardak Tours
Tel: +90 252 284 5374
Fax: +90 252 284 3957
Email: info@kardaktourism.com
www.kardaktourism.com

Kaunos Tours
Email: info@kaunostours.com
www.kaunostours.com/links.php

SAILING DALYAN

Daily life in the pretty riverbank town of Dalyan revolves around the smooth-flowing waters of the Dalyan Çayı river, where boats ply up and down the historic thoroughfare. Cruises and charters set sail all day long from the riverfront, while boats ferry daytrippers back and forth from the resorts of Marmaris and Fethiye. Sailing on the waters of the river and lake is as much a part of the Dalyan experience as fishermen emptying their nets from wooden vessels by the shore. Hiring a boat is easy, with no need to haggle or shop around – the boatmen have formed a co-operative so a standard tariff applies. A night-time boat out on the lake to swim in the moonlight; a seafaring adventure through a maze of reed beds; a simple trip on a rudimentary public boat: Dalyan can provide it all. Meaning 'fishing weir' in Turkish, Dalyan also boasts ample stocks of bass, mullet and sea bream, with fertile waters rich in dolphin and turtle.

Grab a boat from the riverbank for the 40 minute trip to İztuzu beach, a stunning bar of gently sloping sand that remains wholly untroubled by mankind. A breeding ground for loggerhead turtles, the 5 km (3 mile) golden stretch is also known as Turtle Beach and remains an undeveloped safe haven for turtles nesting in the sand. Hire a boatman to glide slowly by the dramatic Lycian tombs hewn into the rock face above the west banks of the river. These weathered façades date back to around AD 400 and are a magnificent illuminated spectacle after dark. Head to the therapeutic natural mud pools of Sultaniye on the shore of placid Köycegiz Lake; an easily navigable jaunt upstream by hire boat. Or, engage one of Dalyan's more adventurous captains for a thrilling waterborne foray into the puzzle-like passages of the Dalyan delta. Ask that he motor round to the entrance of the river mouth for a photo opportunity most travel snappers would hock their best lens for; a pinprick sandy islet with pine trees and beaches beyond, and a weaving waterway trimmed with swaying reeds. Request a slalom around the sandbar and the riddle of narrow channels and into the open river further on. Then get the boat to chug on to the Caunos, a truly gasp-inducing 'pile of old rocks' that offer an insight into a lively and bustling seaport of old. Yachts anchor on the island of Delikli Ada to reach the site in tiny wooden boats in an area known as Sülüklü Göl ('Lake of Leeches') – these fine rumbling ruins date back to 3,000 BC and include a 5,000-seater acropolis.

Navigate thick reed beds to the puzzle-like passages of the Dalyan delta.

UNITED KINGDOM

TIME DIFFERENCE GMT

TELEPHONE CODE +44

CURRENCY Pound sterling

LANGUAGE English

POPULATION 60.6 million

SIZE OF COUNTRY 300,000 sq km
(117,000 sq miles)

CAPITAL London

WHEN TO GO Surrounding seas ensure the UK has a year-round temperate maritime climate with variable, unpredictable weather that can change from day to day. Winters are cool, while summers are warm, if wet. Temperatures rarely dip much below 0°C (32°F) or reach higher than 29°C (84°F), with stiff sea breezes around the coasts.

TOURIST INFORMATION
Visit Britain
Tel: 020 8846 9000
www.visitbritain.co.uk

For a small cluster of islands, the UK boasts a lot of contrasts, with a wide variety of landscapes and diverse cultures whichever direction you travel in. Made up of Great Britain (England, Scotland and Wales) and Northern Ireland, the UK comprises numerous distinct cultures, languages and traditions. Each unique country retains its own architectural heritage and historical legacy. Ancient cities and modern towns are surrounded by rural countryside rich in agricultural communities, while bustling seaside resorts and coastal villages maintain a seafaring tradition. Explore honey-stoned villages, lakes, mountains, glorious national parks, beaches, plunging valleys and even vineyards – and enjoy some of the world's most vibrant and cosmopolitan cities.

FLY FISHING PERTHSHIRE

Although a rod-wielding Ernest Hemingway did much to popularize fly fishing through his works of fiction, the sport is thought to date back to around AD 200. Yet it was the early 1950s that saw large numbers of anglers across the globe become hooked on it. Today, over five million anglers fish the UK's 43,000 km (26,660 miles) of rivers, canals and coastline along with many thousands of ponds, lakes and reservoirs. Fly fishing offers a fusion of exhilaration and stealth-based challenge, as lines spin out under cloud-scudded skies. In Hemingway's *The Old Man and the Sea*, the hero waited 84 days to catch his fish – an all too familiar test of patience and grit.

Although fly fishing has been revolutionized by the development of inexpensive fibreglass rods, synthetic fly lines and monofilament leaders, on the silvery River Tay – Scotland's largest and best known salmon river – many things remain unchanged by time. Traditional fishing techniques continue much as they have done for generations on a multi-faceted river stretch that brims with salmon, brown trout, grayling, pike, chat, perch and roach. A few years ago, barbless hooks were introduced to allow fish to wriggle off without harm – a major change for a region famed for its time capsule preservation. That fly fishermen care more for the health of the fish than slightly increasing their own fishing success, says much about the pride and the pedigree of those that fish the River Tay.

Salmon can be found in the River Tay year round, although peak months are May–June and September–October, with the season running from 15 January–15 October. Other fishing options include some great local hill lochs, while some sections of the river system contain world class coarse fishing. An array of soft grey, stone-built Perthshire lodges provides an atmosphere of gracious, aristocratic living close to the whisky-coloured river during the fishing and shooting season. Set in 22,230 ha (9,000 acres) on the River Tay, the elegant, ivy-clad Kinnaird Estate dates back to the late 18th century. Run by Lady Constance Ward, this grand family mansion sits on some of the finest salmon fishing on the Tay system. Two fishing beats, known as Lower Kinnaird and Upper Kinnaird, have been maintained by the Ward family for generations. A select number of guests are accommodated – royalty amongst them – but most visitors to the Kinnaird Estate are just ordinary, discerning commoners with a fly fishing passion. Ghillie Martin Edgar provides exceptional knowledge of fishing on the waters in and around the estate, offering skilled insight to professional anglers and complete novices alike. Daily fishing rates at the Kinnaird Estate cost from £35 per rod, £30 for equipment hire and £60 for the services of a ghillie.

GETTING THERE

First ScotRail (www.firstscotrail.com) operates a Caledonian Sleeper service between London Euston and Scotland.

CONTACTS

Kinnaird Estate
Tel: 01796 482440
Fax: 01796 482289
Email: enquiry@kinnairdestate.com
www.kinnairdestate.com

Perthshire Tourism
Tel: 08452 255121
Fax: 01506 832222
www.perthshire.co.uk

Visit Scotland
www.visitscotland.com/fish.

Hiring the services of a ghillie is a must for newbies keen to bag a haul.

085

RAT RACING
EDINBURGH

CONTACTS
Rat Race Adventures
Tel: 0845 009 4365
www.ratraceadventure.com

Edinburgh Tourist Board
Tel: 0845 2255 121 (UK)
Fax: 01506 832 222
Email: info@visitscotland.com
www.edinburgh.org

Only the ultra-competitive enter Edinburgh's extreme two-day tough physical challenge.

Edinburgh's rugged volcanic backdrop boasts a mix of sand, sea, cliffs and rolling hills just a stone's throw from the city's urban hub. In the city centre, the towering castle dominates the skyline of the medieval Royal Mile, an instantly recognizable landmark that provides an iconic starting point for the city's thrilling Rat Race adventure. The UK's first ever urban challenge, the Rat Race offers an extreme romp through Edinburgh using crampons, canoes and running shoes, all as the stopwatch ticks. Since its inauguration in 2004, the Rat Race has brought the city to a halt on the third Saturday in July each year, for a two day adventure that spans a wide range of physical disciplines. No support crew or back-up are permitted, and the true nature of the Rat Race course – including its exact location – is kept a closely-guarded secret until just before the event is due to start. All of which means that over 300 three-member teams sign up for Rat Race entry without actually knowing where they're going or what they'll be doing. It's extreme, but fun – and ultra-competitive.

Mixed-sex teams with their eye on a medal can fight it out for a place on the podium, while single-sex teams are permitted to enter purely for the fun of it all. A fee of £29–89 per person (depending on class) provides course maps, race gear, a goody bag, pre-race refresher courses (rope work and watersports), buoyancy aids and the crucial electronic timing chip. The event sells out fast, so early registration is advisable using a downloadable form and credit card. Be sure to have a team name ready, as race organizers will need to log this. Open to anyone who is fit, healthy and aged over 16, the Rat Race centres on running, walking, biking, kayaking, rope-related pursuits, parkour and orienteering – as well as a number of mysterious secret tests. You'll get a feel for what's in store from photographs and postings on the website, including hardy souls abseiling from crane towers and team notes that read: 'Fresh from the Marathon des Sables [a marathon a day for a week in the Sahara desert] and I can't wait!...'

On the first day, expect to get wet, to be driven underground, to climb buildings and scale bridges, trample across fields of nettles and steep rocky paths, and solve taxing logistical conundrums. On the following day you can expect a more demanding foray into the city and beyond. Expect plenty of ropes, boats, bikes and tests of navigation. The so-called 'special stages' could literally mean anything – from throwing hoops blindfolded to surviving the legendary Rat Race slippery wall whilst being pelted with eggs and flour. Winners have the biggest points tally – it's as simple as that.

GETTING THERE
The Blue Planet Aquarium is off junction 10 of the M53. Follow the brown tourist information signs for Blue Planet and Cheshire Oaks. Regular bus services run from Liverpool, Chester, Ellesmere Port and north Wales. If travelling by train, the nearest station is Ellesmere Port, about 3 km (2 miles) away.

CONTACTS
Blue Planet Aquarium
Tel: 0151 357 8804
www.blueplanetaquarium.com

Visit Cheshire
Tel: 01244 405600
Fax: 01244 405601
Email: info@visitchesterand
cheshire.co.uk
www.visitchester.com

DIVING CHESHIRE

As an outlet to the sea south of the Wirral Peninsula, the town of Ellesmere Port on the estuary of the River Mersey has long been associated with seafaring. But in 1998 the town surpassed itself by adding sharks to its aquatic pedigree, offering rare interactive encounters with these razor-toothed predators of the deep.

Ellesmere Port's Blue Planet Aquarium is part of a worldwide marine conservation initiative run in conjunction with PADI and the National Geographic. Divers are lowered into a tank occupied by sand tiger sharks, lemon sharks, nurse sharks, wobbegongs (also known as carpet sharks) and bamboo sharks (a type of long-tailed wobbegong). For good measure, a few southern stingrays have been added to the mix, along with a sprinkling of brightly coloured fish from Caribbean waters to complete this extraordinary bouillabaisse.

Absolute beginners need not worry about a lack of scuba skills, as the PADI-recognized Shark Encounter not only offers a shark meet and greet but also tackles basic diving techniques. It also aims to dispel the man-eating image of sharks to help divers better understand their behaviour. Working on the basis that 'ignorance breeds fear', the Blue Planet Aquarium challenges the common misconceptions about why sharks attack – and how. For example, of the 450-plus species of

shark, only a few are considered to be potentially dangerous to humans.

In their natural habitat, sea fish disperse rapidly when a diver gets too close. In the shark tank however, the residents are all too accustomed to visitors and the most curious will sometimes brush past your nose. The aquarium has handpicked non-aggressive shark species to ensure that the encounter is as safe as it can be, although nobody can rule out the possibility of a rare attack. However, big buckets of mackerel make sure that no shark goes hungry, reassuring when a sand tiger appears to be sizing you up. Everything feels so close in this vast, glass fish tank, where the water may only be about 3 m (10 ft) deep but the sensation is very much that of the deep sea. Sharks are highly sensitive and can pick up fear-generated electric pulses in the water – so if you are aware of your raised heartbeat, they will be too.

A Shark Encounter package costs £199 per person and includes full instruction, scuba gear and tickets for two spectators. Sessions take place daily at 2.15pm or 4.15pm, with a total course length of around five hours. Participants must be aged over 16 and should not fly for 24 hours after completing their dive session. Be aware: the pre-dive briefing doesn't touch on claustrophobia, but the shark tank can feel a little oppressive.

Swim amongst sharks, octopi and stingrays in a dive tank complete with wrecks and reefs.

087

CONTACTS

Angelsey Adventures
Tel: 01407 761777
Email: grant@anglesey
adventures.co.uk
www.angelseyadventures.co.uk

Visit Angelsey
Tel: 08450 740587
Email: info@angleseytourism
association.co.uk
www.visitanglesey.com

Scramble over cliffs, rocks and coastal fissures, all the while being drenched in sea spray.

COASTEERING ANGLESEY

Simple, inexpensive and enjoyed in some of the world's most rugged coastal terrain, coasteering is also surprisingly easy to arrange. Dozens of UK tour operators offer specialist guides with encyclopaedic local knowledge. Rocks, caves, waves and cliffs become an adrenaline-packed adventure course, whether in calm waters or rough seas. To many extreme coasteering die-hards, Wales provides the ultimate coastline for a full day's wave-lashed rocky trek, offering jutting headlands and spiny cliffs on a journey from one bay to the next. Squeeze into a wetsuit and stick on a safety helmet and a pair of old trainers before scrambling, climbing, abseiling, swimming and cliff-jumping along the water's edge over gullies and boulders.

Most coasteering routes snake along the base of cliffs, requiring climbing to escape savage sea spray and impassable rock obstacles. Harder, slippery sections necessitate jumping in to swim on jagged trails that explore every coastal nook and cranny – both in and out of the water. Death-defying leaps from the weathered peaks can

follow demanding clifftop climbs using ropes and a harness. Hanging off craggy promontories by the fingertips chest-deep in surf offers adventure-lovers a real buzz as marine birds circle overhead. Wetsuits, buoyancy aids, helmets and waterproofs are supplied as part of standard tour packages – so all you need to bring is energy and enthusiasm, along with swimming gear, towels and a change of trainers. Be prepared to get wet – a salt water drenching is very much part of the thrill.

Coasteering doesn't require Iron Man stamina, just confidence and good swimming skills. Group members are kitted out and safety briefed before being let loose on the Welsh coast, often for some warm-up activities, such as inflatable dinghy racing or caving. In perfect weather conditions it is possible to push the boundaries to up the ante and make the experience more extreme. Expect mega-abseil challenges into pitch-black rock fissures and daunting jumps to board a boat for a high speed blast to water-filled caves on Anglesey's dramatic unspoilt coastline. Half days cost from around £40, full days from £85.

TREE-TOP ADVENTURE
THE MIDLANDS

Sherwood Forest's 600 year old woodlands are renowned throughout the world as Robin Hood country, where a band of 13th century merry men hid out amongst thick swathes of deciduous and coniferous trees. Today, stunning expanses of ancient oak and birch woodland, interspersed with sandy heath and rough grassland, are protected as a Forest Trust. Incredibly, some of its trees and lowlands are as rare as the earth's endangered rainforests. Sherwood Pines Forest Park, another wooded Nottingham expanse, offers a mix of multi-purpose conifer and broadleaf. Managed by the Forestry Commission, much of the emphasis of the woodlands is on adventure. Two waymarked trails offer forested treks of 2 km (1 mile) and 4.5 km (3 miles), while a puzzle of off-road cycle routes and defined paths total over 10 km (6 miles) – but that's not all. Look up into the tree-tops and you'll spot zip wires linking trunks and branches tucked amongst the leafy canopies. For Sherwood Pines is home to the ultimate brushwood adventure, allowing people to shin up ropes, swing from tree to tree and forest-walk at heights of over 12 m (39 ft).

After being strung up in a harness, participants are free to run wild on an aerial assault course, hauling their bodies up wooden plinths and abseiling through a unique eco-wilderness. Ascend rope ladders into the upper branches of the forest to cross wooden boardwalks and platforms and crawl or slide through various obstacles, trapezes and swings. Cross from tree to tree for over 1 km (0.6 miles) at canopy height, hanging from an extensive cat's cradle of netting amidst the trees. Freefall for a second, then feel the pull of the death slide followed by a power bounce back up the wire in an adrenaline-fuelled rush. Slip or lose your footing and the safety harness will catch you before you fall. Using pulleys and horizontal traverse cables, you'll sail through the treetops on an exhilarating journey. Terrified of heights?

Then use the course to overcome your fears in a personal challenge. Things get more demanding as confidence builds on the home strait.

Some 17 forests in the UK play host to the 'Go Ape' tree-fest. Entrance costs £25 for over 18s, £20 for those aged 10–17, and parking is £3. Tree-swingers keen to sprint around against the clock should start early and aim for a time under three hours. Wear clothes that aren't precious as getting grubby is a certainty. Wear grip-soled ankle boots, fingerless gloves and tie long hair back.

GETTING THERE
If travelling by car, follow brown information signs for Sherwood Pines Forest Park located off the B6030 between Ollerton and Clipstone. Trains to Mansfield can be accessed via the Robin Hood Line operated by Central Trains.

CONTACTS
Go Ape
Tel: 0845 643 9215
Email: info@goape.co.uk
www.goape.co.uk

A head for heights is essential on this aerial assault course.

EXPLORING UNDERGROUND LONDON

CONTACTS
Greenwich Tourism
Tel: 020 8854 8888
www.greenwich.gov.uk

Visit London
Tel: 020 7234 5800
Fax: 020 7378 6525
www.visitlondon.com

To think of London tunnels is to conjure up images of underground tube stations, wriggling below the surface of the city to form a thoroughfare of windswept chutes. Yet London is also criss-crossed by a mass of subterranean subways, from Roman burial chambers and Victorian sewers and pedestrian tunnels to dug-up plague pits, secret government bunkers and the tube system's forgotten limbs. Lying beneath almost every part of London, these long-dry subterranean passageways are said to riddle the bowels of the Houses of Parliament and the royal palaces. Rumour has it that a slog down 400 km (248 miles) of state-owned drainage conduit provides safe migration to Liverpool in the north. Hearsay aside, tourists seeking a below-ground sightseeing tour of England's capital will find plenty of subterranean depths to discover – simply pick up a copy of Stephen Smith's *Underground London: Travels Beneath the City Streets* and head underground.

Thankfully, unless you fancy lifting up a manhole cover to explore the waste pipes of London, you'll not need to pack a first aid kit or a torch or abstain from watching zombie films prior to an excursion. Although British investigative journalist Duncan Campbell was famously able to access an off-limits government bunker from a Bethnal Green traffic island in December 1980, his underground foray was without permission. Tourists, on the other hand, will find that delving into London's tunnelled underworld needn't be illegal. The existence of a warren of unused Victorian chambers offers tourists an altogether less clandestine sortie along abandoned telephone exchanges, concrete viaducts and sub-stations – and contrary to urban myth, there remains no evidence of a £66 million nuclear bombproof bunker by the Jubilee Line.

Subterranean highlights in London include the Greenwich Foot Tunnel, a 19th century conduit that passes under the River Thames in the capital's southeast. Connecting Greenwich with Tower Hamlets to the north, the channel was built to allow dock and shipyard workers to cross the river to their jobs on foot. Access to the tiled, cast iron tunnel is via an entrance shaft, housed inside twin glass-domed cupolas at each end – one in Island Gardens, the other on Greenwich Pier. The southern entrance is close to the preserved tea clipper *Cutty Sark* via a granite entrance shaft served by a lift and spiral staircase, which deliver pedestrians neatly to a tunnel adorned with more than 200,000 glazed, white tiles tarnished by a hundred years of grime. Where the river is at its deepest, the 370 m (1,214 ft) tunnel dips significantly, thus creating a sloping gradient that gives the illusion of the roof pressing downwards. A sense of claustrophobic confinement is allieviated by the endlessness created by the vanishing point of the route's dead straight line, while perfect acoustics make the Greenwich Foot Tunnel a great place to whistle or yodel. Damage from World War II is noticeable at the tunnel's northern end, where patched steel and concrete mark hurried repairs. Because of its depth and location, the tunnel remains cool even on hot days – a welcome respite from the stuffy heat of the city in summer. Kept open by public funds, the tunnel has an attendant-operated lift service from 7am to 7pm from Monday to Saturday and 10am to 5.30pm on Sundays, but is closed on public holidays.

Greenwich's sister foot tunnel at Woolwich opened a few kilometres down the river in 1912, linking the centre of town with the northern limits under the Thames. Stretching 507 m (1,663 ft), it is open to the public and accessed via a glazed-roofed entrance shaft, much like the Greenwich Foot Tunnel. Lifts operate Monday to Saturday, 7.30am to 6pm and Sunday 9am to 4.30pm, or take a time-worn flight of stairs. Pleasing curves and contours meet a slick tile-clad floor in an industrial project that required many tonnes of earth to be excavated by hand, with workers able to dig only around 3 m (10 ft) during a single shift.

Traversing the 19th century Greenwich Foot Tunnel is a subterranean highlight of the capital.

090 SAILING DARTMOUTH

GETTING THERE
The nearest railway station to NONSTOP Sail is Totnes, about 23 km (14 miles) away.

CONTACTS
NONSTOP Sail
Tel: 01803 833399
Email: info@nonstopsail.com
www.nonstopsail.com

Discover Dartmouth
Tel: 01803 834224
Email: holidays@discover dartmouth.com
www.discoverdartmouth.com

With two coastlines and umpteen sheltered harbours, Devon's history is inextricably linked to the sea. Piracy, smuggling and fishing have all played a part in Devon's maritime character, with many of England's most famous seafarers born there, such as Sir Walter Raleigh and Sir Francis Drake. It was from Devon that the Pilgrim Fathers set out in the *Mayflower* in 1620, as did Captain Cook in his voyages to Australia and the southern hemisphere. Sir Francis Chichester carried Devon's sea adventure tradition into the 20th century, when in 1966 he set sail from Plymouth in his yacht, *Gipsy Moth IV*, to solo-circumnavigate the globe. His voyage of 45,885 km (28,500 miles) took 274 days and captured the hearts and minds of the British public – more than 250,000 people cheered him back to shore. In September 2007, Devon made the headlines again when the world's largest sailing yacht swept into Dartmouth harbour. Owned by an American TV mogul, the 93 m (304 ft) long *Eos* dwarfed all other craft in the harbour. More than 200 yachts, worth an estimated £30 million, visit Dartmouth during the three day regatta each year.

Devon's sweeping 695 km (431 mile) coastline boasts hundreds of moorings, marinas, yacht clubs, docks, sailing schools and sailmakers, from Lymouth to Westward Ho and Tavistock to Lyme Regis. A number of operators offer adventure sailing trips and yachting courses, including Dartmouth-based specialist NONSTOP Sail, an RYA accredited sailing school. It now only shows total beginners the ropes, but it also improves the skills of regular sailors. The company, which runs adventure sailing trips around Britain and across the Atlantic, added two new Dehler 39s to its fleet in 2007. Both have since competed in the local regatta circuit as well as the prestigious Fastnet Race, crewed by a Devon-based team.

NONSTOP'S weekend students arrive for a Friday evening safety briefing from skipper Geoff Evans. After a night onboard in the deep water port of Dartmouth, they are given an introduction to sailing. This includes plenty of practical know-how relating to boat handling (what's a kedge?), wind conditions (when to gybe?) and how to tie a double loop bowline and splice. A short passage to the former shipbuilding harbour town of Salcombe gives an opportunity to explore this age-old maritime settlement. Students then get to practice their new-found nautical skills first hand whilst heading back to Dartmouth's choppy waters on the Sunday. Courses run 11 months a year (Feb–Dec), priced from £200.

Learn kedging, gybing and knot-tying skills aboard a deep water schooner passage.

CONTACTS
Roe Valley Country Park
Tel: 028 7772 2074
Fax: 028 7776 6571
Email: roevalley2@doeni.gov.uk
www.eshni.gov.uk

Derry Visitor
Tel: 028 7126 7284
Email: info@derryvisitor.com
www.derryvisitor.com

Discover the natural beauty of Northern Ireland by exploring the countryside on foot.

WALKING LONDONDERRY

Set on the banks of the River Roe, the town of Limavady lies 27 km (17 miles) east of Londonderry's old city and owes its name to the Gaelic term *leim an mhadaidh* – meaning 'leap of the dog'. Local legend has it that canine endeavour saved the town from an unexpected enemy attack. A dog jumped a gorge on the gushing River Roe to raise the alarm and warn villagers – and Limavady was born.

Well-used by canoeists, the River Roe eventually empties into the Atlantic Ocean and is home to the annual Doggy Paddle event in April. Straddled by the Roe Valley Country Park, the river plunges through spectacular gorges and, after heavy rainfall, surges through mixed woodland and ravines. Riverbank trails wind through dense wildflower carpets of damp-loving vegetation that thrive in year-round moist shade. Alluvial floodplains lead to meadows and rocky crags, and foxes, badgers, otters and over 60 species of bird have been spotted within the park's environs. Canoeing, rock climbing and orienteering are common activities in the valley – once Ulster's first domestic hydroelectric power station, built in 1896.

Hikers will find that the Roe Valley Country Park centres on a magnificent double line of very old and beautiful oak and birch trees. These follow the course of the River Roe and are snaked by footpaths on both riverbanks. A trio of bridges allow crossings en route for those keen to switch views. It is more than possible to spend a day stomping along the river along a mix of trails that range from gentle and sodden to steep and wet, passing grazing cows and rocky gorges along vibrant meadows of bluebells. After a downpour, the quiet River Roe transforms into a raging, fast-flowing torrent that crashes over rocks in a roaring mass, dispensing heavy spray across the woods. On calm, clear days look out for herons, white dippers, sparrow hawks and the blue flash of a kingfisher. An hour-long butterfly-filled riverside path weaves from O'Cahan's car park near the Gorteen House Hotel through open, grassy, pastoral land. Pick up a free map and cut across small footbridges and sluice gates below O'Cahan's Rock. Then it's up to the old castle before criss-crossing a large stone bridge and linking up to the water's edge – a popular site for outward bound challenges when river levels are at their peak.

IRELAND

TIME DIFFERENCE GMT

TELEPHONE CODE +353

CURRENCY Euro

LANGUAGE English and Irish Gaelic

POPULATION 4.1 million

SIZE OF COUNTRY 70,280 sq km
(27,409 sq miles)

CAPITAL Dublin

WHEN TO GO Ireland's prevailing warm, moist
Atlantic winds and temperate climate characterize
a landscape lavished with rainfall. Mild winters lead
to cool summers, with May to September the
driest period. Short, wet, foggy days predominate
from November to February.

TOURIST INFORMATION
Discover Ireland
Tel: 020 7518 0800
Fax: 020 7493 9065
www.discoverireland.com

This lush, green, rugged island in the North Atlantic Ocean is separated from Britain by the choppy Irish Sea. Flat, low-lying plains are fringed by a ring of coastal mountains, with Carrauntoohil the highest peak at 1,041 m (3,414 ft). Numerous islets, peninsulas and outcrops hem Ireland's craggy shoreline, with the River Shannon flowing south to north to the sea. Undulating hills offer some of the most varied and unspoilt scenery in Europe, while 5,600 km (3,472 miles) of coastline offer plenty of quiet sandy beaches. Bizarre volcanic lunar landscapes lie lapped by fertile waters rich in marine life, while capital Dublin's lively pub scene boasts dozens of Irish folk bars in which to enjoy the *craic*. Northern Ireland, in the northeast, is part of the United Kingdom (see page 132).

SEA FISHING DUBLIN

Ireland is fast emerging as one of the world's most exceptional low-cost sport fishing destinations. Traditionally, the northwest of the country has claimed the fishing crown. Yet, with an extensive coastline stretching from Carlingford Lough's terrific tope to the fantastic flounder of Wexford, sea anglers are increasingly flying into Dublin on a weekend jaunt. Fishing bases to the north of the city include the up and coming harbour town of Balbriggan, along with neighbouring Loughshinny, Rush, Skerries and Howth Head. These strategic launch points offer good access out to sea from May to October. Top draws include mackerel, whiting, codling, pollack, dab, mullet, tope and ray. Conditions tend to be blustery with plenty of pull, so those in the know stick to ragworm and lugworm as bait. Howth Head has a well developed fishing infrastructure with proper docks, charter boats and bait shops. Nearby Dollymount Strand is renowned as an autumn and winter hotspot, with the waters around the lighthouse on the North Bull Wall rich in coalfish, rockling, whiting and bass. Yet it is arguably Dún Laoghaire that remains the most popular deep sea angling spot, north of the Bay of Dublin. A small fleet of chartered fishing vessels cluster around the harbour, primed to ferry a loyal clientele out to do battle with codling, mackerel, mullet and flatfish.

To the south of Dublin, the peaceful coastal settlements of Dalkey Island and Killiney Bay offer prime fishing just a stone's throw from the capital city's hustle and bustle. Hemmed by two lively harbours, Dalkey Island boasts a ready supply of small boats for fishing trips and regular charters. Killiney Bay used to be rustic fishing village and it still has the unmistakable charm of a working maritime town, although it is now a preferred second home for pop stars and government bigwigs. In Bray, locals fish for conger eel from the relative comfort of a rain-lashed jetty, while both turbot and sole are plentiful in the waters off sleepy Greystones. 22 km (14 miles) from Wexford, Kilmore Quay has become a devoted deep sea angling centre, a pretty nautical hub dubbed 'the graveyard of a thousand ships' due to its surrounding sunken wrecks. In Dublin Bay, try your luck at gurnard, bullhuss and smoothound, or do battle with the region's monster mackerel, some

of which weigh in at a whopping 14 kg (30 lbs).

Deep sea fishing in Ireland is a lively, social affair, even before a line is cast. Expect the skipper to have a repertoire of fishing anecdotes as long as a spool of tangle-free fluorocarbon – as well as a drop of something warming. Pack a set of waterproofs and a sense of adventure, and be sure to keep some energy in reserve. When combat commences with a heavyweight of the deep, muscles and limbs are tested to the max. Battling one-on-one at sea is one of offshore fishing's inscrutable attractions, as blasting squalls and driving sea spray add a frisson to the battle. In Ireland, saltwater angling is challenging, thrilling and dramatic, and nothing makes a fisherman happier than to feel the rod double over as the reel screams. As fingers cramp and legs tighten to anchor the body to the spot, the serious angler prepares for a test of his time-honed skills. Yet the extraordinary demands placed on physical strength and stamina are matched by some soul-refreshing encounters. Sometimes a catch can take several hours to boat, by which time angler and fish share a mutual respect.

CONTACTS
Eastern Regional Fisheries Board
Tel: +353 1278 7022
Fax: +353 1278 7025
Email: info@erfb.ie
www.fishinginireland.net

Dublin Tourism
Tel: +353 1605 7700
www.visitdublin.com

Ireland's eastern coast is rich in marine life, from mackerel and mullet to turbot.

CONTACT
Dingle Tourism
Tel: +353 669 151 188
Email: info@dingle-peninsula.ie
www.dingle-peninsula.ie

Dingle Horse Riding Holidays
Tel: +353 669 152 199
Email: info@dinglehorseriding.com
www.dinglehorseriding.com

Expansive shallow water bays make for exhilarating rides.

CROSS-COUNTRY HACKING DINGLE

David Lean's beautifully-shot film *Ryan's Daughter* encapsulated the charm of the natural beauty of the Dingle Peninsula, one of Ireland's Gaeltacht regions where the Irish language remains in daily use. Lush, green mountain trails and sandy beaches typify this rugged Celtic terrain: a dramatic checkerboard of topographical textures atop the crashing Atlantic waves. Soaring peaks and a ribbon of country roads are lined with golden gorse and flowering fuchsia, while ragged, rocky islands lie drenched in brackish spray. Rolling pea-green meadows and forests offer myriad tracks to explore on foot or on the back of a fine Irish steed. Renowned for their stamina, versatility and gentleness, Irish horses are proud, dependable and companionable, from the tall, placid Irish draught and the spirited, intelligent Connemara to the energetic Irish hunter, the elegant piebald and the surefooted Irish cob. Little wonder Ireland equine tradition has earned it the name 'Land of the Horse'.

Dingle is best suited to riders with some experience, although confidence in the saddle counts for a lot on half- and full-day treks. Several highly reputable stables nestle in the undulating countryside, looped by hundreds of kilometres of first-class riding trails. Fossil-ridden hillsides, ancient stones and ruins and sweeping ocean views are just some of the fascinating sights to be enjoyed past heather-clad hillocks, bird-scattered marshes and juicy pasture. Trek down mountain slopes overlooking Dingle Harbour after some expert tuition in the skills of Irish horsemanship, and make new equine friends on hacks through a fairytale countryside steeped in mythological legend. For the ultimate horse riding holiday pedigree, seek out AIRE (the Association of Irish Riding Stables) accreditation, Fáilte Ireland (the National Tourist Board) affiliation and membership with Equestrian Holidays Ireland. Most operators offer a range of handpicked horses to offer riders a choice of breed, temperament, colour and size, usually up to 16.2 hands. Generally speaking, equipment and tack is part of the package (although you may prefer to pack your own worn-in helmet and boots), as is the experience of a knowledgeable guide. Rides can range from steady treks along level trails to full-on advanced hacks in open countryside. Experienced riders will discover plenty of opportunity to quicken the pace with an exhilarating gallop along the shore before cooling off in the waves. Hacks involve jumping and flatwork to keep both rider and horse wholly stimulated both physically and mentally, reaching flying speeds over 40 kph (25 mph). Cross-country canters demand extraordinary skill and strength through terrain that only the hardiest riders can tackle, across scenery denied to buses and cars strewn with scrubby trees and hedgerows.

Riding horses of legendary Irish stock in such exhilarating rural splendour unites strangers in a close camaraderie. Groups tend to be small, so friendships blossom in the saddle. Even language barriers do not interfere with a good time in a physical pursuit enjoyed by a wide variety of ages and nationalities. Tutorials are typical Irish-style affairs, conducted over pints of stout and pots of tea. Rusty riders are fully briefed in the demands of upcoming trails over lunches of sandwiches, scones, apples, cheese and soda. Maps flagging bridle paths and routes laced with lakes are freely available for solo riders keen to delve into fields

flecked with grey boulders and specks of yellow and purple flowers, on a backdrop of the Slive Mish Mountains. At Coomasaharn Lake, a popular spot for worn-out riders in need of respite, the sunlight's intensity reflects in the water to lull the exhausted into a dreamy doze. Rather aptly, the name for this body of water is Irish for Horseshoe Lake, set as it is in the foothills of the Coomacarrea, a horseshoe-shaped 3,000 m (9,840 ft) chiselled mountain that soars from the water into the sky. Petroglyphs adorn the sculpted peaks of these eerie crags, mirroring the map's knotty scrawls of the onward high speed trails. Those preferring a gentler tempo can amble along enjoying Peninsula views, whilst scouring the surf for a glimpse of Dingle's resident dolphins. Bring comfortable clothes, such as a light fleece jacket and some warm weather gear. Sunglasses and suncream are essential, even in spring and autumn. To embrace Ireland on horseback is to embrace the peculiarities of its weather, so be sure to also stick a decent set of waterproofs in your bags: Dingle isn't a luscious, rich, luminescent green without good reason.

Rolling meadows provide an idyllic landscape to explore on horseback.

ICELAND

TIME DIFFERENCE GMT

TELEPHONE CODE +354

CURRENCY Iceland Krona

LANGUAGE Icelandic

POPULATION 299,000

SIZE OF COUNTRY 103,000 sq km
(40,170 sq miles)

CAPITAL Reykjavik

WHEN TO GO Iceland enjoys a cool temperate
ocean climate, thanks to the Gulf Stream, with
average July temperatures around 12°C (54°F)
and fairly mild winter conditions. Snow becomes
rain in spring, but is rarely more than a shower.
Peak season is the bright, crisp months of
May and June.

TOURIST INFORMATION
Icelandic Tourist Board
Tel: +354 535 5500
Fax: +354 535 5501
Email: info@icetourist.is
www.icetourist.is

Iceland's mystical landscape boasts some of Mother Nature's greatest triumphs, from tremendous icecaps, mammoth glaciers and spouting geysers to steaming solfataras, volcanoes and cascading waterfalls. Home to numerous birds and a prime location for whale watching, Iceland's mild summers and snow-shrouded winters are ideal for the adventurous visitor. Canter across Lapland on horseback, dive into glacial lagoons, trek across rugged mountain peaks or swim against raging currents in fast-flowing icy rivers. All-consuming sunsets see the sky morph from egg yolk-gold to an oily inky-blue, splashed with purple and crimson. You can experience the exhilaration of 24 hour daylight from mid-June to mid-July each year during northern Iceland's celestial White Nights.

HORSE RIDING REYKJAVIK

Why Icelandic horse species are 10 cm (4 in) smaller than a decade ago, nobody quite knows, but what these slender equines lack in stature they more than make up for in brawn. Strong, small and willing, Iceland's horses have been central to traditional culture for generations, with few bonds as lasting as that between a man and his steed. Today, over 75,000 Icelandic horses offer visitors an opportunity to experience the extraordinary sub-Arctic terrain of their homeland as part of a free running herd. Riding in a loose pack of up to 60 horses across unspoiled open landscapes studded with glaciers and geysers is a rare treat for riders unused to boundless freedom and space. Galloping over rocky passes and cantering across wide, empty savannahs provides a rigorous adventure, combining an exhausting physical challenge with some of the most dramatic scenery on the planet in the 'Land of Fire and Ice'.

Iceland's rugged remoteness has made riding long distances over several hours the norm, so traditional culture has a long history of using remounts (a supply of fresh horses) to supplement the journey. Groups of riders with two or three horses often herded their remounts together to allow them to run loose as a reward for their willing hard work earlier in the journey. Chestnut brown, flaxen or silver in colour – often with sooty smudges and creamy dappling – the easy going Icelandic horse is calm on the ground and courageous under saddle. At around 12.4–14.3 hands, this compact mass of surefooted muscle relishes expending energy in abundance, speeding without fatigue for vast stretches with a smooth gait.

Weekending visitors need not travel far from Reykjavik's city centre to join a herd of freely running horses, as Icelandic farmers are found in highland pastures a few hours' drive away. Hvammur Farm, run by amenable couple Haukur and Sonja, continue to use the traditional methods employed by Viking settlers over 1,000 years ago. Driving young horses onto Iceland's remote upper meadows for the warm, summer months, they allow riders to tag along. Speed is wholly controlled by the herd, and ensuring that no horse is left behind, this spirited pack of horses makes an exhilarating dash across the beautiful, ever-changing wilderness of the Vatnsdalur Valley to lush, green, highland pasture. At the end of a long day in the saddle, spend the night in family-run lodges, mountain huts or under canvas and sing the songs of farmers over talk of round-ups for an unforgettable experience.

GETTING THERE
Keflavik International Airport is 48 km (30 miles) from Reykjavik. All flights are linked to Flybus ground transportation services that connect to city centres, resorts and tourist facilities. The nearest village to Hvammur Farm is Blönduós, 244 km (151 miles) from Reykjavik.

CONTACTS
Hvammur Farm
Tel: +354 452 7174
Email: haukur74@mmedia.is
www.isdirect.de/unterseiten

Is Hestar
Tel: +354 555 7000
Fax: +354 555 7001
www.ishestar.is

Join free-running horses on a surefooted Icelandic steed to ride loose-pack across highland pasture.

GETTING THERE
The Silfra rift is in Thingvellir National Park, approximately 50 km (31 miles) from Reykjavik. Keflavik International Airport is 48 km (30 miles) from Reykjavik.

CONTACTS
Black Tomato
Tel: 020 7610 9008
Email: info@blacktomato.co.uk
www.blacktomato.co.uk

Iceland Excursions
Tel: +354 540 1313
Fax: +354 540 1310
Email: iceland@grayline.is
www.icelandexcursions.is

Thingvellir National Park
Tel: +354 482 2660
Fax: +354 482 3635
Email: thingvellir@thingvellir.is
www.thingvellir.is

This gaping underwater canyon is filled with water filtered by porous volcanic rocks, ensuring gin-clear sparkling waters.

GLACIAL DIVING SILFRA

It has been dubbed the coolest place to dive on Earth – and with water temperatures of around 2°C (36°F), Silfra's nickname is pretty spot-on. Mist-shrouded glacial waters and brooding ancient lava beds typify the rugged terrain, just 40 minutes outside Reykjavik's urban sprawl but a whole world away. Borne out of a crevice created by a geological shift that divides the European and American continental plates, Silfra's gaping underwater chasm expands by around 2 cm (0.8 in) each year. This cavernous gully fills with melted water from the frozen icecaps of the Hofsjokull Mountains, filtered by porous volcanic rocks. So dramatic is the clarity that waters shimmer and glitter – hence the name 'Silver Lady' (or Silfra as it is known in Icelandic). Awe-inspiring cut-glass waters in their purest form offer an astounding level of visibility, with transparency up to 100 m (328 ft) commonplace.

Offering an ethereal ambience of an unworldly aquatic land, diving in Silfra is a surreal, dizzying experience. Nature stands little chance of supporting much aquatic life at such low temperatures, hence the water's purity. The result is a space-like dreamy weightlessness that has an intergalactic quality as you dive into its icy depths. Numerous specialist dive operators offer trips out

to the three main sites of Silfra Hall, the Cathedral and Silfra lagoon. Although the clock allows for all three to be dived in a day, the icy chill prevents most divers from doing so. Thermal wetsuits are highly effective in the keeping the body warm, but hands are particularly prone to numbing in the cold. Even seasoned cold weather divers limit their underwater exposure, using flasks of hot water to thaw out numb fingers every 35 minutes or so. Dive spots are accessed via scenic walks across the ice-encrusted tundra, where several deep ponds are linked by inter-connecting tunnels amidst lava crags. Canyons plunge to depths of 10 m (33 ft), below surface waters illuminated by shafts of yellow sunlight. Sharp ravines and twisted volcanic spurts rub shoulders with two continents, nudging the corner of the Cathedral and the entrance of the Silfra lagoon. Vast cracks run through the bed of the lake in a dramatic testament to the power of Mother Nature, a force that allows 24 hour 'daylight' diving in June and July. Droplets and bubbles dance like elaborate swaying crystal chandeliers in Silfra's mild currents. For James Bond-style propulsion, use a DPV scuba scooter: it adds a further frisson to an extraordinary adventure, allowing deeper access to the remote aquatic wilds of Iceland.

NORWAY

Few countries in the world are as active and sports-orientated as Norway, a nation where the great outdoors is utilized to the max. Norwegians first used skis over 4,000 years ago, and today any potentially skiable surface is worthy of an attempt. Over half of the Norwegian population have ready access to a cabin in the mountains. Ski days are a family occasion or a weekend social outing, while mid-week forest walks and country walks are mixed with fishing, cycling, rollerblading, horse riding, kayaking and snowboarding. Norway's adoration of the great outdoors has made unspoiled nature a highly-prized national symbol, the virtues of which are upheld with religious zeal. Getting out in the fresh air is as much a part of the country's national identity as smoked salmon and peace-brokering. Even in Oslo, city-dwellers have over 2,000 km (1,240 miles) of ski trails in surrounding forests.

TIME DIFFERENCE GMT +1

TELEPHONE CODE +47

CURRENCY Norwegian Krone

LANGUAGE Norwegian

POPULATION 4.52 million

SIZE OF COUNTRY 385,155 sq km (150,210 sq miles)

CAPITAL Oslo

WHEN TO GO Despite an extreme northerly position, Norway's mainland climate is surprisingly mild. The four seasons offer a considerable diversity of climate, with hot summer days and mountain skiing possible in the same 24 hours. Winters are cold but lose their bite in late April, when the parks, cafés and beaches spring back to life.

TOURIST INFORMATION
Visit Norway
Tel: 020 7389 8800
Fax: 020 7839 6014
Email: infouk@invanor.no
www.visitnorway.com

096

SKIING OSLO

GETTING THERE
A fast train from Oslo airport to the city centre takes 19 minutes and departs every 10 minutes.

CONTACTS
Skiforeningen (Norwegian Ski Association)
Tel: +47 2292 3200
Email: skif@skiforeningen.no
www.skiforeningen.no

Visit Oslo
Tel: +47 8153 0555
Email: info@visitoslo.com
www.visitoslo.com

Skiing through Marka Forest.

Skiing enthusiasts short for time needn't travel several hundred kilometres to the Norwegian mountains in order to enjoy an adventurous holiday on the slopes. Fresh air, lush hills and forests (called *markas*) are just a 30 minute subway ride from downtown Oslo. Spanning 170,000 ha (419,900 acres), the coniferous Oslo-Marka forest surrounds the city to the west, north and east to form an eco-recreation zone; a beautiful expanse of skiing, skating, walking, running, cycling, fishing, hiking and cycling trails. As Oslo's most popular weekend adventure, over 75,000 people ski the Marka Forest on a fine winter Sunday along 2,600 km (1,612 miles) of snaking scenic trails. There are also over 500 km (310 miles) of cross-country tracks – 125 km (78 miles) of which are floodlit – as well as 11 world-class ski jumps and eight slalom slopes. Yet such is the rural sprawl of this vast, green space that it retains a feel of remote seclusion – even on the busiest weekends.

Oslo-Marka's well-groomed ski routes are meticulously signed, with easy access to trail heads and all trails marked with wooden directional signs lettered in red, thanks to Oslo's local ski association (*Skiforeningen*). Deeper forays and longer tours into the forest's central core, however, do require a map. Tourist offices across Oslo provide skiing maps, guides and details of timber lodges in the woods, as well as details of ski hire and tour companies. The maps also offer lots of practical information about the areas you're about to explore, with summer trails marked in blue. Traditional cross-country skiing is high on the list of Oslo-Marka's biggest thrills, along with the Tryvann Winter Park's downhill runs and slalom trails. Seven popular routes are detailed using subway stations as start and end points, ranging in distance from 10 to 26 km (6–16 miles) across a variety of trails, many of them departing from Frognerseterem. Each route makes suggestions for lunch stop-offs in Oslo-Marka's many fire-warmed log cabin cafés, although packing hot drinks and basic provisions in a backpack is sensible for those wandering further off the beaten track. Conditions for cross-country skiers can vary enormously depending on the weather, from hard-going mega-physical exertion to easier-paced treks. A valley-to-valley ski trek from, say, Sorkedalen to Maridalen or Lommedalen to Sorkedalen can make an exciting alternative to a standard loop. Be sure to allow plenty of time to absorb the solitude and quietude of Oslo-Marka's great outdoors, from its sparkling frozen lakes and snow-frosted pine forests to its icy creeks and spectacular views.

GETTING THERE
NSB run a train from Bergen
to Dovrefjell – see www.nsb.no
for details.

CONTACTS
Musk Ox Safari Company
Tel: +47 7240 0800
Fax: +47 7240 0801
www.moskussafari.no

*Arctic musk oxes are rare,
so keep a wide angle lens
at the ready in this bleak,
treeless land.*

ARCTIC SAFARI DOMBAS

The Arctic musk ox is a rare and enigmatic beast found in the wilds of central Norway; a shy and reclusive unkempt bovine goliath that weighs in at least half a tonne. An oddball mass of pungent, shaggy hair with the strange looks of a sheep–bull hybrid, the Arctic musk ox is found in just four regions in the world, including the countryside outside of Dombas. Named for the gland on their forelock that emits a strong-smelling secretion when rubbed against a branch or rock, the musk ox is easily encountered off the beaten track. From mid-June to late August each year, musk ox safaris delve into a bleak, treeless void north of Lillehammer on a six hour quest. Abandon all images of African-style jeep safaris that transport you to within a few metres of the creature in comfort: this expedition takes place on foot. Long, isolated uphill treks lead from one remote wooden hut to another, so only hardy hikers should consider the route to the so-called Roof of Norway. Unpredictable weather conditions can also be tricky to judge – at any time of year.

Founded in 1974, the Dovrefjell National Park occupies 1,693 sq km (660 sq miles) across three Norwegian counties, 35 km (22 miles) north of Dombas. The harsh, scrubby terrain of stumpy willow – similar to the Welsh moors and Scottish highlands – has been dubbed Europe's last remaining wilderness, a glacier-sculpted moss-shrouded landscape where plant life predates the last ice age. Undefined trails meander in a disorientated riddle across gorse-covered rocks and soft earth. Sparkling pools ripple as a chilly wind gusts across the climbing slopes in this untamed, preserved ecosystem. Wild reindeer, wolverine and various large birds of prey, such as eagles and falcons, have their home here. Having arrived as recently as the 1930s, the Arctic ox musk is the new kid on the block on aged terrain.

At about 1.5 m (5 ft) in stature, musk oxen can be dangerous, with long, curled horns jutting from a thick mat of woolly hair. At ease in peaceful isolation, they can become agitated by noise and aggressive when crowded. Though large and stubby, a musk ox is capable of reaching speeds of about 30 kph (19 mph) – considerably faster than the average human. They are best viewed from a distance as they graze contentedly – they'll be too far away for a decent Polaroid, so be sure to keep a good wide-angle lens at the ready. Costs are from £25 per person for a six hour safari.

SWEDEN

TIME DIFFERENCE GMT+1

TELEPHONE CODE +46

CURRENCY Swedish Krona

LANGUAGE Swedish

POPULATION 9 million

SIZE OF COUNTRY 449,964 sq km
(175,486 sq miles)

CAPITAL Stockholm

WHEN TO GO Considering its northerly geographic location (at the same latitude as parts of Greenland and Siberia), Sweden enjoys a favourable climate with mild, changeable weather influenced by continental high pressure from the east. Sunshine brings hot days in summer and brightens cold winters. White nights (24 hour sunlight) characterizes land within the Arctic Circle from late May until mid-July. Winter, however, sees daylight diminish to around 5.5 hours a day in northern areas.

TOURIST INFORMATION
VisitSweden
Tel: 020 7108 6168
Email: uk@visitsweden.com
www.visitsweden.com

Sweden draws plenty of cultural influences from neighbouring Denmark and Lapland in the Arctic north, adding simple country pleasures to a swish urban mix. Sweden's sleek modern cities ooze sophistication, yet Sweden's heart is in the unfussiness of the mountains, beaches and offshore isles. Bordered by the Baltic Sea, the Gulf of Bothnia, the Kattegatt and Skagerrak Seas, Finland and Norway, Sweden connects to Denmark via the Öresund tunnel and a bridge. As the fifth largest country in Europe, Sweden is largely concentrated in the urban areas of Gothenburg and Stockholm, leaving vast swathes of pine forests, fishing lakes and mountains wholly undisturbed: an unworldly vision during the 'Midnight Sun' in summer and the below-horizon winter rays.

FISHING GOTHENBURG

The waters of the Åsunden Lake are some of Sweden's most temperate, with bath-warm depths on a gorgeous beach. Spanning 32 km (20 miles), the lake is renowned for its first-class fishing thanks to a plentiful stocks of pike, perch, bleak, burbot, vendace, ruffe and zander. A string of angling supply shops and bait vendors are located close to the shore, where maps detailing Åsunden's prime fishing spots are also readily available. It is located in Ulricehamn (reputed to be Sweden's oldest town), which sits at the convergence point with the in-flowing River Atran. Like the rest of Sweden, Ulricehamn boasts the right of common access – a long and historical birthright to experience the nation's natural environment freely. It is a legacy that is enjoyed to the full on Åsunden Lake's sun-dazzled expanses, with Gothenburg's urban sprawl a world away, 100 km (62 miles) to the east.

Although fishing for pike-perch is forbidden during spawning (end of May to early June), very few other restrictions apply. Sweden's summer fishing season runs from mid-May to the end of September, so simply pick up a fishing licence from the local tourist office (for about £3.50 per day) and head out to the shore. Many tourist offices organize package fishing tours, but you can also do it alone. Use anything from jerkbait and livebait to fly fishing during the mayfly period, and if you're packing your own gear bring a more powerful rod to cope with heavier fish. You're also likely to be casting reasonable distances and will be fishing at 9–11 m (30–36 ft), so pack 14–10s (hooks) with the flexibility to scale down to 16s and 18s if conditions dictate.

Umpteen boat charters, rod hire booths and fishing charters ply for trade in the lake environs, and local shopkeepers sell picnic-style snacks and drinks with fishermen in mind. Those keen to stick close to the shore will find a limitless number of spots in which to wait patiently for a bite with a rod. For a bigger rush, anglers can opt to fly fish or spin from a boat or float-tube, or do battle in waist-high waters with waders on. Hiring a small boat for a full day on the water will set you back around £4.30, with lakeside windbreaks and barbeque areas available for a nominal fee. Once your bucket is full, take your freshly caught bounty to Åsunden Lake's very own fishmonger for gutting. Then it's just a case of heating up the grill.

GETTING THERE
Åsunden Lake is situated in the city of Ulricehamn. Buses 100, 200, 777, 830 and 857 depart from Gothenburg central bus station to Ulricehamn bus station.

CONTACT
Ulricehamn Town Hall
Tel: +46 321 59 50 00
Email: info@ulricehamn.se
www.ulricehamn.se

Ulricehamns Turistbyrå
Tel: +46 321 59 59 59
Fax: +46 321 59 59 62
Email: turist@ulricehamn.se

Åsunden's prime angling spots offer peaceful remoteness and excellent fly fishing.

KAYAKING STOCKHOLM

GETTING THERE
For more information on Stockholm's
archipelago ferry service, see
www.stockholmtown.com.

CONTACTS
Dalarö Kajak, Dalarö
Tel: +46 85 015 0180
Email: info@dalarokajak.se
www.dalarokajak.se

Horisont Kajak AB
Tel: +46 76 808 8825
Email: info@horisontkajak.se
www.horisontkajak.se

With its 30,000 islands, the Stockholm archipelago ranks amongst the world's most spectacular huddle of islands, stretching over 100 km (62 miles) from Nynäshamn in the south to the Söderarm in the north. A string of outer islets lie to the immediate east of this route, forming a sparse windblown barrier to the eastern Baltic and protecting inner waterways. Just 150 atolls remain uninhabited in an archipelago with a permanent population of around 6,000. During the summer, the seascape fills with kayaks, schooners and sailboats as Stockholmers flee the city to ply the waters. For no more than the price of a Swedish shrimp sandwich, a fleet of bright white steamboats transport mainlanders from Stockholm across the archipelago's bays and channels to lush, pine-tree covered islets. The Waxholm Company sells a ticket good for two weeks' unlimited travel on more than 20 routes – near-perfect when supplemented by a water taxi and canoe.

Sweeping expanses of sheltered cruising waters and hundreds of anchorages ensure that the Stockholm archipelago contains one of the world's highest concentrations of leisure boats – but pick the right island and it is hard not to believe you aren't blissfully alone. Sailors and boaters from all over northern Europe descend on the region from June to August, although the rock-scattered, largely unmarked sea isn't something that the uninitiated take lightly. A good set of seafarers maps (such as *Batsportkort*) ensure that the archipelago is well charted, with buoyed routes clearly marked. A plentiful range of companies offer boat charters, with guided island hops and tailored tours available for small groups. Renting a kayak, on the other hand, allows total flexibility to explore the region at your own pace, with many of the archipelago's hidden gems unreachable by larger craft. Paddling along at 5 kph (3 mph) is just the speed a human was designed to travel – what's more, barely a kilometre passes without yet another island hoving into view, an added convenience when travelling under your own steam.

A four hour round-trip out to Kymmendö departs Stockholm at breakfast time, skirting the base of the cliffs to journey in and out of curvaceous bays. Against a backdrop of the city's citrus-coloured buildings, under a trademark luminous sky, the route's mill pond waters lead to deep pools and Kymmendö's scenic shores. Nearby Dalarö Skans is a shorter 7 km (4 mile) sprint, but is most exciting in the evening glow. An imposing lighthouse stands next to a 17th century stone fortification lit by lanterns and looped by pretty lanes lined with houses decorated in gingerbread style. To explore Vaxholm's smorgasbord of visual delights, hop aboard the steamboat from Stockholm – it's a beautiful 60 minute trip – and you'll pass all manner of sailboats and cruise ships, each one proudly flying the Swedish flag. Vaxholm's colourful seafront clapboard gives the island a sleepy, bygone feel.

Umpteen guided kayak tours help newcomers avoid the sea's more treacherous elements and offer trips with a wildlife bent. Some offer plenty of opportunities to birdspot on the primary waterway from the Baltic to the capital. Herons, eiders, gulls, terns and eagles are found around the rocky crags on the edge of the islands, where it is easy to paddle in clear water through islets and barren skerries to fish for pike, perch and Baltic herring.

For the locals, the most exhilarating part of the archipelago is the necklace of islands east of the outer islands, a group only accessible in perfect weather. Much like the rest of the region, these pinprick islands are free of souvenir stands and burger bars, protected by Swedish pride and long-lasting island heritage. However, these 'outer' outer islands are somehow wilder, untamed and thrown together – a tangle of atolls to which boats blunder in before wondering if there is a safe passage out. Some look like over-sized broccoli stems sprouting out of the depths. Others boast the lumpiness of a badly bruised potato, while some sport tiny spiky forests the size of a large tea tray. Kayakers will find that they can paddle with ease as the wind takes them, manoeuvring into shallow waters that are inaccessible to other boats. The real adventure is paddling in high winds to the outermost skerries on wrinkly waters, a hair-raising journey on unmarked rocky stretches where GPS would take away most of the fun. The Utskar ferry plies the outer islets of the archipelago every Tuesday and Friday through summer, but you'll need to pack your own kayaking gear and camping supplies. Swedish law dictates a person can pitch a tent just about anywhere – a real boon for a kayaking free spirit. Budget for kayak rental at £15–25 per day (or £100 for a double kayak for four days) or around £45 for a day tour.

Smaller atolls, coves and islets are easily accessible by kayak.

HUSKY DRIVING JÄMTLAND

GETTING THERE
SAS is the only airline offering routes to Östersund in Jämtland. Getting to Vålådalen is easiest by hire car – the drive takes about an hour.

CONTACTS
Nature Travels Ltd
Tel: 01929 463774
Email: booking@naturetravels.co.uk
www.naturetravels.co.uk

Stunning scenery and an exhilarating ride are just two of the pleasures of husky driving.

Sitting in the heart of Sweden, the region of Jämtland comprises an expanse of majestic mountains and forests punctuated by glassy lakes, ponds and ice-cold rivers. Covering around 12 per cent of Sweden, Jämtland is home to just 1.5 per cent of the country's total population and offers over 34,000 sq km (13,260 sq miles) of undisturbed wilderness that is home to ice lakes, glaciers, snow-covered fells and frosted pines. While there are many exciting ways to explore Jämtland's extraordinary hinterland, driving a sledge with Arctic huskies offers minimal disruptions to the landscape. In this silent world, the sound of creaking snow is the only audible distraction, along with the thrilling whoosh of the sledge runners on snow and the ever-eager panting dogs.

Jämtland's sledging tours are physically demanding, placing strain on the arms and shoulders and requiring good levels of basic fitness. Stamina and control are essential when driving a dog team across snow – an exhilarating and adventure-packed journey that gets progressively easier as the huskies settle into their stride. A three- or four-night trip allows sufficient time for some basic training for would-be 'mushers' ahead of meeting the pack. Then it's up with the lark the following morning to set off along crisp woodland trails across frozen lakes and snow-filled valleys. Expect much straining at the leash as the dogs wait impatiently for you to take your foot off the sled brake – they will also bark incessantly until you do. Routes climb up across the highlands to afford gasp-inducing views of a crystal-covered wilderness dappled by sunlight. Distances of 100 km (62 miles) are achievable in a day across good ground, in calm weather, at optimum pace.

As home to Scandinavia's four greatest predatory animals, Jämtland's coniferous forests hide brown bears, wolves, wolverines and lynxes. Moose and reindeer are often sighted, along with dozens of freshwater fish species in streams so clear that the water is safe enough to scoop up and drink. Tour prices include guides, equipment, training and clothing (a fleecy balaclava and extra-padded thermal jumpsuit) along with warming drinks, essential in a region that experiences lows of -46°C (-50°F). Longer tours allow for a greater amount of dog running, although basic command and harnessing techniques are easily absorbed in a few hours. The small village of Vålådalen is a popular starting point for mushers, with snow-laden trails that lead through an ancient forest and wildlife-rich nature reserve. Eastwards via Lundörstugan the huskies exploit a downhill run to race on even ground, requiring top-notch control at full pelt as your cheeks turn pink, then blue. Views over the Lundörrpas are worth idling over, snowdrifts permitting, before a fast-paced sprint past mirror-like lakes edged with pine on the return leg to Vålådalen, to thaw out in a log cabin sauna.

FINLAND

TIME DIFFERENCE GMT +2

TELEPHONE CODE +358

CURRENCY Euro

LANGUAGE Finnish

POPULATION 5.3 million

SIZE OF COUNTRY 337,030 sq km
(131,442 sq miles)

CAPITAL Helsinki

WHEN TO GO Bright spring March–April months lead to magical summers of long, light-filled days as city-dwellers exodus to the country en mass. September–November is when Iceland starts to prepare for winter, while December–February is snowy and icy although rarely without some sunshine.

TOURIST INFORMATION
Visit Finland
www.visitfinland.com

Finish Embassy of London
Tel: 020 7838 6200
www.finemb.org.uk

As a nation, Finland is almost entirely shaped by its climate; exploding in a riot of colourful festivals and exhilarating pursuits in summer and revelling in winter snow and ice. Renowned for its down to earth natural purity in both its scenic splendour and human character, Finland is more than a three-quarters covered in thick, dense coniferous forest. A first-class network of national parks offer outdoor enthusiasts a never-ending list of possibilities, from ice fishing, snowshoeing, hiking and cross-country skiing to husky-sledding and enjoying some Finish R&R in a traditional wood-fired sauna. Helsinki, the nation's buzzing capital, boasts historic Swedish-Russian influences, located on a peninsula reaching into the Baltic Sea.

ICE SWIMMING KEMI

Renowned throughout Finland as a town of ice and sea, Kemi is the gateway to Lapland adventure where snow-bound treks and snowflake dreams come true. Home to Finland's world-famous Ice Castle – a Guinness Book of Records entry reconstructed with each year's snowfall – Kemi sits on the edge of the frozen water's edge, surrounded by vast snowfields. At just 30 degrees north of the Arctic Circle, Kemi is every bit the rugged expedition hub, frequented by sledge-drivers, reindeers, husky trains and snowmobiles. It is also the launch point for the Sampo Icebreaker, the only vessel of its type in the world to transport tourists out on the northern Gulf of Bothnia's vast swathe of ice-capped sea.

In temperatures hovering around zero, icebreaker passengers don their space-age thermal snowsuits, goggles and helmets for the 45 minute snowmobile ride across snowy plains to the 3,450 tonne Sampo Icebreaker. At around triple the size of a standard cargo ship, the Sampo is distinguishable by its rounded bottom, a robust plough that ramps the ice up as it cuts through 5 m (16 ft) depths. A series of ear-splitting cracks accompanies each crushing, forceful thrust and engine roar. Otherwise the landscape is eerily silent, with the sound of vast floating mini-icebergs muffled by the icefield's frozen crags.

It takes four hours to inch through around 20 km (12 miles) of ice in the gloriously bruised and battered Sampo. Four engines push the ship's mega-bulk through the ice in Finnish Lapland from the middle of December to the end of April. During the icebreaker cruise, the most diehard adventurers are offered a healthy dose of sub-zero excitement on the frozen Arctic landscape amidst crackling frost and starry skies: swimming in the Gulf of Bothnia's bitterly cold, icy waters, which provides the ultimate Sampo thrill. Simply slip into a skin-tight orange thermal wetsuit and slide into the sea to float alongside giant chunks of ice. With all the body covered, apart from the face, the sensation is one of a tingly weightless – so exciting that you barely feel the cold. Dwarfed by a hulking vessel of solid steel in a dimming light, the added spectacle of the *aurora borealis* can only make the experience of floating in an over-sized sorbet more surreal.

GETTING THERE

Trains provide the fastest overland transfer to Kemi from Helsinki, with a non-stop service that takes 8 hours, 20 minutes. A domestic flight is quicker and cheaper, though, with numerous daily flights with Finnair that take 1 hour, 15 minutes. From Tampere, trains take about 8 hours. Domestic flights from this airport would need to be via Helsinki.

CONTACTS

Sampo Arctic Icebreaker
Tel +358 16 256 548
Fax +358 16 256 361
Email: sampo@kemi.fi
www.sampotours.com

Kemi Tourist Information Centre
Tel. +358 16 259 465
Fax: +358 16 259 675
www.kemi.fi

Taking a dip in the Gulf of Bothnia's frozen waters is the ultimate Arctic thrill.

INDEX